Have we Christians been led astray,
dumbed down, and drawn . . .

Off Target

18 bull's-eye exposés

JOHN NOĒ, Ph.D.

Off-Target

By John Noē, Ph.D.

Unless otherwise noted, all Scripture quotations are from the Holy Bible, *New International Version* © 1973, 1978, 1984 International Bible Society. Used by permission of Zondervan Bible Publishers.

Published by:

East2West Press
Publishing arm of the Prophecy Reformation Institute

5236 East 72nd Street
Indianapolis, IN 46250 USA
(317)-842-3411

Cover: Tom Haulter

ISBN: 978-0-9834303-2-2

Library of Congress Control Number: 2011945759

Bible. New Testament Revelation. Old Testament Revelation. Prophecy. End Times.

Dedication

To all the many over the years
who have disagreed with me
and felt I was leading people astray,
dumbing them down, and drawing them off-target.

.

May God give us all his
"Spirit of wisdom and revelation,
so that you [we] may know him better" (Ephesians 1:17)
and draw us back on-target with Him
and into the bull's-eye of his Word
and practice of the authentic Christian faith.

Contact Us:

EAST2WEST PRESS

Pioneering the next reformation

www.east2westpress.org

Publishing arm of . . .

PRI

**PROPHECY
REFORMATION
INSTITUTE**

**5236 East 72nd Street
Indianapolis, IN 46250**
www.prophecyrefi.org
jnoe@prophecyrefi.org
Ph. # 317-842-3411

Contents

Introduction – Beliefs and Consequences 1

We've Been 'Tamed' / 'Why Are Christians Losing America?' / One More Off-Target Statistic—the Exodus of Young Adults / Into the Bull's-eye

Exposé #1. Divine Perfection in Two Creations 21

Exposé #2. The Kingdom of God 37

Exposé #3. The Gospel 53

Exposé #4. Hell 61

Exposé #5. The 'Last Days' 77

Exposé #6. Second Coming / Return 91

Exposé #7. Rapture 101

Exposé #8. Antichrist 113

Exposé #9. The Contemporary Christ 117

Exposé #10. Book of Revelation 129

Exposé #11. Battle of Armageddon 145

Exposé #12. Israel   153

Exposé #13. Conflicting End-time Views   165

Exposé #14. Doing the Works of Jesus   181

Exposé #15. Doing Greater Works than Jesus   189

Exposé #16. Origin of Evil   205

Exposé #17. Eternal Rewards and Punishment for Believers   219

Exposé #18. Your Worldview   231

Conclusion – Bull's-eye Theology   237
Onto the Next Reformation

More Books from John Noē – 241

What's Next? – 247

What They Are Saying – 249

Introduction

Beliefs and Consequences

Truly, have we Christians been led astray by our own leaders; dumbed down in our theology by ideas, interpretations, teachings, doctrines of men, and traditions that will not stand up to an honest and sincere test of Scripture, and consequently drawn off target in the practice of our faith? In other words, have we Christians become our own worst enemy? These questions are not pleasant to ponder. But ponder we must because beliefs have consequences.

Please be assured that I am not down on Christianity—just the opposite. I'm down on what we have done to it. Inside these pages we will re-explore what really is authentic Christianity versus today's institutionalized and compromised versions that we've come to comfortably know and accept. Admittedly for some, this reading experience may be uncomfortable. For others, it will be right on-target, a proverbial breath of fresh air, and, perhaps, a godsend.

Throughout this book, I will contend that we Christians indeed have been led astray, dumbed down, and drawn off-target—and by some of our favorite pastors, teachers, authors, TV evangelists, and seminary theologians, many of whom we have known, loved, and trusted. The result—as you will see—has been the widespread acceptance of substandard versions of Christianity. These off-target and substandard versions have been so repeated, perpetuated, and Polly-Parroted that most of us think our particular version is the real and true faith.

By dumbed-down I mean watered-down, diluted, devalued, diminished, depreciated, degraded, and denigrated, doctrinally and functionally. Fact is most, if not all, of our modern-day versions of Christianity pale in comparison with the vibrancy and effectiveness of the Christianity that was preached, practiced, and perceived in the 1st century and turned the hostile world of that day and time "upside down" (Acts 17:6 *KJV*). They also pale in contrast to the faith that brought our forefathers to America to found this country and establish its great institutions based upon Judeo-Christian principles.

But today's versions of Christianity are vastly different. Our many self-inflicted degradations led Dallas Willard in his highly acclaimed book, *The Divine Conspiracy*, to raise these three, most-relevant, and apparent questions:

1) "Why is today's church so weak?
2) Why are we able to claim many conversions and enroll many church members but have less and less impact on our culture?
3) Why are Christians indistinguishable from the world?"[1]

Willard further lamented that "those who profess Christian commitment consistency show little or no behavioral and psychological difference from those who do not."[2] Many others have likewise observed that "there is no significant difference between the way born-againers live at an ethical level as compared with those who are nonreligious."[3]

These off-target and substandard versions have been so continually repeated, perpetuated, and Polly-Parroted that most of us think our particular version is the real and true faith.

Another fact is, over the last 50 to 75 years or so, American Christians have given away almost all of the institutions our forefathers in the faith, who came to this country, founded—the schools, the

---

[1] Dallas Willard, *The Divine Conspiracy* (San Francisco, CA.: HarperSanFrancisco, 1997), 40.
[2] Ibid., 43.
[3] David Wells, quoted in Chris Stamper, "Authors by the Dozen," *World* magazine, July/August, 2002, 53.

universities, the branches of government (federal, state, and local), and being the moral influencer in society. And we gave it away to the ungodly crowd without a fight. Remarkably, we were not pushed out by more powerful anti-God forces or superior godless beliefs. We simply withdrew, and into the vacuum poured the secularists. Bottom line is, we Christians are paying an awful price for our self-inflicted deficiencies.

A prime reason for this change is that the dominant, eschatological (end-time) worldview in conservative Christian circles switched from one of historical optimism to one of historical pessimism. That is, in the mid 20th century, the postmillennial worldview of America's founders was replaced as the majority report among evangelicals by the dispensational premillennial worldview. This relatively new view in church history (originated in the 1830s by John Nelson Darby) believes the world is supposed to get worse and worse before Christ returns. Its ascendancy to dominance perfectly coincides and statistically correlates with the withdrawal of Christians from societal involvement, the rise of godless rule, and the decline of morality and public life here in America.[4]

John W. Chalfant in his book, *America a Call to Greatness* (formerly titled, *Abandonment Theology*) characterizes this great retreat thusly:

> . . . much of the clergy, along with their millions of victimized American Christians following their pastors' lead, have retreated from the battlefront to the social, non-confrontational, noncontroversial reservation [i.e., their church]. They say that Christians should confine their religious activities to politically noncontroversial roles and keep their Bibles out of the political process.[5]

Chalfant pinpoints dispensationalism's emphasis that "these are the 'last days'" as being the number one reason why many modern-day Christians—in stark contrast to our predecessors in the faith—now believe that "any efforts we make to restore righteousness to this nation will be in vain and need not even be undertaken."[6]

---

[4] See "Some Statistical Evidence" in John W. Chalfant, *American A Call to Greatness* (Longwood, FL.: Xulon Press, 2003), 83-90.

[5] Ibid., 142.

[6] Ibid., 143. Unfortunately, Chalfant's book also advocates a Christian or Biblical worldview without mention or inclusion of a mighty kingdom of God. In my opinion, this is equivalent to and about as effective—for rallying the

The much revered evangelist, Billy Graham, in a recent article titled "The End of the World" in his *Decision* magazine preaches we are "heading toward a catastrophe. . . . We can't go on much longer morally. We can't go on much longer scientifically. The technology that was supposed to save us is ready to destroy us." He reports that the "Doomsday Clock" kept by "The Bulletin of the Atomic Scientists . . . . At this writing . . . stands at seven minutes to midnight – two minutes closer to potential destruction than the clock read in 1998 and seven minutes closer than it did in 1995."[7]

Popular *Left Behind* co-authors Tim LaHaye and Jerry Jenkins agree with Dr. Graham. In their recent book, *Are We Living in the End Times?*, they cite "twenty reasons for believing that the Rapture and Tribulation could occur during our generation." To emphasize their tone of contemporary urgency, they further claim that "ours is the first generation that has the technology and opportunity to uniquely fulfill many prophecies of Revelation."[8]

John MacArthur, another prominent dispensational author and pastor, has been trying to convince Christians that "'Reclaiming' the culture is a pointless, futile exercise. I am convinced we are living in a post-Christian society—a civilization that exists under God's judgment."[9] He also argues that "people becoming saved. That is our only agenda . . . . It is the only thing that we are in the world to do."[10]

Amazingly, fellow dispensationalists Tim LaHaye and David Noebel think MacArthur is off target. In their co-authored book *Mind Siege* they concede that "There is plenty to do in all spheres of life. The importance of Christians entering the cultural sphere . . . cannot be overlooked or

---

troops (the Church), taking back lost territory, and producing cultural change, nowadays—as a dog barking at the moon.

[7] Billy Graham, "The End of the World," *Decision*, January 2004, on www.billygraham.org/article (1/14/04).

[8] Tim LaHaye and Jerry B. Jenkins, *Are We Living in the Last Days* (Wheaton, IL.: Tyndale House Publishers, 1999), back cover.

[9] John F. MacArthur, *The Vanishing Conscience: Drawing the Line in a No-Fault, Guilt-Free World* (Dallas, TX.: Word, 1994), 12.

[10] Quoted in John Zens and Cliff Bjork, "A Better Society Without the Gospel? The Unbiblical Expectations of Many Christian Leaders," *Searching Together* 27:1, 2, 3 (Spring-Fall 1999), 12.

underestimated . . . . Christian parents need to prepare their sons and daughters to invade the fortress of the left."[11]

On the other hand, Gary DeMar, a postmillennialist and Senior Editor of *Biblical Worldview* magazine is highly critical of dispensationalist calls for social activism. He writes, "Unfortunately, while LaHaye's points are well made, his call for any type of social action cannot be sustained over time because of his eschatology." DeMar further claims that LaHaye's short-term and popular eschatological worldview faces a "logical dilemma . . . . on the relationship between Bible prophecy and Christian activism." But he relents that "I would rather have LaHaye's prophetic schizophrenia than MacArthur's prophetic fatalism."[12]

Once again, beliefs have consequences. They affect how we think, how we live, what we do, and how we do it. It shows up in our character, our level of Bible knowledge, our struggles to survive or thrive, and in our engagement or disengagement in or from society. Unfortunately today, our massive dumbing down and forsaking of authentic Christianity has not only produced off-target Christians who are indistinguishable from unbelievers in terms of thoughts, words, and deeds, it has also resulted in Christians who are weak, anemic, and causal about their faith as well as apathetic, ineffective, and impotent in being salt and light in the world as Jesus called all Christians to be (Matt. 5:13-16). Sadly, most modern-day Christians seem to have lost their saltiness and darkened their light (if they ever had it). It's like Jesus further explained, "every good tree bears good fruit, but a bad tree bears bad fruit" and "by their fruit you will recognize them" (Matt. 7:17, 19). Even Edmund Burke, the 18th century British statesman, once warned in this commonly known quote, "The only thing necessary for evil to triumph is for good men to do nothing."

. . . beliefs have consequences. They affect how we think, how we live, what we do, and how we do it.

---

[11] Tim LaHaye and David Noebel, *Mind Siege: The Battle for Truth in the New Millennium* (Nashville, TN.: Word, 2000), 228.

[12] Gary DeMar, "Give Up, Caught Up, or Get Up?" *Biblical Worldview*, November 2003, on www.americanvision.org., *Biblical Worldview* Archive.

Bottom line is today's led-astray, dumbed-down, and off-target Christian theology has resulted in substandard versions of the faith that prominently exhibit an abandonment psychology and retreat pathology among most Christians. Is this a case of the blind leading the blind? Or, is it the result of a succumbing to more sinister forces and opposing beliefs? You be the judge. But this well-recognized derogation and paradoxical predicament is the essence of the problem this book addresses and to which it offers a constructive solution—as you will see.

We've Been 'Tamed'

Disparities between modern-day and historical versions of our faith are not lost on the opponents of Christianity. Jewish secular humanist, Alan Wolfe, for instance, in his book titled, *The Transformation of American Religion: How We Actually Live Our Faith*, takes note and makes major emphasis of this change. He concludes that "faith in the United States, especially in the last half century or so, has been further transformed with dazzling speed." Consequently, "culture has transformed Christ[13] . . . . American faith has met American culture—and culture has triumphed."[14]

Wolfe summarizes that "in short, American religion has been tamed."[15] He cheerfully advises his secularist colleagues who might "worry about faith's potential fanaticism"[16] that they have nothing "to fear" because "believers in the United States are neither saviors nor sectarians."[17] They have essentially "succumbed to the individualism and . . . narcissism, of American life."[18]

In a review of Wolfe's hard-hitting book, syndicated newspaper columnist and Christian Cal Thomas terms it "must reading" that offers "some sobering conclusions" and is a "stinging indictment of contemporary Christianity." Thomas recommends that "people looking

---

[13] Alan Wolfe, *The Transformation of American Religion* (New York: Free Press, 2003), 2.
[14] Ibid., 3.
[15] Ibid., inside cover leaf.
[16] Ibid., 4.
[17] Ibid., 5.
[18] Ibid., 4.

for reasons why the church has lost power and real influence need look no further than Wolfe's book." He credits Wolfe as having "discovered the source of the church's contemporary power failure." It is the fact that "people who call themselves evangelicals increasingly dislike sharing their faith with others for fear that doing so might 'make them seem unfriendly or invasive.'" In citing Wolfe's contention "that in the battle between faith and culture, 'American culture has triumphed,'" Thomas rightly points out that "It was supposed to happen the other way." He ends his article with this piece of poignant advice:

> If Christians really want to see culture transformed, Wolfe's book, especially, shows they need to begin with their own transformation. Only then do they have a prayer of seeing cultural change. To expect it to happen the other way around is futile.[19]

Similarly, *Christianity Today* magazine in an editorial review of Wolfe's book admits "the cultural success of evangelicalism is its greatest weakness." *CT* editors seem to agree with Wolfe as he "paints a picture of a privatized religion that lacks confidence and is eager to avoid offense." They term this modern-day reality "toothless evangelicalism" since most evangelicals have grown accustomed to "'practicing the culture' rather than 'practicing the faith.'" They recognized "that Bible study has been so personalized as to effectively block its implications for radical social transformation; the way the fear of offending others has reduced most witness to 'lifestyle evangelism.'" The review closes with "a call to serious Christianity" and concludes that "something must be done." That something "must nurture an evangelicalism that is truer to its robust heritage" and that has a "demanding vision for both individuals and society."[20] To these concluding insights I add a hearty, "amen!"

"American faith has met American culture —and culture has triumphed."

[19] Cal Thomas, "American culture has triumphed over religious faith," *The News-Press* (Fort Myers, FL.), 2 October 2003, 9B.
[20] Editors, Where We Stand: *CT's Views on Key Issues*, "Walking the Old, Old Talk," *Christianity Today* (October 2003): 34-35.

National Review magazine's review of Wolfe's book focused on "those who fret about the danger of the 'Christian Right' lurking within our borders." They agreed with Wolfe "that there is 'no reason to fear that the faithful are a threat to liberal democratic values.'" They laud that "it's great that a scholar of Wolfe's stature is willing to stand up" and put forth "the principle that a vigorous exercise of religious faith poses no threat to the constitutional separation of church and state." They cite Wolfe's three reasons for this principle: 1) "the reason people of faith should not be feared by the body politic is that religion has been watered down, robbed of both supernatural mystery and intellectual vigor." 2) "The evangelicals in their megachurches, Wolfe says, are more interested in emotion and experience than in theological disputation." 3) "Evangelicalism" has entered "a 'Faustian pact' with the culture."[21]

Lastly, an *Associated Press* article reviewing Wolfe's book and "allegations of 'culture war'" highlights that "Wolfe is writing for fellow secularists, whom he depicts as frightened that their devout neighbors are undermining democracy." It reports that Wolfe calms their fears relaying that "the culture has reshaped the evangelicals more than vice-versa" and that "American religion has been so transformed that we have reached the end of religion as we have known it."[22]

'Why Are Christians Losing America?'

The following excerpt was originally part of an article titled "Why Are Christians Losing America?" authored by yours truly and published in *MovieGuide* magazine (Sept. 2007). This title and question was originally the front-cover headline and the non-footnoted-intermittent quotations below are from several articles in WorldNetDay's *Whistleblower* magazine, April 2005 *(WB)*. This excerpt is presented here in its original outline format:

---

[21] Michael Potemra, "That Old Time Religion," *National Review* (15 September 2003): 46-47.
[22] Richard N. Ostling, Associated Press, "Author: America is harmonious in matters of faith," *The Indianapolis Star*, 30 October 2003, E1, 8.

Two suppositions are contained in this discussion question:

1) America is being lost.
2) Christians are responsible.

Or are we since . . .

- "Four out of five Americans describe themselves as Christians?
- 45% of us attend worship services on any given weekend?
- The popularity of Mel Gibson's *The Passion of the Christ* and Rick Warren's book, *The Purpose-Driven Life*?
- America appears to be bursting its seams with vibrant Christianity."

And yet . . .

"America's popular culture, its laws, public education system, news media, entertainment industry, and other major institutions have become progressively *un*-Christian – even *anti*-Christian."

On 4th of July we sang "God Bless America," while much of America is doing everything it can to sabotage that.

The reason Christians are losing America is . . .

"Christians have been seduced . . . hoodwinked . . . sold a bill of goods . . . are operating under a misguided and simplistic interpretation of scripture . . . . Christianity – the deepest, most meaningful and awe-inspiring religion ever – has been ***dumbed down*** . . . ."

Consequently . . .

- "only 9% of Christians have a biblical worldview."
- "'born-again' Christian adults in the U.S. think and act virtually the same as non-believers . . . almost no difference." (recent George Barna study cited)

Whistleblower's answer to how we've been "dumbed down" and how "to turn America around – to take it back – " is . . .

"Take back your churches . . . [as] the springboard to taking back the culture." They call for laymen to lead a "new pulpit revolution . . . ." Think about it. When was the last time you heard a sermon on:

- A great social issue of our time?
- The last time your church engaged in the political debate?
- How many churches are active in the cultural war?
- How many pastors are leading prayers for . . . our nation's soul?"

"The churches remain the last, best hope Americans have for bringing about a rebirth of Western Judeo-Christian culture."

Perhaps Tony Evans has best captured this dilemma thusly:

"Let me put the problem to you in the form of a question. How can we have all these churches on all these street corners, filled with all these members, led by all these preachers, elders, and deacons . . . and yet still have all this mess in America? Something is wrong somewhere!"

"But when we turn the education of our children over to the state, and the state removes biblical ethics from its curriculum, what you get is the mess we have now."

  – Tony Evans, *What a Way to Live!* (Nashville, TN.: Word
    Publishing, 1997), 294, 76.

What do you think?

The Church in Nazi Germany
—Are We Repeating the Mistakes of the Past?—

The Christians in Germany learned only too late that the people of God in Christ cannot disengage from the culture in which they live. We cannot withdraw to the comfortable security of our beautiful sanctuaries and sit in our padded pews while the world all around us goes to hell. For to do so is a betrayal of the Lord whose name we bear and is a denial of the power and efficacy of his Word, the Word that He has given us to proclaim.

In Germany, as here in the United States, one of the most clever tools in the enemy's arsenal used to silence and intimidate Christians, to drive them out of the public square was the lie of the separation of Church and State. . . .

So Hitler called together the most important preachers in the land . . . . to reassure them, and intimidate them, if he could, to silence their criticism so he could go on with his plans for the country . . . . He told them their state subsides would continue, their tax exemptions were secure, that the church had nothing to fear from a Nazi government.

And finally, one brash young preacher who was there . . . had had enough. He was going to tell the truth even if that truth was not popular. And he pushed his way to the front of the room until he stood eye to eye with the German dictator. And he said, "Herr Hitler, our concern is not for the Church. Jesus Christ will take care of his Church. Our concern is for the soul of our nation." It was immediately evident that the brash young preacher spoke only for himself, as a chagrined silence fell over that room and his colleagues hustled him away from the front.

Hitler with a natural politician's instinct saw that reaction and he understood exactly what it meant. And, he smiled as he said to himself almost reflectively, **"The soul of Germany, you can leave that to me." And they did.** They kept their religion and their politics strictly separate from one another. And as the innocent were slaughtered and as the nation was led down the path to destruction, they looked the other way and they minded their own business. And their country was destroyed [in twelve short years].

I would submit to you today that we in America find ourselves in a frighteningly similar predicament. Once again, the innocent are being slaughtered in a 26-year holocaust [over 40 million boys and girls] that makes Hitler look like a humanitarian by comparison. Once again, a nation is being led down the path of destruction and, once again, by and large, God's people are looking the other way.

– An excerpted transcription from: Laurence White, *For Such a Time as This*, (Colorado Springs, CO.: Focus on the Family, BR292/22119, 1998, 1999), audio cassette, side 1.

'War on Christianity'
Bill O'Reilly – 'Talking Points'

June 2, 2004 – When the anti-Christian campaign by the ACLU claimed Los Angeles County as another victim in forcing them to take a small cross off its seal, *Fox News* commentator, Bill O'Reilly, had this to say:

"The harsh truth is that many American Christians don't care about what is happening . . . . Talking Points wants you to know that we are rapidly losing freedom in America. Judges are overruling the will of the people and fascist organizations like the ACLU are imposing their secular will. And, when was the last time you heard a priest, minister, or rabbi talk about this? For me, the answer is simple. . . . Never! And that's a memo."

What do you think?

Fatalistic, False Views of the Future

The current and dominant worldview in American evangelicalism is that the world will, and is supposed to, get "worse and worse."

This pessimism produces a "why-fight-we're-on-the-next-flight" mentality. But how does this fatalistic view match up with Isaiah 9:6-7's description of the future of the messianic kingdom? (It doesn't.)

"This faulty religious teaching, says John Chalfant, is the only way to explain why so many well-meaning Christians are paralyzed into inaction." (*WB*, 17):

"It comprises what is left today of the militant, power-filled, full-dimensional Christian faith of America's Founders after decades of erosion, watering down and trivializing of God's action mandates by America's Abandonment Clergy."

– John W. Chalfant, *Abandonment Theology* (Winter Park, FL.: America – A Call to Greatness, Inc., 1996, 1999), 5.

"For this type of 'Christian,' there's no need to stand up to evil, because they're 'saved by grace, not works' (despite repeated biblical admonitions that 'faith without works is dead'). No need to obey God's commands, because they're already saved, so why bother? No need to try to help make it a better world, because they're going to be 'raptured' soon and those who remain behind can sort out the mess. Is it any wonder the church–and America–are in such trouble?" (*WB*, 27)

Why the Moral Majority failed after only twenty years

Moral Majority Founder, Jerry Falwell, summarized the failure and demise of this activist organization in this manner:

> "I see things getting worse and worse and worse. All we're doing—all we've ever been able to do—is to have the church put its thumb in the dike, but it's inevitable that it's going to come out. We are supposed to keep it plugged up as long as we can, be a restraining influence. We prevent spoilage . . . . But we're kidding ourselves if we think there's any program, any third party . . . or anything we can do to straighten things out right now . . . . these things that we have in the country are beyond repair."
> – From Cal Thomas, Ed Dobson, *Blinded by Might* (Grand Rapids, MI.: Zondervan, 1999), 276.

The problem of sounding "an uncertain sound" is —"For if the trumpet give an uncertain sound [i.e., message], who shall prepare himself to the battle?" (1 Cor. 14:8 KJV). Perhaps, the Moral Majority did not have a sound or strong enough theological foundation that would support the level of activism to which it aspired?

What do you think?

So Here We Are . . .

"The compartmentalization and trivialization of Christianity . . . has ushered in a generation of shallow, ineffectual, and invisible Christians . . . . America's churches have been subverted" (*WB*, 29)

Consequently, thousands of American evangelical churches are culturally neutralized, comfortable, and content with a dumbed-down version of genuine Christianity. Thus, they are committed to:

- presenting a kingdom-deficient gospel
- marketing mediocrity
- laboring in lukewarmness
- and being culturally impotent

In short, according to Jewish secularist Alan Wolfe, Christianity has been "tamed" and "culture has triumphed." (In his book, *The Transformation of American Religion* (New York: Free Press, 2003), inside flap, 3.)

"As a result, Christian faith [has] become increasingly personalized, privatized, and marginalized" (Brian D. McLaren, *The Last Word and the Word after That* (San Francisco, CA.: Jossey-Bass, 169). Even worse, if possible, Christians are not only losing America but we are also losing our kids in droves. And many Christians and churches don't even want to talk about it.

So who is responsible? We are! And we are not being properly and scripturally led. (A few exceptions do exist.) It seems, that once again, the traditions of men have nullified the Word of God in this area (Mark 7:13; Matt. 15:6).

Our Options: What Can We Do?

1) **Nothing** . . . business as usual?

2) **Brow beat** – moral exhortation?

3) **More prayer** – al a 2 Chronicles 7:14? – But it takes more than prayer to meet God's requirements for national blessing here!

4) **Transformational Imagination** – an educational and missional process of enticing, following the model of Jesus' central teaching, and restoring the heart of his earthly ministry—**big problems call for big solutions.**

5 STEPS FOR RESTORING . . .

the preaching, teaching, and practice of the kingdom-of-God worldview (in its fullness) to the Church and to the world.

Step #1 – *Unlearning* popular misconceptions.

Step #2 – *Grounding* the kingdom theologically—the *timing, nature*, and *scope* of its everlasting form.

Step #3 – *Applying* the kingdom to today's world—i.e., the transformation of both self and society.

Step #4 – *Confirming* why it is so important for every believer to be active and fully involved in advancing God's kingdom (seeking justice), here and now, on this earth.

Step #5 – *Prioritizing* this calling as the Church's TOP, No. #1 agenda, because . . .

- It was the #1 agenda of Jesus (Mark 1:15; Matt. 6:33)
- It's why the Church and Christians are here on this earth

But what do you think?

> *"We Christians cannot continue to avoid knowing what we already know: that something is rotten in the state of our religion."*

> *"True prophets (those who bring a new word from God to assist in the current process of emergence) are crucified; false prophets (those who promise shortcuts that will cause regression or stagnation) are made rich and famous."*

> *"The eschatology of abandonment is being succeeded by an engaging gospel of the kingdom."*
> – Brian D. McLaren, a *Generous Orthodoxy* (Grand Rapids, MI.: Zondervan, 2004), 268, 285, 237.

(End of excerpt)

One More Off-Target Statistic—the Exodus of Young Adults

Leslie Leyland Fields in a hard-hitting article titled, "The Myth of the Perfect Parent," specially highlighted this damning statistic:

> It appears that many of us are not succeeding. The exodus of young adults from evangelical churches in the U.S. is well reported . . . . The Barna Group reported in 2006 that 61 percent of young adults who had attended church as teenagers were now spiritually disengaged, not participating in worship or spiritual disciplines. A year later, LifeWay Research released similar findings, that seven in ten Protestants ages 18 – 30 who had worshiped regularly in high school stopped attending church by age 23. Regardless of which studies are the most accurate, there is little doubt that many youth who were raised in the church do not necessarily stick around.[23]

Ken Ham, president/CEO and founder of Answer in Genesis-U.S. and the Creation Museum, in his hauntingly titled book, *Already Gone*, dramatically illustrates the reality of this tragic exodus this way:

> I dare you. I dare you to try it this Sunday. Look to the right, and look to the left. . . . Look at the children and look at the teens around you. Many of them will be familiar faces. . . . imagine that two-thirds of them have just disappeared from your church. . . . Why? Because they are *already gone*. . . . The numbers are in . . . . A *mass exodus is underway. Most youth of today will not be coming to church tomorrow.* Nationwide polls and denominational reports are showing that the next generation is calling it quits on the traditional church.[24]

Ham believes that this exodus of young people from today's churches is due to their not being properly trained and educated in the faith. He terms Sunday school programs of today "statistical failures" because "there is a major problem with *how* they were taught." The Church "should be 'equipping the saints for the work of the ministry' in

---

[23] Leslie Leyland Fields, "The Myth of the Perfect Parent," *Christianity Today*, January 2010, 24.

[24] Ken Ham & Britt Beemer, *Already Gone* (Green Forest, AR.: Master Books, 2009), 21-22.

an unbelieving world . . . to defend the Word of God from the very first verse against the skeptical attacks of this age."[25]

He further explains:

> Unless the facts behind the Christian faith are clearly and convincingly communicated in a way that students can learn and remember, their faith will not stand the assault of doubt from the world. It's not enough to just tell students, 'Believe in Jesus!' Faith that is not founded on fact will ultimately falter in the storm of secularism that our students face every day.[26]

Ham is right on target here. It's an "issue of belief" from Genesis to Revelation that undermines the authority and relevance of Scripture in the minds of our youth. But he advises "if we can do a better job of teaching proper belief, we will at least increase the possibility that these kids will return after they have children."[27]

The Church "should be 'equipping the saints for the work of the ministry' in an unbelieving world . . . to defend the Word of God from the very first verse against the skeptical attacks of this age."

Ham knows that beliefs have consequences. And if we don't change this exodus trend, Ham argues the consequence will be, "we are less than one generation away from being a nation of hollow, empty, churches"— like post-Christian England and much of Western Europe. To his credit Ham recognizes that: "the church is sick and it needs to be told the truth," is "trapped in tradition," and many Christians have become "casualties of burnout from man-made religious institutions" and churches "driven by denominational and congregational expectations rather than Scripture."[28]

---

[25] Ibid., 44, 45, 111.
[26] Ibid., 49.
[27] Ibid., 57, 62.
[28] 79, 109-110, 155, 157.

I concur with Ham's overall assessment and his call for a "vibrant new vision for unleashing God's Word" by making "a tangible connection between faith and fact."[29] This connection is exactly what you will find in this book's 18 bull's-eye exposés.

In this regard and in a recent *Christianity Today* article, Anthony D. Baker appropriately asks, "Can we afford to engage in business as usual if business as usual—doing the same thing Sunday after Sunday—is sinking the church?" He, too, cites statistics and concludes that "the Christian faith is broken."[30]

Into the Bull's-eye

Like 18 arrows flying straight to a target, this book bull's-eyes one of, if not the major and bottom-line reason for the above, disheartening, and daunting statistic of the exodus of young adults from today's churches. And that is, we Christians do not have our faith right—at least in the 18 key and foundational belief areas we will be addressing.

I make no pretense, however, that these 18 areas are exhaustive. You may be able to think of other areas for inclusion. But these 18 areas are significant. They form this book's 18 exposés (or chapters). For ease of comprehension, each exposé is formatted thusly: an opening statement introducing its topic and followed by sections explaining the Theological Problem, What Scripture Says, Elaborations, and Sources.

This book also serves as a sampling, a tasting, and a teaser from a smorgasbord of relevant and significant topics, which comprise my publishing agenda from East2West Press. Therefore, each exposé either contains material from one of two already published books or presents a preview of a future book (see "More Books from John Noē" pp-241-244 and "What's Next?" pp-247-248). Obviously, each book covers or will cover the topic in much greater depth and breadth. The estimated publication year for the future books are cited under the "Sources" sections in each exposé. We at East2West Press are committed to this

---

[29] Ibid., 158.

[30] Anthony D. Baker, "Learning to Read the Gospel Again: How to address our anxiety about losing the next generation," *Christianity Today* (December 2011): 30 and in quoting Stanley Hauerwas.

publishing and next-reformation agenda because we recognize that we Christians are to:

> *Preach the Word; be prepared in season and out of season; correct, rebuke and encourage—with great patience and careful instruction. For the time will come when men will not put up with sound doctrine. Instead, to suit their own desires, they will gather around them a great number of teachers to say what their itching ears want to hear. They will turn their ears away from the truth and turn aside to myths (2 Tim. 4:2-4)*

This bull's-eye-aimed admonition from the Apostle Paul almost nineteen centuries ago still strikes dead center and as true today. It targets one of if not the prime reason we Christians have been led astray, dumbed down, drawn off target and consequently "left behind" by many in today's world. This is why I am claiming that these 18 exposés comprise the theological bull's-eye for the next reformation and reawakening of the Christian Church. Once again, however, I am not insinuating that these 18 areas comprise the entire gamut of needed and further reform. But they are hugely significant as you will see!

This book also serves as a sampling, a tasting, and a teaser from a smorgasbord of relevant and significant topics, which comprise my publishing agenda from East2West Press.

That is all the introduction this book really needs. But in closing, I will make one prediction. If this further reformation and reawakening occurs, the above cited and damning statistic will change, dramatically and for the better. It will transform how we Christians think, who we believe we are, what we do, and how we do it—and for the betterment of all humankind—so help us God.

Once again, however, you be the judge.

Exposé #1

⊱━━━━━━━━━━━━━━━━━━━━━━━⟶

Divine Perfection in Two Creations

The God of the Bible is the God of order and design. Everything He created He did so with a plan, purpose, timeframe, and mathematical precision. For those who have eyes to see, his guiding hand is evident in every part of his two creations—from macro to micro, the largest to the smallest. This attribute of God has been called the stamp or fingerprint of divinity. I chose to call it simply divine perfection.

Theological Problem:

The different creations spoken of in the Bible are: 1) the physical creation; 2) the redemptive creation (Isa. 51:15-16 *KJV*). The first is composed of atoms and molecules. The second is comprised of covenants. Both dramatically manifest divine perfection. Unfortunately, most Christians and their churches deny this attribute of divine perfection in the redemptive creation. They claim that God's "appointed time of the end" has been "delayed." Critics claim it has proved "false." But who should we believe—God and his divinely inspired Word or uninspired Christians?

What Scripture Says:

Seven hundred years before Christ, the God of the Bible inspired the ancient prophet Habakkuk to write: "For the revelation awaits an appointed time; it speaks of the end and will not prove false. Though it linger, wait for it; it will certainly come and will not delay" (Hab. 2:3). One century later, God gave another Hebrew prophet, Daniel, the two most spectacular and explicit time prophecies ever given to humankind. Like bookends, these two prophetic time periods pinpointed and bracketed the exact time in human history for the coming of the Messiah to earth and Habakkuk's "appointed time . . . of the end." It all happened, right on time, certainly came, and came with a plan, purpose, timeframe, and mathematical precision. That's divine perfection!

Elaborations:

1) Why the world will never end.
2) How the perfect ending *for* the world came right on time.
3) Three different entities called "heaven and earth."
4) Divine perfection in God's end-time plan.
5) A 'new' paradigm of thought and faith.
6) Our greater responsibilities herein.
7) Why the future is bright and promising.
8) The basis for the next reformation of Christianity.

Sources:

The Perfect Ending for the World by John Noē
The Privileged Planet: How Our Place in the Cosmos Is Designed for Discovery by Guillermo Gonzalez and Jay W. Richards
Darwin's Black Box: The Bio-chemical Challenge of Evolution by Michael Behe
The Last Days According to Jesus by R.C. Sproul

(1)
Why the world will never end.

Ever since the first caveman stuck his head outside his hole, peered up into a night sky, and saw a comet streaking across the heavens, we humans have always felt and many of us have believed that this world is going to end someday, if not someday soon. As a consequence, many have tried to predict when this proverbial "end of the world" would occur. But it has not happened. And it will *never* happen. Nevertheless, and once again, "end-of-the-world" ranting and ravings are parading across our paths. Harold Camping, president of the Family Radio Network, is the latest "prophet" of this ultimate doom.

Not surprisingly, the media went "gaga" over Camping's failed prediction of May 21, 2011. Some reporters no doubt, were motivated by this opportunity to further mock and discredit Christianity. But Camping didn't give up. He recalculated and reset his date to October 21, 2011. The media pounced on this date, as well, but not as hard. It also failed. But (as of this writing) we still have the next date, December 21, 2012 date to contend with—based on calculations from the Mayan calendar. If you are unaware of this predicted and soon-coming apocalypse, rent the movie—appropriately titled, *2012*. Unfortunately, all humankind, throughout the ages, has paid and is paying a horrendous price for our multi-centuries-old trail of false-and-failed, end-of-the-world predictions.

Nonetheless, many today are wondering if "our time," could really be it? The correct, biblical, and historical answer, as we shall soon see, is, "No!" The reason is: the one thing all end-of-the-world doomsayers have in common and will always have in common is they are simply: *"failed prophets of a false premise."*

Contrary to what most of us have been told and taught, the Bible—the most published and read book in the world—proclaims that our world is "without end." This truth is contained within the biblical phrase "from the beginning of the world . . . . throughout all ages, world without end, Amen" (Eph. 3:9, 21 *KJV*, and many more). This verse is the source of the well-known doxology of the Church, the *Gloria Patri*:

> Glory be to the Father and to the Son and to the Holy Ghost
> As it was in the beginning is now and ever shall be.
> World without end. Amen

Many other biblical scriptures support this truth (see for instance: Eccl. 1:4; Psa. 78:69; 93:1 96:10; 104:5; 119:90). Fact is, the *only antidote* for *all* "end-of-the-world" ranting and ravings is the realization of these two historically defensible and scriptural revelations: 1) Our world is without end. 2) The perfect ending *for* the world came right on time.

Sources:

The Perfect Ending for the World by John Noē
The Day and the Hour: Christianity's Perennial Fascination with Predicting the End of the World by Francis X. Gumerlock
A History of the End of the World by Jonathan Kirsch
When Time Shall Be No More by Paul Boyer

(2)
How the perfect ending *for* the world came right on time.

The key word to note here is the small word in italics—*for*. It is not "of." Big difference! Not only did this end *for* the world come right on time. It's past and not future; its "last days" are behind us, and not present or ahead of us. And this end or goal *for* the world is consistently proclaimed throughout the Bible. In the New Testament, the Greek word often translated as "end" is *telos*. It means either a goal or a termination. In this case it was both (see Matt. 24:14).

The one thing all end-of-the-world doomsayers have in common and will always have in common is they are simply: *"failed prophets of a false premise."*

Outstandingly, this end came right on time. It occurred *within* Jesus' "this generation" (a forty-year period) exactly *as* and *when* He specified (Matt. 24:3, 34; Luke 21:32; Mark 13:30), and exactly *as* and *when* every New Testament writer and the early Church expected as they were guided into all truth and told what was yet to come (John 16:13). No gaps, no delays, no interruption of time frames, and no strained explanations are needed. All was fulfilled precisely, sequentially, and chronologically within human history and as prophesied centuries in advance. It wasn't, however, the end of the material cosmos. It was the end of the Jewish covenantal world and its age (see 1 Cor. 7:29, 31; Heb. 8:13; 9:8-10; 1 Pet. 4:7, 17, and many more).

Bible scholars Drs. William W. Klein, Craig L. Blomberg, and Robert L. Hubbard, Jr. in their hermeneutical textbook titled, *Introduction to Biblical Interpretation* recognize that . . .

> The historically defensible interpretation has greatest authority. That is, interpreters can have maximum confidence in their understanding of a text when they base that understanding on historically defensible arguments . . . . We should seek the most likely *time* for the fulfillment of a prophecy in history.[1]

This end's precise past-fulfillment is both well-grounded scripturally and deeply rooted in documented history. Truly, this is *The Perfect Ending for the World* and great good news—socially, culturally, politically, environmentally, and theologically. It's also the ultimate apologetic (defense) for the existence of God, the climax of the rest of the greatest story ever foretold, and the basis for the next reformation of Christianity.

Truly, truly, this great good news for the world is the *only antidote* to the long, sad, and tragic tradition of endsaying (saying the "end of the world" is near). All other explanations simply fall far short and are bad news.

Sources:

The Perfect Ending for the World by John Noē
Introduction to Biblical Interpretation by Klein, Blomberg, and Hubbard, Jr.
Last Days Madness by Gary DeMar
The Last Days According to Jesus by R.C. Sproul

---

[1] William W. Klein, Craig L. Blomberg, and Robert L. Hubbard, Jr., *Introduction to Biblical Interpretation* (Dallas, TX.: Word Publishing, 1993), 149, 310.

(3)
Three different entities called "heaven and earth."

"But doesn't the Bible say that God is going to destroy heaven and earth and create a new heaven and earth someday?" The answer is: yes, it does. But something most people, including Bible scholars, *do not know* is—*three different entities* in the Bible are called "heaven and earth." One "heaven and earth" would never pass away. Another had already passed away. A third would soon pass away and be made new. If this sounds like a riddle, perhaps, it is. It is also a biblical truth and historical fact. Sadly, much confusion prevails.

"God has *not* created the new heaven and new earth yet," a pastor-friend of mine insisted. With a wave of his hand out the window, he leaned back in his chair and sighed, "I believe the Bible says that there will be an end to all this someday." But will there so be?

The biblical and historical resolution to the riddle is this. The "heaven and earth" that would never pass away is *the physical creation* (Gen 1:1). The one that had already passed away was *Babylon in the 6th century B.C.* (Isa. 13: 1, 13; Hag. 2:6-7). The third one that would soon pass away and be made new was *Old Covenant biblical Judaism* (Deut. 32:1; Isa. 1:2-3; 51:13-16; Heb. 12:26-27).

Thus, the Bible's "new heaven and new earth" is not a re-creation of the physical universe. It's the complete arrival of the new covenantal order on Planet Earth. And its Holy City, the New Jerusalem, is the ultimate reality, the ultimate joy, and beloved community for God's overcoming people here on this earth! I suggest you read about it, anew, in Revelation 21 and 22.

Sources:

The Perfect Ending for the World by John Noē
The Works of Josephus translated by William Whiston
Josephus the Essential Writings by Paul L. Maier

(4)
Divine perfection in God's end-time plan.

"Surely the Sovereign LORD does nothing without revealing his plan to his servants the prophets" (Amos 3:7). And so God has perfectly revealed his end-time plan, purpose, and timeframe through his prophets. We of biblical faith could solve many of our disagreements by reconsidering the time-integrity of the major end-time prophecies and by becoming better acquainted with the nature and historical accuracy of their fulfillment.

In the 6th century B.C., God supernaturally gave the Old Testament prophet, Daniel, the two most spectacular and explicit time prophecies ever given to humankind. They are "Daniel's 70 weeks (of years)" and the "time of the end." You'll find them in Daniel 9:24-27 and 12:4-12, respectively. Like bookends, these two prophetic time periods bracketed the exact time in human history for this coming of the Messiah and Habakkuk's "appointed time . . . of the end." They foretold the climactic events that would signal the consummation—i.e., the end or goal (Greek word, *telos*) of God's redemptive plan for humankind.

In retrospect, then, the prophecy of Daniel's 70 weeks (490 years):

- *Commenced* in 457 B.C. with the decree of Artaxerxes.
- Was *determined* in A.D. 30 at the cross.
- Was *confirmed* by the New Covenant for 3½ years before and 3½ years after the cross.
- *Concluded* in A.D. 34 when the Gospel had been preached to the Jews and was now freed to go to the Gentiles.

The entire prophecy transpired in a mathematically precise, uninterrupted 490-year period. No valid rationale exists for interrupting the time segments, splitting apart the years, inserting gaps, elongating weeks, or postponing, delaying, minimizing or tampering with the fixed time period in any manner. Thus, the front bookend of the end-time, age-changing transition period—Daniel's 70th week—certainly came and was perfectly fulfilled. Perfectly! It's a mainstay of messianic authentication, a mathematical demonstration for the divine inspiration of the Bible, and an unanswerable argument for critics of the Christian faith. This is why the Apostle Paul could and did write that Jesus came and died "at just the right time" (Rom. 5:6).

Likewise, <u>Daniel's 1290-1335-days, time-of-the-end prophecy:</u>

- *Commenced* in July of A.D. 66 with the cessation of the twice-daily Temple sacrifices for Caesar and the Roman people.
- 1,290 days later, early in the year of A.D. 70, a *major abomination* took place in the Temple that all Jerusalem could see.
- 45 days later (1335 days following the previously cited Temple cessation of sacrifices), the abomination that causes desolation was *set up*—the Roman general, Titus, "set up" three encampments within three miles of the walls on the hills surrounding and overlooking Jerusalem.
- In April of A.D. 70, the Roman army began the fourth and final siege of the Jewish-Roman War of A.D. 66-70. In September, it was *over*. The city, the Temple, and the whole of biblical Judaism was *utterly destroyed* and left *desolate*.

Thus was also fulfilled Jesus' most dramatic end-time prophecy: "Look, your house is left to you desolate" (Matt. 23:38). "I tell you the truth, all this will come upon this generation" (Matt. 23:36; 24:34). And it all did.

Seriously, doesn't a straightforward approach to Daniel's prophecies and the preciseness of their literal, exact, chronological, and sequential fulfillment make more sense than the popular view that interrupts the time context? By the straightforward method, Daniel's prophecies were fulfilled long ago. Only by tampering with the text can we force a postponement and arrive at a yet-future fulfillment.

Most Christian endsayers, however, insist that the prophetic time clock stopped ticking when the Jews rejected the Messiah and crucified Him on the cross. So they interrupt Daniel's 70 weeks and insert a time gap of indeterminable length between the 69th and the 70th week. Next, they lift the 70th week out of its 1st-century, time-period context, stretch it like a rubber band over 19 centuries and counting, and plop it down somewhere out in the future. This seven-year period, which was designated by the text as the time the Messiah would confirm a covenant with the Jews, is now recast into being a future 7-year period of tribulation upon the Jews, who are then ruled by the Antichrist. In this bizarre scheme, the Antichrist rises from one of the nations of a so-called revived Roman Empire and confirms a supposed covenant with the geopolitical and secular nation of Israel.

The biblical fact is, no scriptural warrant or valid precedent exists for such abusive treatment or manipulative handling of God's Word. No imposition of gaps, interruptions, or delays can be scripturally or historically justified. This type of tampering with Scripture has crippled the Church and resulted in erroneous and disastrous date-setting. Ironically, the futurist-literalist endsayers profess a good and valid phrase: "when the normal sense makes sense, seek no other sense." It's unfortunate that those who subscribe to this bit of good sense are doctrinally and/or emotionally committed to violating it here. But times are changing. A new paradigm and reformation is underway.

Sources:

The Perfect Ending for the World by John Noē
Biblical Hermeneutics by Milton S. Terry
The Days of Vengeance by David Chilton
The Parousia by J. Stuart Russell

(5)
A new paradigm of thought and faith.

The recovery of a world that is "without end, Amen" is an idea whose time has come. Its power to influence the human psyche and thus the future course of history cannot be overestimated. In this author's opinion, the unleashing of this truth is destined to change the cultural and theological landscape. Entire schemes of religious and non-religious teaching focusing on a future end of the world have run their course; their prophecies have not come true. Instead of striving to hang on till the end, we can have a strong reason to undertake dynamic roles in the present, both individually and corporately, for a better future and for the benefit of current and coming generations.

Pioneering a new idea, however, is rarely a popular work, at least at first. Historically, the "powers that be" usually reacted angrily whenever confronted with an upsetting truth. Voltaire, the 18th-century French philosopher, hit it on the head when he surmised, "Our wretched species is so made that those who walk on the well-trodden path always throw stones at those who are showing a new road."

Our road is really not new, but so old and so neglected that it seems new. Thus, it will likely suffer the usual reactions of anger and disbelief. Admittedly, the idea of a world without end is a threat to the status quo, which is dominated by a traditional termination futurism, be it Roman Catholics or Protestants. They view "evil" as simply too much for God to overturn and transform. Therefore, God "must" destroy the planet before He makes it "anew." But after a reformational idea bursts onto the public scene and awareness spreads, a paradigm shift begins to take place as people at the grassroots level begin to realize how much the value of the new outweighs the detriments of the old.

But times are changing.
A new paradigm and reformation is underway.

Our paradigm answers our most basic question: what is real? If one's paradigm is the correct way of seeing the world, then one's judgments, decisions, and actions will be correlated and productive. If it's distorted or incorrect, they will be skewed. Our view of the world and the future is a paradigm. As we've seen, millions have been programmed into believing in an end-of-the-world paradigm. But this new, open-ended paradigm will force us to reexamine and rethink other end-time assumptions, prophecies, and beliefs, and our role in an unending world. If, indeed, this world is a world without end, and eternally established by a Creator God, isn't our role in taking care of it, and of each other, even more significant? Doesn't this provide more reason, motivation, and responsibility to pass it along to future generations in a better condition than we found it?

Sources:

The Perfect Ending for the World by John Noē

(6)
Our greater responsibilities herein.

Ideas and beliefs have consequences. And 'end-of-the-world' predictions and tirades are pervasive. They have infected the whole world. Even when viewed as nonsense, the cumulative effects of this incessant pounding and their urgent warnings still take a toll. Few are immune. And incredibly, millions keep falling for it. So check this highlighting recap out:

- ✓ Socially, it leaves its mark on the human psyche and on our dreams and goals— especially on those of our youth.
- ✓ Culturally, it diminishes our willingness to make commitments and get involved in social injustice and human needs issues, or to invest in long-term efforts to transform institutional structures. After all, if the future is fixed and terminal, why bother? So many who otherwise would be diligent stewards and productive workers tend to sink into helplessness, piety, and/or isolation.
- ✓ Politically, many fear the personal views of end-time Bible prophecy might influence the foreign policy decisions of the President of the United States and other world leaders— especially concerning the Middle East.
- ✓ Environmentally, it's a major reason why environmentalists face an uphill struggle—again, if there is no future for the future, why bother "polishing-brass-on-a-sinking-ship?"
- ✓ Theologically, wolf-cries of nearness and missed times and dates have been an embarrassment and discredited the Bible and the whole Church, making it appear like a joke in the eyes of the world. Therefore, many reason, why take Christianity seriously about anything?

The alternative and positive worldview of a world that never ends could blast many out of their complacency and motivate us to make a more viable and significant difference in our world for the benefit of present and future generations. Why so?

- ✓ Socially, because one's view of the future determines one's philosophy of life.

✓ Culturally, because the proliferation of end-of-the-world tirades and dates in American life is a significant reason why the optimism and activism of the 19th and early 20th century has changed to pessimism and withdrawal today.
✓ Politically, because world leaders need to know their efforts for world peace are not in vain but attainable, and have solid reasons to support that optimism.
✓ Environmentally, because a world that never ends demands we earthlings take better care of it than a world that's about to end, which is what we keep hearing from so many different sources, nowadays.
✓ Theologically, because the Church's long string of end-saying, fatalistic pundits is in dramatic contrast to and flies directly in the face of the optimistic beliefs of our forefathers in the faith who came to this country and founded its great institutions under Judeo-Christians principles. Sad to say, many Christians today would rather contemplate "the End" than pitch in with the job at hand.

Not surprisingly, this dramatic change of paradigms in thought and belief herein being proposed will necessitate that we moderns become more responsible for passing our world onto future generations in better condition than we found it—socially, culturally, politically, environmentally, and theologically.

The . . . worldview of a world that never ends could blast many out of their complacency . . . .

In conclusion, endsaying (crying out "the end is near") must be termed for what it is—not just a deceptive con game but an age-old crime against humanity. It must be refuted, reformed, and replaced with solid substance, positive hope, and confidence in the future. This is exactly what readers of this author's book will find throughout its pages.

Sources:

The Perfect Ending for the World by John Noē

(7)
Why the future is bright and promising.

Today, as we stand poised just inside the doorstep of a new millennium, I believe we are also on the threshold of a new reformation and an even greater awakening than has occurred in the past. The words of the 16th-century Reformers couldn't ring more true or louder: (*semper reformanda*) "The Church is reformed and always reforming."

Fact is, we moderns have not reached the point where reform is no longer needed. And in this author's opinion, the divisive, defeatist, pessimistic, strained theories, and side-stepping interpretative devices of end-time Bible prophecy (eschatology) encompass the next major area ripe for reform. These falsehoods have distracted us from our high calling—both an earthly and heavenly calling much higher and greater than we've been led to believe. When realized, this reformation will change the way the Christian life is lived out. No longer will dolefully sitting round waiting for Jesus to come back be acceptable. No longer will watching the culture deteriorate into godlessness be permissible. No longer will 6 to 7 out of every 10 children raised in the faith and leaving the faith by age 23 be tolerable.[2] With this next reformation and reawakening, all this will change.

But reformation can be messy. It always has resisters and attackers. This next reformation will be no exception. Some will keep on preaching and teaching some things not found in the Bible simply because they are committed to it, have built their ministries upon it, and would be embarrassed or find it awkward or career-threatening to "change horses in the middle of the stream." Others will come against me and fellow co-reformers. But for many of you, who seek after truth and long for a more firm foundation upon which a genuine biblical faith can be better built, it will be a godsend and a breath of fresh air. This is the further reformed faith that must be re-presented in the Church and taken to the world.

As has been true of other reformations, this one will require a new way of thinking, new perspectives, and a paradigm shift away from some of the traditional and defective positions currently holding sway. As such, we must follow the scriptural admonition to "Test everything.

---

[2] Statistic from: Fields, "The Myth of the Perfect Parent," *Christianity Today*, January 2010, 24. See quote in Introduction p-16.

Hold on to the good," (1 Thess. 5:21). Our failure to do this in the past has put us in our current eschatological dilemma of so many failed prophecies and conflicting positions. This is the sad but present-day status of our faith at which much of the world scoffs. But how long can we continue stretching out the biblical "last days" and perpetuating imminency of Jesus' so-called "return" before biblical faith completely loses its meaning and value?

The time for further reformation has come. Its potential is huge. A more responsible apocalypticism is within our grasp. In this regard, I am very appreciative and much indebted to Dr. James Earl Massey, Former Sr. Editor of *Christianity Today* magazine and Dean Emeritus of the School of Theology, Anderson University, for his endorsement of my original work and first edition of the book from which most of this material comes. As he foresees and wrote, "Noē's book just could be the spark that ignites the next reformation of Christianity." Then where do we go from here?

First, we must be willing and have the courage to admit that we were wrong and have misunderstood some very important, foundational aspects of Scripture and our faith. This is a necessary prerequisite. For far too long, far too many have been far too vocal and in far too great a frenzy to get out of here (the Rapture) and get the world destroyed. This fear-based, traditional, "orthodox" doctrine has been a fool's paradise. It is an outright misunderstanding, misconception and misrepresentation of God's redemptive plan of the ages. Please be assured, we have nothing to fear from the biblical end that was and last days that were—only positive things to gain, and much to celebrate because of them. Therefore, endsaying with its long record of negative impact upon the Church and the world must be relegated to the ash heap of history.

The time for further reformation has come. Its potential is huge

Next, we must fan the spark of reformation into a flame, and the flame into a raging fire of purification. Our current eschatological system needs a major overhaul. Minor tweaking of the four major, competing, confusing, and conflicting positions will not fix the problem. Like Copernicus' model of planetary motion, which upset the current thinking of his day, we, too, will have to unlearn more things in order to relearn them correctly. Therefore, I propose the following four-step process for this next reformation.

Sources:

The Perfect Ending for the World by John Noē

(8)
The basis for the next reformation of Christianity.

Four Steps to Bible Prophecy Reform

Step #1. Acknowledge that the physical world is never going to end. By "world" I mean planet Earth, the cosmos, and humanity. The *terra firma* and all else has been eternally established, and is sustained by our Creator God. He has charged us with the responsibility of keeping it, protecting it, and passing it along to future generations in better condition (spiritually, physically, socially, culturally, politically, environmentally, and theologically) than we found it.

Step #2. Honor the plain, face-value meaning of all prophetic time statements, timeframes, and imminency expectations—no gaps, no gimmicks, no delays, no twisted meanings, no deceptions. Our fundamental error has been the failure to understand the historical context of the 1st century for the fulfillment of all end-time biblical prophecies. Therefore, we have lifted "the perfect ending for the world" out of its divinely appointed timeframe and exchanged our divinely determined heritage for a hodge-podge of flawed human hopes.

Step #3. "Contend for the faith that was once for all delivered to the saints" (Jude 3). "Once for all" here means exactly the same as it means in Romans 6:10 when applied to Jesus' death; in Hebrews 9:12 with Jesus entering the Most Holy Place to pour out his blood; in Hebrews 9:26 with Jesus' appearance and sacrifice of Himself; in Hebrews 10:10 with us being made holy by the sacrifice of his body; and in 1 Peter 3:18 with Christ dying for our sins.

Hence, the past tense use of this phrase can only mean one thing. Biblical faith is a finished faith; the Messiah's two great works, that of the kingdom and salvation, are complete. This is the firm foundation that must be restored, better understood, and more fully realized. We need to take an honest look at history and see how all promised eschatological events happened and all redemptive realities were completely established and made everlastingly available by the time Jerusalem was destroyed and the Jewish age ended circa A.D. 70 - 73. Nothing more remains to be done. But plenty remains to be accomplished because of this perfect fulfillment.

Step #4. Unify the current competing, conflicting, confusing and divisive system of four major eschatological views into one view via a "solution of synthesis." The four major views of end-time prophecy are: preterist, premillennial, amillennial, and postmillennial. Each contains strengths and weaknesses. Thus, each needs to and must participate in this reform. A "solution of synthesis" would keep the strengths and dump the weaknesses of each view and unify the strengths into one meaningful, coherent, and consistent view that is more Christ-honoring, Scripture-authenticating, and faith-validating than any one view in and of itself. (See Exposé #13.)

In conclusion, the time is ripe and the climate prime to finally recognize and face up to the fact that Christianity in the modern world is not as strong as it could and should be. This must and can be changed. It starts with getting our faith right. *On with the Prophecy Reformation!*

Sources:

The Perfect Ending for the World by John Noē
Dictionary of Biblical Prophecy and End Times by Hays, Duvall, and Pate
Encyclopedia of Biblical Prophecy by J. Barton Payne

Exposé #2

The Kingdom of God

Next to the Person of Christ, the kingdom of God is the most important and all-encompassing concept of Scripture. So much is contained within it. Fact is, get the kingdom of God straight and many other, vital, and interrelated realities of the Christian faith readily fall into place. Miss it, even slightly, and you're liable to be way off on these many other aspects. That is how pivotal the kingdom of God is.

Theological Problem:

The kingdom of God was the central teaching of our Lord Jesus Christ, at the heart of his earthly ministry, and central to his worldview and that of his first followers—the New Testament writers and the early Church. It was the very essence of 1st-century Christianity. But today, the kingdom is no longer the central teaching of most of his Church, at the heart of its ministry, nor its worldview or very essence. RED FLAG! *What has happened? What has changed?*

Once again, Dr. Billy Graham aptly demonstrates this omission deficiency in his syndicated newspaper column addressing the question of why we Christians "Celebrate Christ's birth:"

> Yes, Christmas should be a time of celebration—the celebration of the coming of God's son into the world for our salvation. . . . He came as a baby, but he grew up to become God's appointed sacrifice for our sins

by his death on the cross. And because he rose from the dead we have hope now and for eternity.[1]

Of course, what Dr. Graham writes is true. But notice that he makes no mention of the kingdom. The kingdom has been edited out. Therefore, his statement is only partially true. And as Christian Overman writes, "The most effective lies are those which come as close to the truth as possible. That's no lie."[2]

The most blatant example of Dr. Graham's kingdom-deficient worldview and theological bias, however, comes from his column in today's paper (as I write). I quote his sentence exactly and fully:

> In his first sermon, Jesus declared, "The time has come. . . . Repent and believe the good news!" (Mark 1:15).[3]

Here the kingdom of God is literally edited out by a three-dot ellipsis. Mark 1:15 actually reads in the NIV, "'The time has come,' he said. 'The kingdom of God is near. Repent and believe the good news!'"

What Scripture Says:

At the very start of his earthly ministry, "Jesus went into Galilee proclaiming the good news of God. 'The time is fulfilled [has come] . . . the kingdom of God is at hand . . . .'" (Mark 1:14-15 KJV [NIV]). What "time" (*kairos* meaning "set," "proper time," or "season") was Jesus talking about that He claimed was "fulfilled?" Many Bible scholars maintain that "it is impossible to know the time." Consequently, they wrestle with the tension of the kingdom being both present and future, and insist that the "time of apocalyptic consummation remains in the future." Or does it?

---

[1] Billy Graham, "My Answer," *The Indianapolis Star* (Indianapolis, IN), 3 December 2011, E-4.
[2] Christian Overman, *Assumptions That Affect Our Lives* (Bellevue, WA.: Ablaze Publishing Co., 1986, 1996, 2006), 95.
[3] Billy Graham, "My Answer," *The Indianapolis Star* (Indianapolis, IN), 26 December 2011, E-4

Elaborations:

1) When would the everlasting kingdom come?
2) How we lost Jesus' kingdom—so what?
3) False kingdom views in the Church today.
4) Not postponed.
5) Not 'already / not yet.'
6) Not just initiated or inaugurated.
7) How long would Jesus' kingdom last?
8) What truly is the kingdom?

Sources:

A Once-Mighty Faith (future book – est. 2013) by John Noē
The Divine Conspiracy by Dallas Willard
The Great Omission by Dallas Willard
The Presence of the Future by George Eldon Ladd
Assumptions That Affect Our Lives by Christian Overman

(1)
When would the everlasting kingdom come?

Six centuries before Christ and in two parallel dream-visions (Daniel 2 and 7), God set the time parameter *within human history* for the establishment of the eschatological and everlasting form of the kingdom of God on this earth. In Daniel 2 for instance, Daniel both declared and interpreted the king's dream of a *statue* with *four sections* (head of gold, chest and arms of silver, belly and thighs of bronze, and legs and feet of iron and clay). He said these symbolize four earthly and succeeding kingdoms or world empires. They were: Babylon, Medo-Persia, Greece, and Roman. Daniel next isolated the time parameter thusly:

> *"In the days (time) of those kings*, the God of heaven will set up a kingdom that will never be destroyed, nor will it be left to another people. It will crush all those kingdoms and bring them to an end, but it will itself endure forever" (Dan. 2:44, *italics mine*).

"It is impossible to know the time."

Problem is, most commentators and Christians cannot accept the natural, plain, and straightforward meaning of Daniel's inspired prophetic words. Why not? Because "the days of those kings" *ended in A.D. 476!* And there is no other, future-coming kingdom prophesied in Scripture.

Source:

A Once-Mighty Faith (future book – est. 2013) by John Noē

(2)
How we lost Jesus' kingdom—so what?

Our forefathers in the faith (including most of America's founding fathers) came to this country not just to escape religious persecution, but under a divine mandate to expand the kingdom of God. The kingdom was absolutely central to their worldview. Propelled by this kingdom worldview, they fought the Revolutionary War with the motto "No king but King Jesus!" They also founded the great institutions of our country—the government, the schools, the universities—under Judeo-Christian principles—and Christianity was the moral influencer in our society. But within the past 50 to 75 years or so we modern-day Christians here in America have given away almost everything our forefathers founded, and without a fight. *What has happened? What has changed?*

The answer is, we in the Church changed our worldview—from the optimistic, kingdom-of-God worldview of the world getting "better and better" to one of it getting "worse and worse." In other words, we lost our kingdom orientation. And when we started losing the kingdom and our positive worldview, we also started losing the culture and our children in droves. The statistical correlation is significant.

Sources:

A Once-Mighty Faith (future book – est. 2013) by John Noē
What a Way to Live! by Tony Evans
Abandonment Theology / America A Call to Greatness by John
Chalfant
The Transformation of American Religion by Alan Wolfe
When Nations Die by Jim Nelson Black
The Myth of a Christian Nation by Gregory A. Boyd
To Change the World by James Davison Hunter

(3)
False kingdom views in the Church today.

Today the kingdom of God seems caught-up in eschatological mid-air. The majority of evangelicals have been led to believe God has withdrawn his kingdom, and someday it will be established and *visibly* set up in a future Jewish millennial era. Others believe it is here but only partially "in some sense" but question in what sense. Some say it is here but major elements have ceased to function, having been withdrawn by God. Therefore, they do little, if anything, with Jesus' kingdom. On the other hand, Jesus' first followers were accused of having "turned the world upside down" (Acts 17:6; 20:25, 27) with his kingdom. Most, today, however, only give the kingdom of God a small place in their lives and have totally neglected Jesus' admonition to "But seek, ye first the kingdom of God and his righteousness" (Matt. 6:33).

How many coming kingdoms of God (or forms) were prophesied by Daniel and proclaimed by Jesus? The correct answer is, "One." But . . .

Dispensational premillennialists' answer is "four" – 1) Jesus' 1st-century kingdom, 2) the withdrawn or present mystery kingdom, 3) the millennial kingdom, 4) the eternal kingdom.

Amillennialists' answer is "two" – 1) the present kingdom Jesus brought, which is a foretaste of . . . 2) the eternal-state kingdom in fullness.

Postmillennialists' answer is "two or three" – 1) the present kingdom Jesus brought, 2) a future golden age, 3) the eternal-state kingdom.

Cessationist Preterists' answer is "two" – 1) the pre-A.D. 70 version of the kingdom brought by Jesus, 2) the post-A.D.-70, spiritual version with major elements removed (i.e., the charismatic gifts, ministries of the Holy Spirit, and angels).

Whom should we believe—these conflicting Church views or Daniel and Jesus?

Sadly, the kingdom of God remains one of the most misunderstood, misconstrued, confused, abstracted, and contested realities in Christianity. Most churches today rarely mention the kingdom, let alone teach and obey its established and present-day elements. For centuries, even theologians have been divided over both its timing and nature. All this confusion and disagreement has led to a number of bizarre behaviors and avoidance practices.

Sources:

A Once-Mighty Faith (future book – est. 2013) by John Noē
Dictionary of Biblical Prophecy and End Times by Hays, Duvall, and Pate

(4)
Not postponed.

According to the most popular view, the kingdom of God is not here anymore. It was withdrawn and postponed by God when the Jews rejected Jesus and the type of kingdom He was offering and crucified Him. Some acquiesce that it is here but only in "mystery" form. But someday (soon) Jesus will return and set up or establish his kingdom in Jerusalem for a thousand years.

Problem is, if this position is correct, somebody, like the Apostle John or the Holy Spirit, forgot to clue either the Apostle Paul or Peter in that the kingdom had been postponed. For some thirty-five years after this supposed postponement event they both were still preaching and teaching the kingdom as a then-present and relevant reality (see Acts 8:12; 14:22; 19:8; 20:25; 28:23, 31; 1 Cor. 4:20; and more). And so was Jesus after this resurrection (see Acts 1:3; also Rev. 1:6, 9; 5:10). Besides, I pondered, how are Christians today supposed to follow Jesus' admonition to "But seek first his kingdom and his righteousness" (Matt. 6:33), if this kingdom is in a postponed status and not even here anymore? This most-popular explanation does not make Bible sense!

Source:

A Once-Mighty Faith (future book – est. 2013) by John Noē

(5)
Not 'already / not yet.'

Amillennialists contend that Jesus' kingdom of God is only here in some sense, i.e., it's in an eschatological tension between the "already" and the "not yet" regarding its fulfillment and someday future establishment (consummation). Here's how they say this in their own words:

- "the kingdom of God is now hidden . . . . to all except those who have faith in Christ . . . . but some day it shall be totally revealed . . . . when the final phase of the kingdom is ushered in by the Second Coming of Jesus Christ." [4]
- We await the kingdom's "final establishment . . . at the time of Christ's Second Coming,"[5] as well as the "final judgment" and "final stage"[6] "at the end of history"[7] "at the end of this present age . . . . at the time of Christ's Second Coming."[8]

---

[4] Anthony A. Hoekema, *The Bible and the Future*, (Grand Rapids, MI.: Eerdmans, 1979, 1991), 52.
[5] Ibid., *ix*.
[6] Ibid., 1.
[7] Ibid., 253.
[8] Ibid., 255.

- Today we are "living between the times" of the "'already of the coming of the kingdom" and "the 'not yet' of its consummation." [9]
- This interim time is the time of the "semirealized kingdom." [10]
- "The Bible favors the idea that the present dispensation of the kingdom of God will be followed *immediately* by the kingdom of God in its consummate and eternal form." [11]
- "God's great plan . . . . includes not only the salvation of individuals and the redemption of the church but also the reestablishment of God's kingdom of righteousness, peace, and justice in a new heaven and a new earth." [12]
- "whose Kingdom rule is already established and not yet fulfilled [13] . . . . the coming of Jesus . . . [was] his inauguration of the Kingdom of God [14] . . . . We are constantly faced with the 'not yet' existence of the Kingdom of God." [15]

The huge problem here is, Scripture never uses this type of qualifying terminology, and for good reason.

Sources:

A Once-Mighty Faith (future book – est. 2013) by John Noē
The Bible and the Future by Anthony A. Hoekema

---

[9] Guenther Hass, "The Significance of Eschatology for Christian Ethics," in David W. Baker, ed., *Looking into the Future: Evangelical Studies in Eschatology* (Grand Rapids, MI.: Baker Academic, 2001), 326.
[10] Vern S. Poythress, *Understanding Dispensationalists*, (Phillipsburg, NJ.: P& R Publishing, 1987, 1994), 36.
[11] J. Marcellus Kik, *An Eschatology of Victory* (Phillipsburg, NJ.: Presbyterian and Reformed Publishing Co., 1971), 3, in a quotation from D.H. Kromminga, *Millennium in the Church*, 257, 258.
[12] Paul G. Hiebert, in Forward to, Arthur F. Glasser, *Announcing the Kingdom* (Grand Rapids, MI.: Baker Academic, 2003), 8.
[13] Ibid., 123.
[14] Ibid., 141.
[15] Ibid., 343.

"The Significance of Eschatology for Christian Ethics" by Guenther Hass, in David W. Baker, ed., *Looking into the Future: Evangelical Studies in Eschatology*
Understanding Dispensationalists by Vern S. Poythress,
An Eschatology of Victory by J. Marcellus Kik,
Announcing the Kingdom by Arthur F. Glasser

(6)
Not just initiated or inaugurated.

Amillennialists further try to explain that Jesus only initiated or inaugurated the kingdom during his earthly ministry. But someday He will return and finish the job—i.e., consummate it. The problem here is, what does the phrase "set up" in Daniel 2 really mean (see #1 above again) regarding the establishment of the everlasting form of the kingdom and when that would happen "in the days (time) of those kings?"

If we follow basic hermeneutical principles, it is not difficult to determine what the Hebrew word *quwm* (pronounced "koom" and translated as "set up" in Daniel 2:44) really means:

1) *Quwm* means to: "appoint, establish, make, raise up, stand, set (up)" (*Strong's Exhaustive Concordance of the Bible*). According to *Vine's An Expository Dictionary of Biblical Words*, its primary meaning is "to arise, stand up, come about . . . . It may denote any movement to an erect position." The only qualification *Vine* mentions is "when used with another verb, *qum* [sic] may suggest simply the beginning of an action." But *quwm* is not so used with another verb in Daniel 2:44.

2) Daniel uses this word nine times in his very next chapter (Dan. 3:1, 2, 3, 3, 5, 7, 12, 14, 18). This verb describes King Nebuchadnezzar's erection of a ninety-foot-high image of gold on the plain of Dura—i.e., he "set up" this image.

3) Nebuchadnezzar did not just begin to or only *partially* "set up" this ninety-foot-high image. Nor did he merely *announce* that he

was going to do it, or only *initiate* it, or only *inaugurate* it. He finished the job. He established the image. He completed and fulfilled his plan and project. Nor did he come back later and remove an arm and a leg, or any other parts. It stood established, completed, and erect. This comparative usage and illustration is in such close proximity, contextually, that it must not be ignored or diminished.

Likewise, the *one*, "never [to] be destroyed," and to "endure forever" kingdom in Daniel 2:44 was "set up"—i.e., established, completed, fulfilled, and consummated—"in the days of those kings." I suggest that this literal meaning and realization is absolutely demanded by the text. And, its eschatological and worldview implications are profound!

Further validating this above understanding is the popular dispensational-premillennial, eschatological view. Its proponents recognize this same literal meaning for the Hebrew word translated as "set up." But then they must conceive the false ideas of "a revival of the Roman Empire" and a rebuilt temple to accommodate their yet-future fulfillment of Daniel's prophecy.[16]

Moreover, and please make special note of this fact, the reason Scripture does not use "already/not-yet" partial language is because this kingdom arrived in human history fully established in the form of human flesh (see Luke 17:20 – "in your midst" is best translation; and Col. 2:9). From there it has only increased (Isa. 9:6-7).

Sources:

A Once-Mighty Faith (future book – est. 2013) by John Noē
Strong's Exhaustive Concordance of the Bible
Vine's An Expository Dictionary of Biblical Words

---

[16] John F. Walvoord, *Major Bible Prophecies* (Grand Rapids, MI.: Zondervan, 1991), 162-164.

(7)
How long would Jesus' kingdom last?

No longer do scholars as well as plain and ordinary Christians need to be puzzled about what Jesus meant when he spoke of the kingdom. Nor must we continue submitting to the ambiguity that "no one knows when the kingdom will come in the full, future sense." When Jesus came into Galilee proclaiming the good news of God that "the time is fulfilled [has come] . . . the kingdom of God is at hand " (Mark 1:15 KJV [NIV]), the "time" He was referring to that He claimed was "fulfilled" was the long-promised and intensely awaited kingdom spoken of by Daniel in Daniel 2:44 and 7:14, 18, 22, 27.

It is a fact of history that Jesus lived and ministered "in the days of those kings"—and those days ended in A.D. 476. It is another fact of Scripture that Jesus ushered into human history the *one* and only, greatly awaited, "kingdom [that] will never end" (Luke 1:33; Heb.12:27-28; Matt. 28:18). This was precisely what the Messiah was to do—from his birth to his judgment. Once again, all this was to take place "in the days of those kings:"

> For to us a child *is born*
> to us a son is given,
> and the *government* will be on his
> shoulders.
> And he will be called
> Wonderful Counselor, Mighty God,
> Everlasting Father, Prince of Peace.
> Of the *increase of his government* and peace
> there will be *no end.*
> He will *reign* on David's throne
> and over his *kingdom,*
> *establishing* and *upholding* it
> with justice [judgment] and righteousness [justice]
> ***from that time on and forever.***
> The zeal of the Lord Almighty will accomplish this.

(Isaiah 9:6-7 – *italics-bold emphasis mine* [*KJV*])

Establishing the non-ending, ever-increasing, eschatological kingdom, "in the days of those kings" and "from *that* time on and forever" was a major part of the work Jesus did, precisely as prophesied. Literally, God actually kept his word—his "perfect" and "flawless" word (Psa. 18:30).

I submit that Daniel's two, parallel, and general time prophecies and his time-restrictive words in Daniel 2:44 must be *naturally, plainly,* and *literally* understood and *fully* honored—something the vast majority of Christian commentators, scholars, and lay people alike have not been willing or taught to do. But this straightforward understanding firmly grounds the establishment of the everlasting, ever-increasing, eschatological kingdom of God in human history over nineteen centuries ago.

No other kingdom, form of this kingdom, or ultimate different establishment or fulfillment beyond this *one* is prophesied in Scripture or yet-to-come. There is no scriptural warrant for conceiving of "a revival of the Roman Empire" to accommodate a yet-future establishment and fulfillment of Daniel's prophecy. Nor do we need to await an unscriptural "end of time" for kingdom's final establishment, as has been devised by both amillennialists and postmillennialists. These man-made ideas only cause deception and confusion. Why don't we just believe the Bible and stop trying to stretch prophecy like a rubber band way out into the future?

Interestingly, when Satan tempted Jesus (Matt. 4:1-11), he quoted Scripture out-of-context. We have taken the final establishment of the everlasting kingdom of God on earth out of context as well. The biblical and historical context for the establishment of the *one* and only everlasting and ever-increasing kingdom was clearly "in the days of those kings" which ended in A.D. 476.

No other kingdom, form of this kingdom, or ultimate different establishment or fulfillment beyond this *one* is prophesied in Scripture or yet-to-come.

In my opinion, this timely realization is one of "the secrets of the kingdom of God [that] has been given" (Luke 8:10). Sadly, it has been lost in the Church because it has been covered back up by our traditions, with which we "nullify the word of God" (Matt. 15:6; Mark 7:13). Lifting this fulfillment out of its divinely determined time frame in human history has been the most significant factor for disestablishing the kingdom of God and producing what Darrell L. Guder terms, "the reductionism of the gospel[17] . . . . whose result is a gospel that is too small"[18]—our next exposé topic.

Source:

A Once-Mighty Faith (future book – est. 2013) by John Noē
Kingdom Ethics by Glen H. Stassen and David P. Gushee
The Continuing Conversion of the Church by Darrell L. Guder

(8)
What truly is the kingdom?

One other problem contributing to the confusion that surrounds the kingdom of God is the absence of a scriptural definition. Fact is, neither Jesus nor any biblical writer ever defined the kingdom of God. As perplexing and ironic as this omission may seem, a definition by at least one of them would surely have alleviated much of our modern-day confusion. Nor did any one back then ask for a definition, as far as we know.

But another fact is Jesus' presentations of the kingdom departed radically from the Jewish expectations. In the 1st century many Jews (and Christians yet today) were and are still looking for their Messiah to bring a visible and political kingdom which would overthrow the Roman governmental authorities and elevate Israel to supremacy over all the nations (Acts 1:6). Problem is, Jesus never taught, promised, nor delivered that kind of a kingdom.

Theologian George Eldon Ladd is somewhat helpful in his book, *A Theology of the New Testament*, as he contrasts the kingdom from the all-to-common tendency of identifying it with the Church. He writes:

---

[17] Darrell L. Guder, *The Continuing Conversion of the Church* (Grand Rapids, MI.: Eerdmans, 2000), *xiii*, 71,
[18] Ibid., 102.

The Kingdom is primarily the dynamic reign or kingly rule of God, and derivatively, the sphere in which the rule is experienced. In biblical idiom, the Kingdom is not identified with its subjects. They are the people of God's rule who enter it, live under it, and are governed by it. The church is the community of the Kingdom but never the Kingdom itself. Jesus' disciples belong to the Kingdom as the Kingdom belongs to them; but they are not the Kingdom. The Kingdom is the rule of God; the church is a society of women and men.[19]

Christian Overman deals with the kingdom in its "broadest sense." Hence, he defines it thusly:

In the broadest sense of the word, God's kingdom is that domain over which He is King. Taken in this context, then the kingdom of God is as broad as creation is wide, for there is no realm which exists independently of God's sovereign rule and authority, either in heaven or on earth.

In support of his definition, Overman cites these two Psalms:

- "The Lord has established His throne in heaven, and His kingdom rules over all" (Psa. 103:19).
- "The earth is the Lord's and all it contains, the world, and those who dwell in it" (Psa. 24:1).

He does, however, recognize that "even though it all belongs to God, ever since the first temptation of man, the earth and all it contains have been contested ground. There is an enemy who lays claim to that which is God's. . . a rebel kingdom of his own inside the true King's territory."[20]

Throughout Church history, there have been a variety of attempts to define the kingdom, again because neither Jesus nor any biblical writer ever did. But here is my working definition of what is meant by the *kingdom of God*. First, it is not a political administration, a geographic territory, or an abstract notion. However, it is a rule, it does have a realm,

---

[19] George Eldon Ladd, *A Theology of the New Testament* (Grand Rapids, MI.: Eerdmans, 1974, 2000), 109.
[20] Overman, *Assumptions That Affect Our Lives*, 117-118

and it is a pragmatic and dynamic reality. Simply defined, the kingdom of God is:

The sphere of God's will, reign and rule.

It is located throughout heaven and the cosmos, and wherever on earth the manifestation of his sovereignty, holiness, power, and kingly authority is acknowledged and obeyed. That means it is realized both internally and externally, within and among, to draw human hearts to Him, to bless and discipline his people, and to defeat his enemies. It is to be entered, exercised, and advanced by every Christian who follows Jesus, and experienced in every aspect of society. However, it is not universally recognized, is contested, opposed, and persecuted, and is greatly under-realized.

The *kingdom of God* . . . is not a political administration, a geographic territory, or an abstract notion. However, it is a rule, it does have a realm, and it is a pragmatic and dynamic reality.

For more: listen to podcast for the "Kingdom Christianity" series on www.prophecyrefi.org.

Sources:

A Once-Mighty Faith (future book – est. 2013) by John Noē
A Theology of the New Testament by George Eldon Ladd

Exposé #3

The Gospel

A sk a committed, evangelical Christian what the gospel is and most will respond that it's the good news of: "the death, burial, and resurrection of Jesus."[1] He or she might also add that if you believe this gospel and in Him, then when you die you will go to heaven and not hell. Thus, the gospel is all about "our redemption in Jesus Christ."[2]

Theological Problem:

But this was not the gospel Jesus came proclaiming. Jesus did not come into Galilee preaching Jesus or that He was going to die so that when you die you could go to heaven. Nor was Jesus asking people the question Evangelism Explosion has made so popular for several decades—"If you were to die tonight, do you know where you would go—heaven or hell?" Fact is, the gospel Jesus preached had absolutely nothing to do with redemption and his dying and going to heaven so that when we die we can go to heaven—until approximately the three-year point in his 3 ½-year ministry.

---

[1] Michael Horton, "The Good God Who Came Down," *Christianity Today*, December 2011, 28.
[2] Ibid., 29.

What Scripture Says:

For the first three years Jesus' gospel was all about the kingdom of God on earth, in this life, and as a there-and-then present reality (Mark 1:14-15). And as we have seen, this gospel of the kingdom was also his central teaching, at the heart of his ministry, his worldview, and the very essence of New Testament Christianity. This gospel dealt with the ethical question 'How then should we live?' Today, this gospel of the kingdom is no longer the central teaching of most of his Church, at the heart of its ministry, its worldview, or its very essence. Red flag! What has happened? What has changed? Yes, we do have a problem here, Houston!

It was only at the approximate three-year point in his earthly ministry that Jesus began teaching about his upcoming death and what that would mean—"From that time on Jesus began to explain to his disciples that he must go to Jerusalem and suffer many things at the hands of the elders, chief priests and teachers of the law, and that he must be killed and on the third day be raised to life" (Matt. 16:21).

Elaborations:

1) Gospel reductionism.
2) Steadfast resistance.
3) Dysfunctional Christianity ripe for reform.
4) Redefining the gospel.

Sources:

Hell Yes / Hell No by John Noē
A Once-Mighty Faith (future book – est. 2013) by John Noē
The Divine Conspiracy by Dallas Willard
The Great Omission by Dallas Willard

(1)
Gospel reductionism.

For all practical purposes, Christian evangelicals today, basically and essentially, have abandoned Jesus' gospel of the kingdom (Mark 1:14-15). Instead, they major almost solely on this latter gospel of salvation. This reality has prompted some perceptive Christian writers to vocalize this methodological problem in how we moderns are presenting our faith to the world in these terms:

- Dallas Willard terms this kingdom deficiency, "the great omission" in his recent book by this title and the primary reason "why . . . today's church [is] so weak." [Instead, the Church is preaching the] "gospel of sin management"—in his classic, *The Divine Conspiracy.*[3]

- Darrell L. Guder calls it "reductionism of the gospel"—in his book, *The Continuing Conversion of the Church.*[4]

- Robert Lynn laments that "the gospel we proclaim has been shrunk"—in his article, "Far as the curse is found."[5]

- Scot McKnight worries that "we have settled for a little gospel, a miniaturized version that cannot address the robust problems of our world"—in his article, "The 8 Marks of a Robust Gospel."[6]

- Not surprisingly, therefore, in 2003 Christian researcher George Barna in a poll about who does or doesn't have a biblical worldview—had no kingdom in his definition of a biblical

---

[3] Willard, *The Divine Conspiracy*, 40-41.
[4] Guder, *The Continuing Conversion of the Church*, xiii.
[5] Robert Lynn, "Far as the curse is found" (*Breakpoint Worldview* magazine, October, 2006, 14.
[6] Scot McKnight, "The 8 Marks of a Robust Gospel" (*Christianity Today*, March 2008, 36.

worldview. In other words, Barna edited out or failed to include the central teaching and worldview of our Lord Jesus Christ.[7]

Question: why shouldn't this depreciation of the gospel be viewed in terms of the "other gospel" that Paul warned about in Galatians 1:8-9? Please keep in mind to be an "other gospel" it does not need to be totally different, only slightly.

Sources:

A Once-Mighty Faith (future book – est. 2013) by John Noē
The Great Omission by Dallas Willard
The Divine Conspiracy by Dallas Willard
The Continuing Conversion of the Church by Darrell L. Guder

(2)
Steadfast resistance.

In typical evangelical fashion, however, Brian Jones in his book, *Hell Is Real (But I Hate To Admit It)*, steadfastly maintains that his reductionistic, shrunken, and little gospel is *the* gospel by insisting that "Christianity is a religion meant to solve a sin problem. It is not a religion meant to solve all the problems of this world. . . . our ultimate mission is not to make this world a better place to live . . . . Our mission is to give every human being on earth the news that their relationship with God can be restored through Jesus' death on the cross."[8]

Why shouldn't this depreciation of the gospel be viewed in terms of the "other gospel" that Paul warned about in Galatians 1:8-9?

[7] Barna Research Online, "A Biblical Worldview Has a Radical Effect on a Person's Life" (www.barna.org/cgi-bin/PagePressRelease.asp., 1 December 2003), 1-2.
[8] Brian Jones, *Hell Is Real (But I Hate to Admit It)* (Colorado Springs, CO.: David C. Cook, 2011), 106.

But scripturally and factually, Jesus' presentation of the gospel was a both/and proposition and not an either/or. Later, and to his credit, Jones admits "it's never either/or in Scripture"[9] and asks a most pertinent question: "What business is Christianity in?"[10] My answer is: How about Jesus' nutshell admonition in Matthew 6:33 to put it most succinctly? "But seek first his kingdom and his righteousness . . . ." Let's please note—and according to David Neff, Editor in Chief of *Christianity Today* magazine—that the Greek word usually translated as "righteousness" in this verse is *dikaiosune* and can also and "easily mean *justice*. . . . Unfortunately, the translation *righteousness* has overtones of personal piety . . . . We need a stronger contrast between these works of piety and what constitutes the essence of the kingdom of God."[11]

Sources:

A Once-Mighty Faith (future book – est. 2013) by John Noē
Hell Is Real (But I Hate To Admit It by Brian Jones

(3)
Dysfunctional Christianity ripe for reform.

Perhaps, it's our modern-day versions of Christianity and each of us—who no longer feel the urgency to make evangelism their [our] top priority—who need re-challenged and stretched to re-think and change our approach to world missions and personal evangelism. Perhaps it is we who need to become fully consistent and compatible with Jesus' gospel as He presented it. And his gospel was *both* the presence of the redeeming reality of the kingdom of God—i.e., as God transforming this world and everything in it with our involvement in helping to make this happen—and the future coming salvation of individual lives.

This whole and full gospel contrasts dramatically with the "miniaturized version" whose focus is only upon obtaining "fire insurance," securing a "get-out-of-hell-free card," and opening up an

---

[9] ibid.
[10] Ibid., 107.
[11] David Neff, "Signs of the End Times," *Christianity Today*, August 2001, 48.

afterlife option or providing an election for a chosen few. Honestly and seriously, why don't we call this gospel reductionism and consequential evangelistic lukewarmness for what it is: "a dysfunctional and dumbed-down version of Christianity that's ripe for reform?"
Sources:

A Once-Mighty Faith (future book – est. 2013) by John Noē
The Upside~Down Kingdom by Donald B. Kraybill
The Reality of the Kingdom by Paul Rowntree Clifford
The Reformation Manifesto by Cindy Jacobs

(4)
Redefining the gospel.

Let's face it, "our traditional focus . . . as an evangelistic tool" has been "on hell . . . to escape" its "eternal fires"—as Sharon Baker charges in her book, *Razing Hell*.[12]

Hell has been and still is the great negative incentive, prod, spur, hammer, and driving and motivating imperative for world missions and personal evangelistic efforts. Thus, hell is touted as "part and parcel of the good news!"[13] Throughout most of Church history, it has also been credited with being a, if not *the*, major deterrent in trying to shape moral behavior for Christians and non-Christians alike. In other words, and as Baker well puts it in question form, "Do we so passionately need a corporate scapegoat to prove our righteousness and goodness, to feel as though we have a handle on how to abolish and punish evil, to feel peace about our own eternal destination?"[14] Apparently, we do.

So how are we Christians doing with our "hell-to-be-shun-heaven-to-be-won-no-second-chance" oriented evangelism approach? Not very well according to most sources. But if we sincerely desire to see present-day Christians do a better job of evangelism and missions, the gospel itself will need to be realigned in harmony with Jesus' presentations in the

---

[12] Sharon Baker, *Razing Hell* (Louisville, KY.: Westminster John Knox Press, 2010), *xiv*.
[13] Ibid., 66.
[14] Ibid., 67.

Gospels. That means we will need to develop a better understanding of God's kingdom, his justice, and our roles in advancing that kingdom "on earth as it is in heaven" (Matt. 6:10b). That means we must rediscover the whole, full, and true gospel that Jesus as well as the Apostle Paul presented (see Acts 28:31; 20:25-27; 19:8).

This whole and full gospel contrasts dramatically with the "miniaturized version" whose focus is only upon obtaining "fire insurance," securing a "get-out-of-hell-free card," and opening up an afterlife option or providing an election for a chosen few.

So what difference do you think a kingdom-oriented-salvation-coupled gospel such as Jesus was presenting, modeling, and conferring would make in how people in our world today respond to the Christian faith? What difference do you think this would make in how interested and willing Christians might be to share this redefined gospel with others? What difference do you think this reconstituted gospel that exhorts us to live out Jesus' full teaching of the kingdom of God—especially in the area of compassion for the weak, needy, vulnerable, and oppressed—would actually have in how most Christians live their earthly lives? Would the results be about the same, lower, or greater than the current response to the reductionist, shrunken-down, and dying-go-to-heaven-and-avoid-hell gospel we are supposed to be presenting now? What do you think?

Sources:

A Once-Mighty Faith (future book – est. 2013) by John Noē
Razing Hell by Sharon L. Baker
Hell Yes / Hell No by John Noē

Exposé #4

Hell

Every week in churches all around the world multiple millions sit snug in their pews believing that when they die they will go to heaven to spend an eternity of bliss with God because they are born again and saved. Meanwhile, the vast majority of humankind—untold billions of others—will go down into the flames of hell after they die because they have not believed in Jesus, repented and been forgiven for their sins, and are not Christians. In hell they will suffer awful, painful, and conscious punishment and torment, forever and ever, with no hope or chance of escape.

Theological Problem:

Hell is also a huge problem for a lot of people, Christians included. Its horrible and haunting concept has thoroughly permeated and embedded itself in almost all areas and aspects of our society. Nobody is immune. Fact is, this traditional belief and afterlife curse is so ingrained in the collective consciousness of society that it is now variously and negatively termed:

- "One of Christianity's most offensive doctrines."
- "The ultimately intolerant doctrine."
- "Invented by church leaders to 'keep the people in line.'"
- "Theology's H-word, a subject too trite for serious scholarship."

- "It's like capital punishment for a traffic violation."
- "There is no good news if there is no bad news."

But is there really an afterlife place and reality of eternal conscious punishment and torment called "hell?"

What Scripture Says:

Nowadays, the Bible is considered the primary source of "hell" proclamations, denunciations, and slang phrases. And most Bible scholars confidently assure us that "hell is vividly described in the pages of the New Testament." But d*o you know what the Bible actually says or literally mentions about "hell"?*

The correct answer: **NOTHING! ZERO!**

What's going on? Do you see a problem here?

Elaborations:

1) Hell cartoon.
2) How many Americans believe in hell?
3) What does the Bible actually say about hell?
4) What did Jesus actually say about hell?
5) Where did hell come from?
6) The greater issue.
7) The 'all' controversy.
8) Thinking outside the box—like God.
9) The twelve demands of Scripture.
10) The synthesis solution.

Sources:

Hell Yes / Hell No by John Noē
The Last Word and the Word After That by Brian D. McLaren
Razing Hell by Sharon L. Baker

Erasing Hell by Francis Chan and Preston Sprinkle
Love Wins by Rob Bell

(1)
Hell cartoon

The beginning of the book, ***Hell Yes / Hell No* . . .**

Introduction

You've Gotta Be Kidding . . .
Right?

*H*ell *yes!*" What better way to kick off a serious book about a sobering subject, and as the cover suggests, a vast gray area of theology and controversy, than with a bit of light-hearted, hellacious humor?

Pickles by Brian Crane   September 04, 2009 ⏮ ◀ ▦ ▶ ⏭

(*The Indianapolis Star*, 9/4/09 – Used by permission)

But, "*hell no*," I'm not kidding; by *gosh,* hell is a *heck* of a problem. What images race through your mind when this subject comes up? How have those images influenced your life, positively or negatively? Have they affected the lives of others you know or love? Have those images and beliefs changed during your life? If so, how so? Has the idea of an eternal hell troubled, comforted, confused, worried, or delighted you? How have you grappled with it?

All joking aside, hell is a huge problem for a lot of people. Its terrifying and haunting concept has thoroughly permeated and embedded itself in almost all areas and aspects of our society. Nobody is immune.

Source:

Hell Yes / Hell No by John Noē

(2)
How many Americans believe in hell?

According to pollster George Barna:

- "76 percent of Americans believe in heaven, and 71 percent believe in hell.
- Only 32 percent believe that hell is 'an actual place of torment and suffering.'
- 40 percent believe it is 'a state of eternal separation from God's presence.'
- 64 percent believe that they will go to heaven,
- Only 0.005 percent believe that they will be sent to the flames."

U.S. News and World Report (31 Jan. 2000) generally agreed. Their survey showed that:

- "64 percent of Americans think there is a hell.
- 25 percent don't.
- And 9 percent don't know.
- More believed in hell in 2000 than did in 1990 or in the 1950s."[1]

---

[1] Results of these two surveys were quoted from Brian D. McLaren, *The Last Word and the Word after That* (San Francisco, CA.: Jossey-Bass, 2005), 104.

A 2008 Pew Forum on Religion and Public Life survey "showed that 59 percent of Americans believe in hell as a place of eternal punishment for all those who did not repent of their sin. . . . Although this number has decreased from 71 to 59 percent over the last decade."[2]

Regardless of which survey is more accurate, these results show how deeply entrenched traditional views of hell still are. And given the 0.005 percent figure above, one must wonder how effective of a deterrent the threat of an eternal hell really is? Another paradoxical fact is, hell is one of the main reasons most Christians are so lackadaisical about their biblical responsibility and disinclined to share their faith with other people. One would think the opposite would be true—that if they really believed in hell, you couldn't stop them from constantly warning their family, friends, relatives, everyone about it and explaining how to avoid being burned in the flames. Then why don't most Christians do this?

Do you know what the Bible actually says or literally mentions about "hell"?
The correct answer: NOTHING! ZERO!

Sources:

Hell Yes / Hell No by John Noē
Hell Under Fire by Christopher W. Morgan and Robert A. Peterson
What's So Great about Christianity by Dinesh D'Souza
The Shack by Wm. Paul Young
The Last Word and the Word after That by Brian D. McLaren
Razing Hell by Sharon Baker

---

[2] Baker, *Razing Hell*, 186. "You can read the article online at http://pewforum.org/news/display.php?NewsIE=16260)."

(3)
What does the Bible actually say about hell?

Try this little numerical exercise. Write down this series of numbers on a piece of paper: 570, 54, 32, 14, 13, and 0. Now, here are two questions:

1) Does the Bible ever "call" or literally mention "heaven?"

Correct answer: YES! There are **570 matches** in the original King James Version for original language words translated as "heaven." And Scripture takes us to heaven—describing it in Isaiah 6, Daniel 7, and Revelation 4, 5, 6 for instance. The Apostle Paul also talks about a man he knew who was caught up to the "third heaven." There is no disagreement about any of this.

2) Do you know what the Bible "calls," says, or literally mentions about "hell"?

Correct answer: **NOTHING! ZERO!** And Scripture never takes us to hell by describing it to us. Any yet many scholars confidently assure us that "hell is vividly described in the pages of the New Testament."

The Italians have a saying, "traduttore, traditore." It literally means, "translator, traitor." Or more freely, "all translators are traitors." In this vein, here is a revealing statistic in the form of a graphic illustration regarding translation matches for the word "hell" throughout both the Old and New Testaments in a few notable translations, along with their original publication dates:

> **54 matches** in the original King James Version (1611)
> **32 matches** in the New King James Version (1982)
> **14 matches** in the New International Version (1978)
> **13 matches** in the New American Standard Bible (1971) and
>   American Standard Version (1901)
> **0 matches** in Young's Literal Translation (1862)—i.e., the word
>   "hell" is not found once.

What's going on? Why such great discrepancy among Bible translations? Do you see a trend here or sense a problem? Clearly, these differences indicate something is wrong, or at least changing. So, are any of these translators traitors, as the Italian saying goes? The reason for this variance from 54 to zero is there are no equivalent Hebrew words in the Old Testament or Greek words in the New Testament for the present-day term, concept, and eternal place of damnation variously and differently translated (or perhaps mistranslated) as "hell."

Sources:

Hell Yes / Hell No by John Noē
Hell Is Real (But I Hate to Admit It) by Brian Jones
Surprised by Hope by N.T. Wright
Love Wins by Rob Bell
God Wins by Mark Galli

(4)
What did Jesus actually say about hell?

Jesus is credited by most Christian writers and scholars as being "the chief proponent of the doctrine of hell." But is He? And "Jesus believed in hell." But did He?

The word Jesus most often used that is most often translated as "hell" was *Gehenna*. And *Gehenna* was and still is today a real, literal, familiar, and this-world place with a long, sad, sordid, and well-known past history. In Jesus' day, it was located in the immediate vicinity of Jerusalem. Biblical scholars traditionally insist that "over time *Gehenna* also became the name of the place where sinners were punished after death." But why did it?

One of the biggest problems with *Gehenna* being an other-worldly, afterlife place is, it was and still is a proper noun and the name of a real, literal, familiar, this-world place. Just like the Mount of Olives, the Judean Desert, Calvary, Bethlehem, or Gethsemane, all these places were and are still located in the immediate vicinity of Jerusalem. Today, *Gehenna* is a beautiful and partially but densely populated suburb of this modern-day city.

In Bible times, however, *Gehenna* was a horrific place and reeked of a horrible stench. Why? Because, allegedly and arguably, it was the local city garbage dump of Jerusalem. Hence, fires were kept burning to dispose of the garbage and worms ate this waste as well as the carcasses of sacrificed animals deposited there from the Temple (see Heb. 13:11), and the bodies of criminals who had been executed (see Jer. 31:40a). All these things and more were tossed into this fiery garbage dump.

Additionally, *Gehenna* had been the place of pagan sacrifices and burnings of Israeli children as they were offered to the gods of Baal(s) and Molech (see Jer. 7:30-31; 19:2, 4-5; 32:35). Let's also make special note from these just-referenced, Old Testament passages that these sacrifices and burnings were not "commanded" nor "mentioned" by God. They never "enter [his] mind." And God termed these acts "evil" and "detestable." Nowadays, and perhaps ironically, the Church has, or soon will have, God Himself doing these same "evil" and detestable" acts to multiple billions sentenced and cast into an eternity of fiery punishment and suffering in a *Gehenna* "hell."

***Gehenna* was and still is today a real, literal, familiar, and this-world place with a long, sad, sordid, and well-known past history.**

To this day, this same valley surrounds old Jerusalem on the southwest side and bears the name *Gehenna*. You can go to this "hell"—Jesus' hell—without dying. Israel's Ministry of Tourism hopes that you will. It conducts daily tours and would be delighted to assist you in making your travel plans.

Fact is, *Gehenna* is *Gehenna* and not hell. Making it hell won't stand up to an honest and sincere test of Scripture and history. Not surprisingly, today, the message of hell is under attack or fire, so-to-speak, as never before, and mostly from within Christianity's own ranks, and rightfully so.

Sources:

Hell Yes / Hell No by John Noē
Surprised by Hope by N.T. Wright

(5)
Where did hell come from?

What's the opposite of these words: "to torment and punish forever?" How about "to cover, conceal, and protect for a temporary period of time?" Shockingly, perhaps for some, this latter phrase is the etymology and original meaning for our modern English word "hell." Moreover, it comes from a pagan source and not from the Bible. It also has little, if any, resemblance to our modern-day images of hell.

Etymology is the study of the origin, history, and derivation of words. *The New Encyclopedia Britannica* confirms this little-known etymology this way: "Hell, the abode or state of being of evil spirits or souls that are damned to postmortem punishment. Derived from an Anglo-Saxon word meaning "to conceal," or "to cover . . . ." *Webster's Dictionary* explains that "hell" comes from middle English, old English, and old high German, (*hel, helle, helan*) and arose during the Anglo-Saxon pagan period (A.D. 400 – 1100).

Our word helmet is derived from this same etymology, root, and meaning. A helmet covers, conceals, and protects the head. It certainly does not torment or punish one's head. Similarly, the word "hel" or "helle" was used in Europe during the middle ages when potato farmers would "hel" their potatoes. That is, during the winter they would cover, conceal, and protect their potatoes by digging holes, putting their potatoes in the ground, and covering them with dirt. These farmers referred to this process as "putting their potatoes in hel"—again, for the purpose of care and protection, and not torment and punishment.

Today, my wife conceals and protects the potatoes she buys at the store by storing them in a dark place so they won't sprout buds and go soft and bad as quickly as they would in a lighted and open area. In some parts of England it is also said that to cover a building with a roof of tiles or thatch was "to hel the building." That job was done by people called "helliers." Therefore, to hel a house meant to cover and protect it with a roof. I'm told that the term heling a house is still used in the New England portions of the United States.

Thus, the origin and basic meaning of the word "hell" had nothing to do with an other-worldly, afterlife place or with a place of eternal torment and punishment with no hope of escape. That connotation or derivation had to come later. But the modern-day meaning evolved, or devolved, depending on your perspective, from referring to the common earthly grave of all deceased human beings into its meaning today of being a nether-world place of eternal conscious torment and punishment for only the damned.

Thus, the origin and basic meaning of the word "hell" had nothing to do with an other-worldly, afterlife place . . . .

Consequently, most of our thinking about hell and hellfire today does not come from either the Bible or from its etymology and historical usage.

Sources:

Hell Yes / Hell No by John Noē

(6)
The greater issue.

Every now and then in Christian circles a strange-sounding idea pops up. It's deemed "heretical" and "not an option for evangelicals because it lacks biblical warrant." In the contemporary church, it's only held by a small and fringe minority. It's the doctrine and belief that eventually everyone who has ever lived on planet Earth will be saved and spend eternity with God.

Upon first hearing, most Christians reject this possibility without a moment's thought. To them, it seems so obviously false. Often they are shocked that anyone would believe such an absurdity, especially people in the Church. After thinking about it for a few moments, however, some agree that God could save everyone if He wanted to, but they insist that He doesn't want to and that the Bible clearly teaches He will not save everyone. At least this is what they have been told, taught, and led to believe the Bible says.

But here's a bigger, broader, and more "hell-of-a-problem" than hell. I call it "the 'all' controversy." In several places in the Bible, God actually says that He wants to save everyone and that He will accomplish everything He desires. Even more troubling—and in my opinion the irony of ironies and the paradox of paradoxes—is that this belief, which sounds so strange to us today, just may have been the prevailing doctrine of the Christian Church during its first five hundred years.

"*Hell no!*" you say. "*Hell yes*, it was!" Christian Univeralists retort. One thing we can know for sure, however, is, this issue is not something we can simply ignore or take too lightly.

It's called "Universalism," and also "Universal Salvation," "Universal Reconciliation," "Final Universal Restoration," or "Final Holiness." But it's not a uniform belief system, as some assume—except for the end product of all people being saved, eventually. Several varieties of Universalism have been and are currently espoused. The differences between varieties basically involve the questions of "how" this saving process happens, "where" it happens, and "why."

Sources:

Hell Yes / Hell No by John Noē

(7)
The 'all' controversy.

As a result of this disagreement over the extent of God's grace and wrath in the afterlife destiny of all people, what we find is that one of the smallest words in the Bible is one of the most difficult to interpret and understand. The dispute revolves around this basic question: when does "all" mean "all" and when does "all" not mean "all?" When does it mean only "some" or "all of some sort?" Make no mistake; this small word "all" is the most significant word in this debate in such verses as these:

*"Therefore, just as sin entered the world through one man, and death through sin, and in this way death came to **all men**, because **all** sinned . . . . Consequently, just as the result of one trespass was condemnation for **all men**, so also the result of one act of righteousness was justification that brings life for **all men**.* (Rom. 5:12, 18)

*"For as in Adam **all** die, so in Christ **all** will be made alive. But each in his own turn . . . ."* (1 Cor. 15:22-23a)

*For God has bound **all men** over to disobedience so that he may have mercy on **them all.**"* (Rom. 11:32)
*"for **all** have sinned and fall short of the glory of God, and are justified freely by his grace through the redemption that came by Christ Jesus."* (Rom. 3:23-24)

*"who gave himself as a ransom for **all men** . . . ."* (1 Tim. 2:6)

*". . . we have put our hope in the living God, who is the Savior of **all men**, and **especially** of those who believe."* (1 Tim. 4:10).

And many more

Sources:

Hell Yes / Hell No by John Noē

(8)
Thinking outside the box—like God.

Battle lines are drawn. Sides are fixed. Arguments are exhausted. From the time of prominent early Church fathers, nothing has been resolved or scripturally reconciled—until now. And, yes, the stakes are high. But something is lacking.

When questions of the ultimate and eternal destiny of billions upon billions of un-evangelized and Christ-rejecting nonbelievers hang in the balance, more is demanded than human opinions, rote repetition of traditionally held beliefs, or the continuance of theological debates. After all, if we have received, accepted, and are now passing along erroneous answers, we may be misleading people, resulting in tragic and eternal consequences.

So as we continue to re-explore the possibility that God's grace, mercy, love, justice, and wrath may be far different and more extensive than our limited earthly view(s), let's re-address how we might be able to honor all the demands of Scripture bearing on this issue and harmonize and reconcile them via a solution of synthesis into one consistent, coherent, Christ-honoring, Scripture-authenticating, and faith-validating view.

Battle lines are drawn. Sides are fixed. Arguments are exhausted. . . . nothing has been resolved or scripturally reconciled—until now. . . . something is lacking.

Regrettably, we humans tend to box ourselves into narrow mindsets. Nowhere may this be truer than in the topic of the eternal afterlife destiny of all people. Let's also remember we are delving into a mystery! (Rom. 11:33-36). Thus, we must not confine or limit ourselves to a traditional, boxed-in way of thinking and believing. Thinking "outside the box," so to speak, means that we think outside the limit of this earthly life and into the unlimited realm of the afterlife. Who of us would doubt that this is how God thinks and acts?

Sources:

Hell Yes / Hell No by John Noē

(9)
The twelve demands of Scripture.

To get us started thinking "outside the box," I have identified and boiled down from all sides in this great debate what I am calling "The Twelve Demands of Scripture for Salvation and Eternal Life." I believe they are clear, emphatic, and inescapable. I also think they are exhaustive. See if you agree with them. Also can you think of any I have missed and that we must also satisfy?

The Twelve Demands of Scripture for Salvation and Eternal Life

1. God's numerous statements that He will do all He pleases (Isa. 46:10-11; 14:24, 27; 55:11; Psa. 33:11; 115:3; 135:6; Dan. 4:35; Job 23:13; 42:2; Heb. 6:17) and "work(s) out everything in conformity with the purpose of his will" (Eph. 1:11; 2 Tim. 1:9). This includes God's "not wanting anyone to perish, but everyone to come to repentance" (2 Pet. 3:9) and "all men to be saved and to come to the knowledge of the truth" (1 Tim. 2:4), so that "all" who die "in Adam" will eventually "all" be saved "in Christ." (Rom. 3:23-24; 5:12, 15, 18-19; 1 Cor. 15:22-23).

2. Grace abounding much more than sin (Rom. 5:15, 20).

3. Jesus being God's only provision for and the means of salvation and eternal life as "the Savior of all men, and especially of those who believe" (1 Tim. 4:10).

4. A special-ness and incentives for those who believe, are saved, and obedient in this life.

5. Salvation only coming to a person after hearing about it (Rom. 10:13-14, 17).

6. Salvation only coming to a person after the Father having "mercy on them all" (Rom. 11:32), "drawing" (John 6:44), "enabling" (John 6:65), "un-hardening" (Rom. 9:18; 11:7-10), and/or "re-grafting" them in again (Rom. 11:23).

7. Salvation only coming to a person after a "willing" and conscious profession of faith and belief, and placing one's trust in Christ and his work on the cross and resurrection from the dead—all people must do this to be saved (Rom. 10:4, John 1:12; 3:15, 36; 6:47; 8:24). Those who do not so "believe" (per #5, #6, #7), are not saved, do not enter heaven, nor have eternal life. Instead, they are "condemned" (Mark 16:16; John 5:28-29; Jude 4) and "God's wrath remains" on them (John3:36).

8. Given the paucity, if not total non-existence, of scriptural support for the orthodox, traditional, and modern-day doctrine and understanding of "hell," we must reconsider this mainstay of Christianity as *not* being part of God's plan of afterlife punishment and/or redemption.

9. But "eternal" judgment, punishment, loss of rewards, and fire are certainly real and part of God's justice and wrath in the afterlife—for both unbelievers and believers. For as the Scriptures state: "The law of the LORD is perfect . . . . the judgments of the LORD true and righteous . . . . By them is your servant warned; in keeping them there is great reward" (Psa. 19:7-11). These must be retained as clear consequences not only of unbelief but also for disobedience. The question is, are these to be understood in retributive terms, in restorative terms, or both?

10. The individual reality frequently spoken of as both "perishing" and "destruction" must also be worked into this synthesis.

11. The fate of the "un-evangelized" (those who never heard about Christ or the gospel of salvation) must be better explained than has been done to date. These include those who died as: unborns, infants, young children, mentally disabled, pre-Christ heathen, and post-Christ heathen.

12. If all the above demands are true and reconcilable in a proposed synthesis fashion, then several other major concepts in modern-day Christianity will have to be readdressed and redefined in better agreement with what the Scriptures actually present and with more accuracy than what is currently being taught and preached today. These include: evangelism, missions, eternal security, the Great Commission, and even the question of what is the gospel.

Sources:

Hell Yes / Hell No by John Noē

(10)
The solution of synthesis.

The great Christian revolutions come not by the discovery
of something that was not known before. They happen when
somebody takes radically something that was always there.
—H. Richard Niebuhr

Is God the Father of all, Christ the Savior of all, and heaven the final home of all, or not? In the sixteenth chapter of my book, *Hell Yes / Hell No*, I boil down "The Twelve Demands of Scripture for Salvation and Eternal Life" into "Seven Points of Synthesis." Please do not misunderstand or jump too quickly into an inappropriate conclusion. Just because these twelve demands can be synthesized does not mean this synthesis is right, or that I'm right. We must never forget that we are dealing with a mystery. But I do maintain that this synthesis contains no contradictions or violations of Scripture.

Sources:

Hell Yes / Hell No by John Noē

Exposé #5

The 'Last Days'

"We are living in the 'last days!'"

"These are the end times!"

"Soon it will be all over!"

"Jesus is coming back!

"We're leaving this world!"

If we've heard it once, we've heard this a thousand times. And it never happens. Since the 1970s—the heyday of Hal Lindsey's book, *The Late Great Planet Earth*—this end-times-gospel has been everywhere it seems. For me, this was not good news. I remember thinking at the time, "Oh, no!" I had just become a Christian. The business my wife and I started five years ago was starting to make money. Our two children were attending grade school. I wanted to see them grow up. I didn't want everything to end, at least not yet.

Theological Problem:

As a new Christian, I was also being told and taught to read and study my Bible. That's when another strange thing started happening.

Verses began popping out, like these two verses from the New Testament book of Hebrews 1:1-2. "In the past God spoke to our forefathers through the prophets at many times and in various ways, but in these last days he has spoken to us by his Son."

So I started asking more questions of those I deemed to be in the know like . . . "Doesn't the writer of Hebrews state here that the biblical timeframe known as the 'last days' was taking place, back then and there—i.e. during the earthly ministry of Jesus and during the time this writer was writing? And if that is true, how can we possibly say that we are now living in the 'last days?'"

"Well, we just are! Look around," I was bluntly informed. "It doesn't take a genius to figure this out. Just look at the moral decay in society and world events—especially those in Israel. How could anyone come up with any other conclusion? Everybody knows we are living in the 'last days.'" Or are we?

What Scripture Says:

Every New Testament reference to the "last days" or to equivalent terms such as "last times" or "last hour," confirms the same thing. And history records that circa A.D. 70, exactly forty years after Jesus' most dramatic end-time prophesy on the Mount of Olives and within the time of one biblical generation that He placed upon its fulfillment, Roman armies led by Titus destroyed the city of Jerusalem and the Jewish Temple. This was the same Temple that was standing when Jesus foretold its destruction—not some third (or fourth), rebuilt temple centuries removed.

Make no mistake—Jesus was no false or fallible prophet. He was the greatest Prophet of all. And even though many may have dealt loosely, if not treacherously, with Jesus' words, He set a definite time limit for the "last days." These "last days" and end times were not a 19-centuries-and-counting extended period. Without exception, they literally refer to that 1st-century timeframe in which the New Testament writers were living, there and then. Hebrews 1:1-2 clearly and firmly affixes Jesus' earthly ministry, as well as the time in which the writer of Hebrews was writing, to the historic and biblical time period termed the "last days."

Elaborations:

1) Jesus' most dramatic prophecy.
2) Confusion abounds.
3) Five side-stepping devices.
4) More startling nearness statements
5) The 'whole world' objection.
6) What the critics charge.
7) Exactness.

Sources:

The Perfect Ending for the World by John Noē
The Last Days According to Jesus by R.C. Sproul
Last Days Madness by Gary DeMar
The Works of Josephus translated by William Whiston
Josephus the Essential Writings by Paul L. Maier

(1)
Jesus' most dramatic prophecy.

One week before He was crucified, Jesus made some startling statements about the end. He left no doubt that something truly significant was about to happen. His prophetic words are paramount to understanding the "last days" and end-time prophecy. Although they have puzzled and perplexed humankind for nearly 2,000 years, they need not. We have only to compare his prophecy with Habakkuk's and Daniel's—and take Him at this word—to arrive at his proper meaning.

While sitting on the Mount of Olives, looking across the valley at the beautiful Jewish Temple, Jesus stunned his disciples by prophesying that this entire complex of buildings, an awesome structure "famous throughout the world" (2 Maccabees 2:22 NRSV), would be totally destroyed. "I tell you the truth, not one stone here will be left on another; every one will be thrown down" (Matt. 24:2). His disciples asked, "When will this happen?" (Matt. 24:3) and He answered, "I tell you the truth, this generation will certainly not pass away until all these things

have happened" (Matt. 24:34). Not only was something significant about
to happen, it was to happen in their lifetime. To top it off, He told them
about many other "last days" or end-time events that would also take
place within that same time period. Included in "all these things" were:

- The end of the age and the sign of his coming (*parousia*) (vs. 3)
- The gospel preached in all the world . . . to all nations (vs. 14)
* The end will come (vs. 14)
* The abomination of desolation standing in the holy place (vs. 15)
* The hearers fleeing for their lives (vs. 16-20)
* A great tribulation, unequaled in history before or after (vs. 21)
- False Christs and false prophets appearing, performing great
  signs and miracles and deceiving even the elect—if that were
  possible (vs. 24)
- The coming (*parousia*) of the Son of Man (vs. 27)
- The sun and the moon darkened, stars falling from the sky and
  the heavenly bodies shaken (vs. 29)
- The sign of the Son of Man appearing in the sky (vs. 30)
- Their seeing the Son of Man coming on the clouds (vs. 30)

This passage of Scripture is recognized as Jesus' longest and most
dramatic prophecy. It is also his most problematic and contested
teaching. It contains the promise of what many considered to be his
biggest, baddest, and best coming of all. Scholars call it the Olivet
Discourse, since Jesus gave this end-time prophecy while sitting on the
Mount of Olives during the last week of this life. I suggest you read
Jesus' prophetic words for yourself before continuing. Three similar but
slightly different versions are recorded in Matthew 24, Mark 13, and
Luke 21.

Sources:

The Perfect Ending for the World by John Noē
The Last Days According to Jesus by R.C. Sproul
Last Days Madness by Gary DeMar
The Works of Josephus translated by William Whiston
Josephus the Essential Writings by Paul L. Maier

(2)
Confusion abounds.

Today, millions of Bible readers and scholars continue to be baffled and confused by Jesus' allegedly cryptic words and his emphasis that those who were there with Him at the time would witness all these climactic end-time events—i.e., "all these things." Most debate centers on what generation Jesus was really talking about when He referred to "this generation." Let's also note that He emphatically warned his first hearers, "Watch out that no one deceives you" (Matt. 24:4). As we shall see, his warning is just as relevant today as it was back then. So, if we take Jesus at his literal word (as they did) and hold to an authoritative view of Scripture, "all these things" must have occurred within the lifetime of his disciples exactly *as* and *when* He said. Nothing short of the credibility of Jesus Christ is at stake. Surely Jesus didn't make a mistake or intend to mislead his disciples. The only other alternative is that He spoke truly—just as He said He did.

Skeptics contend that Jesus' Olivet Discourse is an empty prophecy, since neither Jesus' generation, nor any generation since, has seen its "complete" fulfillment. However, his prophesied stone-by-stone destruction of the Temple complex is historical fact. It occurred in A.D. 70 - 73, precisely within the time period Jesus said. Yet most people of the world have been led to believe that the rest, and most, of Jesus' other prophetic words are still to be fulfilled.

To side-step the plain meaning and utmost importance of Jesus' words, prophecy teachers and futuristic theologians have devised every kind of strained exegesis (an explanation or interpretation of a word, sentence, or passage), linguistic gymnastics, and sophisticated arguments imaginable. Not surprisingly, every attempt over the centuries to evade the force of this passage and place its fulfillment beyond the 1st-century timeframe Jesus specified has brought nothing but embarrassment and discredit to the Church and undermined the deity of Christ and the integrity of the Scriptures.

Sources:

The Perfect Ending for the World by John Noē
The Last Days According to Jesus by R.C. Sproul

Last Days Madness by Gary DeMar
The Works of Josephus translated by William Whiston
Josephus the Essential Writings by Paul L. Maier

(3)
Five side-stepping devices.

Traditionalists assure us that when Jesus "returns" at his so-called "Second Coming" at some point in the future, He will fulfill the rest of his prophecy and destroy this physical world. But is this really what Jesus taught? For those raised in postponement traditions, most have never considered that Jesus might have been speaking of events (note the plural) which were *all* to transpire during the lives of his 1st-century hearers. Consequently, to cover up for Jesus' apparent failure to produce what He promised, and to defend their futuristic-deferment positions, they have employed one or more of five side-stepping devices.

These interpretative techniques usually fall under the guise of "traditional explanations." And many of us have naively accepted one or more of them as orthodox. Each device, however, is a ploy born of theological necessity—this is what they want to believe and are required to believe despite what the text plainly says. Yet none of these devices is textually, exegetically, or grammatically justifiable. They are simply "necessary" to evade, finesse around, distort, or neutralize the plain, face-value meaning and clear relevance of Jesus' prophetic words and time restriction. In other words, they are tied to agendas, and therefore "absolutely demanded." Here are the five, most-widely used, side-stepping devices to wrestle away Jesus' intended meaning from the text:

> **Device 1:** "Generation" must refer to a future generation.
> **Device 2:** "Generation" must mean "race," "nation," or "a kind of people."
> **Device 3:** Dividing Jesus' prophecy into two sections—one past, one future.
> **Device 4:** Change the meaning of the apocalyptic language.
> **Device 5:** Jesus was mistaken or never said these words.

But to the contrary, the imminence of Jesus' "this generation," and whom He meant by "you," lie at the heart of his message on the Mount of Olives. These two chronological and relevancy keys are indispensable to the proper understanding of his prophecy, and all New Testament "last days" and end-time statements as well. His words were not vague or ambiguous. They were clear and time-sensitive. They qualified the time context and nature of fulfillment, and therefore absolutely demanded a 1st-century fulfillment. It's the most natural way of reading and understanding the text.

Sources:

The Perfect Ending for the World by John Noē
The Last Days According to Jesus by R.C. Sproul
Last Days Madness by Gary DeMar
The Works of Josephus translated by William Whiston
Josephus the Essential Writings by Paul L. Maier

(4)
More startling nearness statements.

Yes, something was up back then in Bible times and in those "last days." Something so big and so near that it prompted the 1st-century, Holy Spirit-guided writers of the New Testament (John 16:13) to make or record such additional and startling statements as . . .

- ...the end of all things is at hand (1 Pet. 4:7 *KJV*)
- ...the fullness of time was come (Gal. 4:4 *KJV*)
- ...the time is fulfilled (Mark 1:15 *KJV*)
- ...the fulfillment of the ages has come (1 Cor. 10:11)
- ...the ends of the world [ages] are come (1 Cor. 10:11 *KJV*)
- ...for these be the days of vengeance, that all things which are written may be fulfilled (Luke 21:22 *KJV*)
- ...the time is short (1 Cor. 7:29)
- ...for the world in its present form is passing away (1 Cor. 7:31)
- ...it is the last hour . . . . it is the last hour (1 John 2:18)

What's the scoop? Why were they talking like this? Is it possible that these words literally mean what they say and, therefore, these writers said what they meant? If so, what could have been so monumental and so impending, right there and then and in their lifetime, to justify such emphatic and strong claims? The thoughtful answer to that question is, in this author's opinion, what should be termed the *climax for the rest of the greatest story ever foretold.*

No question about it, the 1st-century followers of Jesus Christ lived in expectation of something big about to happen, very soon. For them, it was the "last hour." But the last hour of what? Was this big event the proverbial end of the world? The end of time? Or the conclusion of human history? Obviously, it was not. So it had to be something else. If nothing of radical magnitude happened befitting this language and imminency (nearness), then these statements were misleading or mistaken, at best—which is exactly the interpretation that has been given to us by many modern interpreters!

Sources:

The Perfect Ending for the World by John Noē
The Last Days According to Jesus by R.C. Sproul
Last Days Madness by Gary DeMar
The Works of Josephus translated by William Whiston
Josephus the Essential Writings by Paul L. Maier

(5)
The 'whole world' objection.

Jesus emphatically specified that "this gospel of the kingdom will be preached in the whole world as a witness to all the nations, and then the end will come" (Matt. 24:14). No way around it, it's what He said. This condition was a prerequisite for "the end" to come.

How then could the end possibly have come circa A.D. 70, when the gospel had not yet been preached in the Western Hemisphere? The great missionary movement of the 18th and 19th centuries hadn't taken place, worldwide communications hadn't been developed, and many nations and people groups in remote tribes had yet to hear the gospel. This fact alone, critics contend, should stop dead in its tracks any idea that the end came circa A.D. 70.

No way around it, it's what He said. This condition was a prerequisite for "the end" to come.

The Bible, however, must be understood on its own terms and in the context of its original hearers. Only then can we properly understand what any portion really means for us today. Therefore, let's carefully note that the inspired writers of the New Testament confirmed, several times, that Jesus' prerequisite was accomplished in their day:

- Using hyperbole and in the context of the Jewish worldview, "every nation under heaven" was assembled on the day of Pentecost (Acts 2:5).
- The Apostle Paul, 31 years later, confirmed that "all over the world this gospel is producing fruit and growing . . ." (Col. 1:6) and that "the gospel that you heard . . . has been proclaimed to every creature under heaven" (Col. 1:23), and that "your faith is being reported all over the world" (Rom. 1:8). This was not Paul's opinion. It is inspired Scripture. A few years after Paul said these words, the end came, right on time.
- For more confirmations, read: Rom. 10:18; 16:26; Acts 1:8; 24:5; Jude 3; also compare with Dan. 2:39; 4:1, 22; 5:19; 7:23; Luke 2:1, 30-32; 24:47; Rev. 3:10.

Why is this scripturally documented fulfillment of Jesus' prerequisite so hard to believe? The answer is simply the power of the traditions of men rides roughshod over the Word of God (Mark 7:13; Matt. 15:6). According to the Bible itself, and prior to A.D. 70, the gospel was preached to all nations and to the world. The Greek word translated "world" in Matthew 24:14 is *oikoumene*, meaning land (i.e., the [terrene part of the] globe, specifically the Roman Empire). In this commonly used and restricted sense, the then-known Roman world, or the civilized world of that time, was also the "world" of the Jews into which they had been scattered. If the entire global earth was meant, the Greek word *kosmos* would have been used, as it is in Matthew 24:21. But it wasn't.

Hence, Jesus' end-coming condition has been scripturally met. This is a truth that has been lost by many today. But early Church father Eusebius clearly understood this linkage and its significance. He confirmed that both the world-wide preaching of the gospel and this end of biblical Judaism were fulfilled:

> Moses had foretold this very thing and in due course Christ sojourned in this life, and the teaching of the new covenant was borne to all nations, and at once the Romans besieged Jerusalem and destroyed it and the Temple there. At once the whole of the Mosaic law was abolished, with all that remained of the Old Covenant.[1]

Let's further note that the fulfillment of this world mission was an absolutely necessary part of God's plan. Since Jews had been scattered over the world (Jas. 1:1), they all had to have the opportunity to accept the gospel or reject it and persecute its proclaimers. In this way they would and did "fill up, then, the measure of sin of your forefathers" (Matt. 23:32; Isa. 65:6-12). That's why the gospel had to go out into "the whole world." The previously cited verses verify this accomplishment. They cannot be lightly dismissed. So let's just believe what inspired Scripture writers said. God had allowed one generation of time—Jesus' "this generation"—for the completion of this missionary task. Once completed, the stage was set. The end could now come. It did, perfectly. It was the end of the Old Covenant, biblical Judaic system, and not the physical creation, which will never end.

Sources:

The Perfect Ending for the World by John Noē
The Last Days According to Jesus by R.C. Sproul
Last Days Madness by Gary DeMar
The Works of Josephus translated by William Whiston
Josephus the Essential Writings by Paul L. Maier
(6)
What the critics charge.

---

[1] Eusebius, *Proof of the Gospel*, Bk. I, Ch. 6, 34-35.

Most Christians don't seem to realize the predicament we are in if Jesus Christ didn't fulfill his many promises to come or "return" within the time parameters He specified. Informed critics of Christianity, on the other hand, have no trouble seeing through the strained attempts of church leaders to explain away "nonoccurrence" in order to protect the credibility and divinity of Jesus in the face of his supposed failure. But let's face it. These critics have a legitimate complaint if Jesus did not do something that He said He would, and within the timeframe He stated. They also are quite aware of both the enigma and dilemma that "nonoccurrence" presents for the Christian Church and the impossibility of escaping it without being disloyal to Christ.

- **Bertrand Russell.** Atheist Bertrand Russell, in his book *Why I Am Not A Christian*, discredits the inspiration of the New Testament by saying:

  > I am concerned with Christ as He appears in the Gospel narrative . . . He certainly thought that his second coming would occur in clouds of glory before the death of all the people who were living at the time. There are a great many texts that prove . . . He believed that his coming would happen during the lifetime of many then living. That was the belief of his earlier followers, and it was the basis of a good deal of his moral teaching.[2]

- **Albert Schweitzer.** In his 19th-century book, *The Quest of the Historical Jesus,* liberal Schweitzer summarized the problem of "Parousia delay" as follows:

  > The whole history of Christianity down to the present day . . . is based on the delay of the Parousia, the nonoccurrence of the Parousia, the abandonment of eschatology, the process and

---

[2] Bertrand Russell, *Why I Am Not a Christian* (London: George Allen & Unwin Ltd., 1957), 11.

completion of the 'de-eschatologizing' of religion which has
been connected therewith.[3]

- **Jewish Critics.** Jewish critics contend that Jesus didn't complete
the whole mission of the Messiah within the timeframe their
prophets had predicted, although some admit He fulfilled some
of it. They allege that Christians invented the idea of a "second
coming" off in the future to cover up Jesus' failure to return as
He promised. This is the Jews' primary excuse for rejecting
Jesus and belittling Christianity.

- Even C.S. Lewis, the respected Christian apologist and author, I
am embarrassed to report, said in 1960 about Jesus time-
restrictive, "this-generation" statement in Matthew 24:34:

> "Say what you like," we shall be told [by the skeptic], "the
> apocalyptic beliefs of the first Christians have been proved to
> be false. It is clear from the New Testament that they all
> expected the Second Coming in their own lifetime. And,
> worse still, they had a reason, and one which you will find
> very embarrassing. Their Master had told them so. He shared,
> and indeed created, their delusion. He said in so many words,
> 'this generation shall not pass till all these things be done.'
> And He was wrong. He clearly knew no more about the end of
> the world than anyone else."
>   It is certainly the most embarrassing verse in the Bible.
> Yet how teasing, also, that within fourteen words of it should
> come the statement, "but of that day and hour knoweth no
> man, no, not the angels which are in heaven, neither the Son,
> but the Father." The one exhibition of error and the one
> confession of ignorance grow side by side.[4]

As we shall see, the embarrassment belongs to C.S. Lewis.

[3] Albert Schweitzer, *The Quest of the Historical Jesus* (New York, NY.:
Macmillan, 1948), 360.
[4] C.S. Lewis, essay "The World's Last Night" (1960), found in *The Essential
C.S. Lewis*, Lyle W. Dorsett, ed., (New York: A Touchstone Book, Simon &
Schuster, 1996), 385.

Sources:

The Perfect Ending for the World by John Noē
The Last Days According to Jesus by R.C. Sproul
Last Days Madness by Gary DeMar
The Works of Josephus translated by William Whiston
Josephus the Essential Writings by Paul L. Maier

(7)
Exactness.

Truly, exactness in the form of timely and precise fulfillment is the most Christ-honoring, Scripture-authenticating, and faith-validating of all the various end-time views in the historic Church. It is also, in this writer's opinion, the ultimate apologetic supporting God's demonstrated attribute of divine perfection.

Hence, this time-restricted period of "these last days" was to encompass the full redemptive work of the Messiah: his birth, anointing, teaching, ushering in of the everlasting kingdom of God, death, resurrection, sending of the Holy Spirit, ending of the Jewish age, and much more, as we shall see.

These biblical "last days" were never to be the last days of the world, planet Earth, human history, or the Church. They *were* the beginning days of the Church, as well as the last days of the biggest thing that was ending at the time or will ever end on Planet Earth—the ending of biblical Judaism and its Old Covenant age. That's why the Apostle Paul reminded his contemporaries that ". . . this world in its present form is [was] passing away" (1 Cor. 7:31) and that "the time is [was] short" (1 Cor. 7:29). For Paul the end was very close. Was he wrong? Or did he understand exactly what he was saying?

These biblical "last days" were never to be the last days of the world, planet Earth, human history, or the Church.

No doubt for most viewers of PRI's website or readers of my books, what I have been presenting is a completely different understanding of the "last days" and end-time prophecy and its fulfillment. But crucial to our understanding are the proper identification of this end-time period and its literal fulfillments. It's a powerful vindication of the perfection of God's prophetic word. Daniel had prophesied that its historical setting and defining characteristic would be "when the power of the holy people has been [was] finally broken" (Dan. 12:7). And this is exactly what happened circa A.D. 70. Jesus' Olivet Discourse prophecy perfectly fits this scenario. Forty years—one biblical "this generation"—had been given to the Israelites to repent and accept their Messiah. Some did. Many didn't. But when the time of God's grace was over, "it is [was] time for judgment to begin with the family of God" or "at the house of God" (1 Pet. 4:17 *NIV-KJV*). This age-ending judgment certainly came during the final portion of Israel's "last days." After A.D. 70 -73, the "last days" were over.

Consequently, a Jewish temple does not need to be rebuilt and destroyed again in our day and time. The perfect ending *for* the world had come, right on time! But what about Jesus' "Second Coming?" Did that happen back then in A.D. 70 as well?

Sources:

The Perfect Ending for the World by John Noē
The Last Days According to Jesus by R.C. Sproul
Last Days Madness by Gary DeMar
The Works of Josephus translated by William Whiston
Josephus the Essential Writings by Paul L. Maier

Exposé #6

Second Coming / Return

No idea has gripped the human imagination more firmly, saturated the Church more completely, or been proclaimed as the hope of the world more frequently than the idea and doctrine of a "Second Coming/Return" of Jesus Christ. Its influence on the thinking of most Christians and non-church people alike has been a driving force in the world. And yet this belief has been both the bane and chief blind spot of Christianity as its persistent nonoccurrence throughout Church history has embarrassed and discredited the faith.

Theological Problem:

The Bible says *nothing* about a "second coming" or a "return" of Jesus Christ. Nor do the historic creeds of the Church. *Nothing*! Why not? Because it's inappropriate terminology.

Also, be assured that we simply cannot afford to be misinformed or confused about such an important element of our biblical faith. Unfortunately, "second coming" and "return" terminology implies only two comings of Jesus, one in the past and the other supposedly in the future. But this limitation does not fit with the testimony of Scripture. The idea of limiting the comings of Jesus to only two and calling the later one the "Second Coming" or "Return," or limiting his comings in any way—past, present, or future—is simply a human notion, man-made terminology, and a post-biblical doctrine kept alive by tradition.

What Scripture Says:

Make no mistake. Jesus' timely coming in judgment, "on the clouds," circa A.D. 70, and in destruction of Jerusalem and the Temple was a biggie! It was his real, personal, and bodily coming and ending of the Old Covenant age. But it was not his so-called "return" or "second coming," nor will any of his comings in the future so be. The late-great theologian, George Eldon Ladd, in his highly acclaimed book, *The Blessed Hope*, acknowledged this most significant fact this way:

> . . . the words 'return' and 'second coming' are not properly speaking Biblical words in that the two words do not represent any equivalent Greek words."[1]

Ladd's admission here is huge and leads to major implications. Fact is, we Christians have been hamstrung for centuries with these two non-scriptural expressions and unscriptural concepts. Biblically, the idea that Jesus is off somewhere waiting to come back at some future time, as well as the idea of limiting the comings of Jesus to only two or three times, or to any at all, is man's idea and not God's.

Elaborations:

1) He never left.
2) What is a coming of Jesus?
3) The many comings of Jesus.
4) Freeing yourself from religious bondage.
5) The deception of the elect.

Sources:

The Perfect Ending for the World by John Noē
The Greater Jesus (future book – est. 2012) by John Noē

---

[1] George Eldon Ladd, *The Blessed Hope* (Grand Rapids, MI.: Eerdmans, 1956), 69.

The Last Days According to Jesus by R.C. Sproul
Last Days Madness by Gary DeMar

(1)
He never left.

The biblical and historical facts are, Jesus is not coming back ever because He never left—as He said (Matt. 28:20b). Therefore, return language is inappropriate and never used in proper translations. And He still comes, many times and in many different ways as He has done throughout both the Old and New Testaments. Consequently, the coming of Christ does not refer to *just one or two* historical events. Nor is there such terminology in the Bible as a "final coming" or "last coming" in a world, kingdom, and Christian age that are all without end.

How can we be even more sure of all this? It's as simple as answering the question, Where is Jesus now? Yet it's as complex as asking, why don't we see Him with our physical eyes somewhere on this earth? Since we don't see him, we have decided that Jesus could not have "returned" and be here with us. Paradoxically, Billy Graham confidently declared to a mass crusade audience on September 2, 1997, "This living Christ is in the world today." Well, is He or isn't He? And if He is, where is He?

The answer to this perplexity is simple yet profound. Authentic Christianity does not stand for an absentee Christ absent the entire length of the Christian age! It stands for a present and active Christ who never left and is truly, wholly, and totally here with us. Of course, at one point in history, after his ascension and during the closing period of the Jewish age ("the last days"), He did leave, physically. This departure was required, and it was the decisive factor for the coming of the Holy Spirit (John 14:2-3, 18-19, 28; 16:7; 2 Cor. 5:8; Acts 2:16-17 f). However, He didn't leave to send Himself back.

And yet some postulate that He "returned" in the sending of the Holy Spirit at Pentecost. But this is scripturally impossible. Not only was the outpouring of the Spirit a separate and distinctly prophesied event in the Old Testament, but no New Testament text acknowledges this event as that fulfillment. Rather, all New Testament writers were still anticipating Christ's age-ending coming as future.

The biblical and historical facts are, Jesus is not coming back ever because He never left —as He said (Matt. 28:20b).

So if Jesus is *now* present, and not off in some distant place waiting to come back, then at some point between his departure and his Presence with us today He either *had to return* or *He never left*. The sequence therefore is either: *present, absence, present* or *present, present, present*. It's *highly* inconsistent for deferment futurists to say that Jesus is with us today and then claim that He has not "returned."

The correct biblical and historical answer is: Jesus never left, just as He said (Matt. 28:20). Hence, He doesn't need to "return" or come back again from anywhere at the end of the Christian age or at the demise of the material universe, as is commonly asserted—one cannot return to a place one never left. John, in the first chapter of the book of Revelation, affirms this reality. He saw Christ standing in the midst of the lampstands (his Church) clothed in his high priestly garments (Rev. 1:13, 20). His continuing Presence has not changed since that time.

What is needed is for us to wean ourselves from the idea that the Presence of Christ must be visible, and to reeducate ourselves on how to better worship, encounter, and enjoy Him in his Presence. Unfortunately, assumptions often blind us to realities.

Sources:

The Perfect Ending for the World by John Noē
The Greater Jesus (future book – est. 2012) by John Noē

(2)
What is a coming of Jesus?

My working definition for "a coming of Jesus" is this: it's a personal and bodily intervention and/or manifestation of Jesus into the life of an individual, a group, or a nation on this earth. And there are many different types of comings for different purposes. They also occur at different times and places. Some are visible appearances; some are invisible interventions. Some are physical (seen, heard, felt); some are spiritual (an internal illumination or revelation); and some are combinations.

Theologian Henry A. Virkler calls them "a special manifestation of His presence."[2] Furthermore, there may be other types of comings with which I am not aware, if for no other reason than not everything Jesus did was recorded (see John 21:25).

Sources:

The Perfect Ending for the World by John Noē
The Greater Jesus (future book – est. 2012) by John Noē

(3)
The many comings of Jesus.

Have you ever wondered why Jesus' birth (around 4 B.C.) is never called his "first coming" in Scripture as Dr. Billy Graham so calls it?[3] It's for a good reason—it wasn't. This misconception only leads to the improper numbering of another coming as his "second coming"—which it isn't either.

God's Word clearly and plainly documents and teaches that the comings (plural) of Jesus run like a thread throughout both the Old and New Testaments. I have documented 38 such comings. For instance, Jesus told his disciples, "I will come to you . . . . you will see me" (John 14:18-19). Scripture documents that He did and they did. Jesus came and

---

[2] Henry A. Virkler, *Hermeneutics* (Grand Rapids, MI.: Baker Books, 1981), 150.
[3] Bill Graham, "My Answer," *The Indianapolis Star*, 12/5/11, E-4

appeared to them many times as is recorded in the Gospels and the books of Acts and Revelation.

Also, please be assured that the comings (plural) of Christ are multifold and ongoing not only throughout both the Old Testament and the New Testament, but also since then, today, and in the future. A discussion of this vital aspect of Christ's Presence and his many countless comings, however, is a subject for a future and forthcoming book unveiling the contemporary Christ. (For a preview, go to "Unraveling the End" MPC series podcasts on PRI's website (www.prophecyrefi.org) and listen to Lesson #8 and #9.)

Jesus' birth (around 4 B.C.) is never called his "first coming" in Scripture.

Now you know why the expression "second coming" is never found. It is non-scriptural terminology. The closest you can come to the phraseology of a "Second Coming" is in Hebrews 9:28: "so Christ was sacrificed once to take away the sins of many people; and he will appear *a second time*, not to bear sin, but to bring salvation to those who are waiting for him" (*italics* added). Contrary to popular belief, this scripture does not limit, number, or confine Jesus' comings to only two times. Rather, it highlights two specific and significant comings, among many, for a special salvation-fulfillment purpose. This "second-time" coming follows the typology of Israel's high priest on the Day of Atonement, which occurred every year. And Christ as both our sacrifice and our High Priest (see Heb. 7:27-28; 9:11-15) had to come and fulfill this typology, perfectly (see Heb. 8, 9, and 10).

Sources:

The Perfect Ending for the World by John Noē
The Greater Jesus (future book – est. 2012) by John Noē
Eusebius: The Church History by Paul L. Maier

(4)
Freeing yourself from religious bondage.

Reluctance to give up the so-called "Second Coming/Return" of Christ idea, doctrine, and terminology must be called for what it truly is: *religious bondage.* In this author's opinion, this area of our faith is also ripe for reform.

First, we should drop the use of this non-scriptural terminology and its unscriptural connotations of limiting Jesus' comings to only two and rendering Him an absentee Lord and Savior. This man-made intrusion has led many astray and greatly nullified "the word of God for the sake of your tradition" (Matt. 15:6; Mark. 7:13). Secondly, we must reeducate ourselves concerning the biblical reality of his ongoing Presence and many countless comings—past, present and future.

Of course, a reformation of this magnitude, though desperately needed, is far easier said and outlined than accomplished. Blind allegiance to entrenched traditions stands in the way. It always has. However, the idea and doctrine of a "second coming/return" has got to go. It simply will not stand up to an honest, sincere, and *sola Scriptura* testing of Scripture, as we are commanded to do (1 Thess. 5:21).

The question then becomes, are we willing to abandon tradition when its terminology and concept have been shown to be scripturally erroneous? For many, the answer will be yes, absolutely. Others, I suspect, will kick up their heels and resist the truth of God's Word. But the many comings of Jesus are a beautiful biblical truth and an ongoing reality in his everlasting kingdom. So let's not be intimidated or brainwashed by the traditions of men.

Are we willing to abandon tradition when its terminology and concept have been shown to be scripturally erroneous?

The plain, simple, yet precious truth of Christ's coming (singular) is many comings (plural). This revelation must be proclaimed in certain and Scripture-honoring terms. He has been and still is present and active in his creation. His comings are one of his ways. Let's stop limiting his comings! He comes! Come Lord Jesus! Again, I will have much more to say on this topic in a future and forthcoming book.

Sources:

The Perfect Ending for the World by John Noē
The Greater Jesus (future book – est. 2012) by John Noē

(5)
The deception of the elect.

Jesus warned his disciples of deception. He said that there would be "false prophets . . . to deceive even the elect—if that were possible" (Matt. 24:24). If this deception of the elect was not possible, why would Jesus even bring it up? He also said that insistence on a visible criterion (nature) for his end-time *parousia* coming was (and still is) part of this deception:

> At that time if anyone says to you, 'Look, here is the Christ!' or, 'There he is!' do not believe it . . . So if anyone tells you, 'There he is, out in the desert' do not go out; or, 'Here he is, in the inner rooms,' do not believe it (Matt. 24: 23, 26).

Some of "the elect" today (the saints in the Church), as well as back then, have succumbed to this visible-criterion deception. Thus, they, too, have been falsely prophesying. How so?

First, by their paralleled misunderstanding of the invisible nature for his promised and time-restricted coming (Matt. 24:3, 30, 34; John 14:19, 22). Also, He told them that "before long the world will not see me anymore" (John 14:19, 22). How long is Jesus' "not . . . anymore, anyway? And yet many saints today are still waiting for a physically visible, worldwide sighting of Jesus in Person, in bodily form, in the sky, in the Israeli desert, in an inner room of a rebuilt temple in Jerusalem, or in some other geographic location to which they can definitely point and in like manner say, "There He is!"

Secondly, by their professing and proclaiming a half-truth faith in a world filled with competing religions and secular ideologies. The truthful half is that the promised Messiah (Jesus) came, lived, died, rose from the dead, and ascended to heaven exactly *as* and *when* prophesied. The untruthful part is that Jesus has not come again to finish the work He started, *as* and *when* He said He would and *as* and *when* He was expected to by his Spirit-guided, first followers and every New Testament writer (John 16:13).

Thus, for 19 centuries and counting, the Church has been attempting to side-step and downplay this time-restricted, 1st-century "failure" and "nonoccurrence." As a result, it has been forced to settle for a faith that has *not* been "once for all delivered to the saints" (Jude 3) and whose "end of all things" was *not* "at hand" in that same 1st-century context in which these inspired words were penned (1 Pet. 4:7 *KJV*).

Consequently, and since the fall of Jerusalem circa A.D.70, most of the Church has been proclaiming a half-truth faith. We must therefore ask, if this half-truth faith has been as effective as God has allowed it to be, how much more effective and God-empowered would be the proclamation and practice of a whole-truth faith—one that really "was [past tense] once for all delivered to the saints" (Jude 3)?

I believe it's time for this reform to take place and for God's people to come out of their 19-centuries-and-counting "deception of the elect." In every generation except one, the Church has wrongly proclaimed the imminence of our Lord's climactic coming on the clouds in age-ending judgment and consummation. No more. Perhaps we should now expand our Easter proclamation to say:

> He's arisen! He's arisen, indeed!
> He's come! He's come, indeed!
> He's with us! He's with us, indeed!
> He still comes! He still comes, indeed!

Sources:

The Perfect Ending for the World by John Noē
The Greater Jesus (future book – est. 2012) by John Noē

Exposé #7

Rapture

"C aught up…in the clouds to meet the Lord in the air" (1 Thess. 4:17). What does it mean? To multiple millions of Christians it means "in an instant, millions of people disappear from the face of the earth, shedding their clothing, shoes, eyeglasses and jewelry."[1]

It's called the "Rapture" and it's a near-frantic preoccupation with the idea of Christians mysteriously being physically levitated off the surface of planet Earth, alive, and whisked away, en masse, on a gigantic flight through outer space to heaven. You can read it on bumper stickers:

- "In case of Rapture, this car will be unmanned!"
- "Rapture: The only way to fly!"
- "He's coming to take me away! Ha! Ha!"
- "Get right, or get left behind!"

This is the view promoted and popularized by the "Left Behind" series—which has been termed "the hottest trend in apocalyptic literature since Hal Lindsey's *The Late Great Planet Earth*."[2] It is also the predominant view in evangelical Christianity.

---

[1] *New York Times,* Front page, October 4, 1998.
[2] Focus on the Family's *Citizen* magazine, December 1998, 6.

Theological Problem:

The so-called "Rapture" was never taught in the Church prior to its invention in the 1830s. And it directly contradicts Scripture.

What Scripture Says:

Jesus specifically prayed against this belief. In his prayer for all believers He prayed that they back then and we today would *not* be removed from the world. "My prayer is not that you take them out of the world but that you protect them from the evil one" (John 17:15, 20). I believe Jesus prayer for all believers is still in effect and that He gets his prayers answered. In perfect consistency, Jesus sent forth his disciples, and us today, into the world (John 17:23) to be salt and light (Matt 5:13-16). Furthermore, He told us that "in this world you will have trouble/tribulation" (John 16:33 *NIV, KJV*). He never said some would escape it.

Another problem is, rapturists think they are going to defy the death rate—which to date is 100 percent—and get out of this world without going through the grave. The Bible, on the other hand, teaches that it's "appointed unto men once to die, but after this the judgment" (Heb 9:27). A Rapture-removal, at best, would be an exception to this, or it's an outright contradiction. Also, an escape from planet Earth is not the subject of any Old Testament prophecy or promise to be fulfilled by the coming Messiah.

Elaborations:

1) Invention of the 'Rapture' idea.
2) A seductive teaching.
3) What else might God have had in mind?
4) Resurrection of the dead ones (plural).
5) 'Bones-are-still-in-the graves' objection.

Sources:

Shattering the 'Left Behind' Delusion by John Noē (out-of-print)
Unraveling the End (future book – est. 2012) by John Noē
End Times Fiction by Gary DeMar
Last Days Madness by Gary DeMar
The Rapture Plot by Dave MacPherson
Rapture Fever by Gary North

(1)
Invention of the 'Rapture' idea.

Rapture-removal is not the historic teaching of the Church. One of the more astonishing facts in the history of eschatological thought, and one that most Christians are unaware of, is that the idea of "a secret pre-tribulation, Rapture removal from the earth of the Church" is a fairly recent theory in Church history. In theological circles, it's a "Johnny come lately." Even the historic creeds, conspicuously, don't mention it. In fact, it was relatively unheard of and never taught until the early 19th century, and it didn't become widespread until the 20th century. Since then, it has spread like wildfire. But the many failed predictions of its coming have made it an embarrassment.

The first known reference may have appeared in two obscure but contestable sentences from a 4th century A.D., 1500-word sermon written in Latin by someone called "Pseudo-Ephraem." If so, this idea went essentially unknown and undeveloped for fourteen centuries. According to most researchers, the idea of a Rapture-removal from planet Earth prior to a "great tribulation" period began to surface in the late 18th and early 19th centuries. Possible but only slight and vague mentions of it may have been published in the writings of a famous Calvinist theologian Dr. John Gill (1748), an early American Baptist pastor Morgan Edwards (1788), a Jesuit priest Emmanuel Lacunza (1812), and Edward Irving, who translated Lacunza's book (1826).

Most scholars, however, agree that the secret Rapture theory was launched into prominence around 1830 by a group of people in Scotland who had become known as the Plymouth Brethren. Under the direction of John Nelson Darby (1800-1882) and others, they began to hold

Prophetic Conferences. Supposedly, during one of those conferences, or from a sick bed during those conferences, a charismatic utterance came forth as a prophetic message from the Lord through a young, fifteen-year-old Scottish girl named Margaret Macdonald. While in a trance, she received a private vision and revelation that only a select group of believers would be removed from the earth before the days of the Antichrist. But she also saw other believers enduring the tribulation—something most rapturists nowadays do not teach.

Soon thereafter, Darby coupled this highly questionable vision of a secret, pre-tribulation Rapture with another idea originated by the Jesuit priest, Francisco Ribera. In 1585 A.D., Ribera was the first to introduce the idea of interrupting Daniel's 70-week, end-time prophecy and inserting a "gap" between the 69th and 70th weeks. This was done to deflect apocalyptic heat from the Reformers who were fueling reformation fervor by claiming the Pope was the Antichrist and the Catholic Church the beast of Revelation. Ribera surmised that the first 69 weeks (483 years) concluded at the baptism of Jesus in 27 A.D., but God had extended the 70th week into the future. Therefore, the Pope and the Catholic Church could not be so accused. Darby grabbed hold of Ribera's severance idea, connected his "Rapture" to the beginning of that final week, and changed that week from a 7-year period of covenantal confirmation to one of tribulation—big difference! (Notably, the Bible never mentions a future 7-year period of tribulation.) He then introduced this now fully developed, pre-tribulation Rapture view (theory) in Europe and later in America. It was popularized in American by inclusion in the notes of the *Scofield Reference Bible* in 1917 and by elaborate End Time event charts published in Clarence Larkin's *Dispensational Truth* in 1918.

Most scholars, however, agree that the secret Rapture theory was launched into prominence around 1830.

Of course, the relative newness of the "Rapture" theory in Church history (180 some years ago) neither proves nor disproves its biblical correctness. But it certainly shouldn't be blindly accepted nor excluded from being questioned and tested (1 Thess. 5:21). Ultimately, the truth can only be found in the Scriptures. But what began as a result of one woman's private vision and charismatic utterance became widely taught, accepted as the truth, and popularized in the thinking of millions. It has become so deeply entrenched that many pastors and Christian leaders assume it is an essential teaching of Church history extending back to apostolic times. It is not. What's more, it is not believed by the majority in the Church today, and with good reasons.

Sources:

Shattering the 'Left Behind' Delusion by John Noē (out-of-print)
Unraveling the End (future book – est. 2012) by John Noē
End Times Fiction by Gary DeMar
Last Days Madness by Gary DeMar
The Rapture Plot by Dave MacPherson
Rapture Fever by Gary North

(2)
A seductive teaching.

As a result, millions of Christians have fallen for a new and seductive teaching. These millions fervently want to believe that some day—and some day soon—they will be removed, alive, from the surface of planet Earth and taken away from their earthly problems and responsibilities. What then will happen to those "left behind?" Supposedly, they will suffer unbelievable havoc and horrors over a 7-year period of tribulation. Sadly, this is the predominant view in conservative, evangelical Christianity. And it has becoming more entrenched and well-known as the phenomenal success of the *Left Behind* craze spread. But make no mistake, ideas and beliefs do have consequences. In this case, they are highly negative.

First, this new theory of a "Rapture" is an affront to Jesus' prayer for all believers that they and we would not be removed from the world (John 17: 15, 20). It's also a disgrace to the great God and his Christ whom we claim to follow because of its highly fabricated and severely flawed system of interpretation that requires abuses and the mishandling of Scripture to support this scenario.

Secondly, what we believe affects what we do, or don't do, and who we are. How sad it is today to see so many of God's people making so much of "the Rapture" as a means of escaping tribulation, and hoping, trusting, and pleading for God to take them out of this world just when they are most needed. Several generations of Christians have already been and are being diverted. Facts are that the modern doctrine of "the Rapture" has produced a withdrawal and abandonment mentality and is in opposition to Christ's prayer for all believers and other teachings as well. Jesus prayed for God to keep his people in the world to carry on his work, not take them out of it. He wants us here working to expand his kingdom and to think long-term about the future of human existence on this planet. But a longing for escape thwarts this purpose and produces too many lazy Christians, who too easily retreat from society and passively wait for Jesus to come back, take them out, and finish the job. They have no hope of things ever getting better until they get much worse. In essence, they have given up on this world, abandoned their calling to be salt and light, and drawn away from involvement. They reason, "Why bother?" because they think this world is about to end and "the Rapture" is very near. Like it or not, it's the prevailing Rapture mentality, and it's a natural response. But as we've seen, it is also a relatively new theory in Church history.

Rightly teaching God's Word is an awesome responsibility. Therefore, just to discredit this new teaching by scripturally refuting what it's *not*, is not enough. We must also discover what verses used to insinuate this "Rapture" truly *were* about and prove what they *mean* for us today and in the future.

Sources:

Shattering the 'Left Behind' Delusion by John Noē (out-of-print)
Unraveling the End (future book – est. 2012) by John Noē
End Times Fiction by Gary DeMar
Last Days Madness by Gary DeMar
The Rapture Plot by Dave MacPherson
Rapture Fever by Gary North

(3)
What else might God have had in mind?

Since there is no direct or explicit teaching to support Christ coming *for* the Church and taking it to heaven, the Rapture-removal doctrine grows out of deductive reasoning (inference) and goes something like this: Since sin and death exist in the material world, God must snatch his saints out of it, destroy it, then create a new and sinless world. Forget about God loving the world enough to give his only begotten Son for it (John 3:16-17). Forget about Jesus' prayer for all believers that we would not be removed from the world. Those Scriptures, according to the Rapture doctrine, are *not* to be taken literally; but the ones about a catching up and snatching away *are* to be taken literally.

Perhaps you have wondered why so many Christians risk so much on their novel idea of a Rapture-removal from planet Earth—versus staying here, living, reigning and overcoming with Christ as we've been commanded to do. God's Word gives example after example and promise after promise, not of "rapturing" his people out of their tribulation, but to see them through it.

Many have also wondered why God would be prophetically obliged to rescue a "church" from the world's mess that the church's neglect and impotency is largely responsible for allowing. Within this past century, the church in America has lost much of its long-range vision and its unique position, moral influence, and leadership in our society. Pessimism and fatalism now prevail in many of its ranks. While we have been awaiting the "Rapture," Satan and his cohorts have been stealing our children, our schools, and almost all of our culture.

It's far past time for us to wake up! The idea of a one-time, future, physical removal of believers from planet Earth is a major factor in this decline. It's also a new theory in Church history and does not reflect the terminology or teachings of the Bible. It's a false hope and a destructive teaching. The biblical truth is, God has chosen to leave his people and his Church in the world for good reasons. But it's easy to see why the idea of a great escape is so deceptively appealing:

1) Many Christians are afraid of dying and will grasp at any hope of avoiding a trip through a dirt grave to reach heaven.

We'll spend more money trying to stay alive than we've ever given to the Lord.

2) This world is an evil place that is beating up on us, and the idea of a Rapture offers the easiest and quickest way out.

3) It offers a most-convenient excuse to avoid our scripturally mandated responsibilities here on earth in this life and to thereby sooth our guilty conscious.

So *what else* might God have had in mind? As we shall see, next, it was something far different and far greater.

Sources:

Shattering the 'Left Behind' Delusion by John Noē (out-of-print)
Unraveling the End (future book – est. 2012) by John Noē
End Times Fiction by Gary DeMar
Last Days Madness by Gary DeMar
The Rapture Plot by Dave MacPherson
Rapture Fever by Gary North

(4)
Resurrection of the dead ones (plural).

All the Scriptures used by popular "Rapture" writers and teachers were actually fulfilled by real and bodily resurrections. These occurred during the 1st century. These occurrences are some of the most ignored, distorted, confused, and misunderstood realities and concepts in Christianity. No more!

Key passages are: 1 Thessalonians 4:13-18 and 1 Corinthians 15. In the Corinthian passage, an order for these resurrections is revealed:

But Christ has indeed been raised from the dead, the firstfruits of those who have fallen asleep. For since death came through a man, the resurrection of the dead comes also through a man. For as in Adam all die, so in Christ all will be made alive. ***But each [every man] in his own turn [order]:*** *Christ, the firstfruits; then, when he comes [at his coming], those who belong to him* (1 Cor. 15:20-23 *NIV*, [*KJV*]).

If it is true, as the "Left Behind" people tell us, that for over nineteen centuries and counting these inspired words of Paul have not been fulfilled, then the nonoccurrence of this event presents a highly problematic dilemma:

1) Paul's words of encouragement turned out to be a cruel misrepresentation in the lives of his original readers.
2) 1st-century believers actually ended up deceiving each other with these words rather than encouraging each other (1 Thess. 4:13, 18). And they died "in vain" not having received what they expected in their lifetime (1 Cor. 15:14).
3) If Paul's Holy-Spirit-guided imminency expectations proved false, how can we trust him to have conveyed other aspects of the faith along to us correctly (John 16:13)?

Let's see if we can arrive at a better understanding, from a *sola Scriptura* standpoint, of the order and time of fulfillment in four successive resurrection stages:

Stage #1 – Jesus' resurrection.

The bodily resurrection of Jesus Christ is one of the most well-attested and well-known facts of human history. No other event has such overwhelming weight of evidence and left such an impact on the world. What is not well-known is that this event marked the beginning of the "last days"/eschatological resurrection of the dead ones (plural).

Stage #2 – More bodily resurrections.

Using harvest imagery and the metaphor of the "firstfruits," more resurrections took place as the bodies of many (not all) Old Testament saints came out of their graves and paraded through the streets of Jerusalem:

> *And behold, the veil of the temple was torn in two from top to bottom, and the earth shook; and the rocks split, and the tombs were opened; and **many bodies** of the saints who had*

*fallen asleep were **raised**; and coming out of the tombs (graves), and **after** his [Jesus'] resurrection they entered the holy city [Jerusalem] and appeared to many* (Matt. 27:51-53 – **bold** is mine).

This event confirms that they were living in the eschatological and biblical "last days," back then and there, because the general resurrection of the dead was now underway. No doubt, this was why the Apostle Paul, during his defense before King Agrippa remarked, "Why should any of you consider it incredible that God raises the dead?" (Acts 26:8). The Greek word translated "dead" here is in the plural—i.e., "dead ones" or "dead persons." This is the proper translation. For more plural usages see: Acts 17:32; 23:6; 24:21; 1 Cor. 15:12, 13, 15, and 16. But resurrection for the rest of the dead ones (the harvest) was still being anticipated as the New Testament was being penned.

Stage #3 – Resurrection Day for the rest of the dead ones.

Thirty years after the above two resurrection events, the Apostle Paul wrote:

> . . . *I believe everything that agrees with the Law and that is written in the Prophets, and I have the same hope in God as these men, that there **will be** [to be about to be] a resurrection of both the righteous and the wicked* (Acts 24:15).

Two of Paul's key words in this passage are *mellein esesthai*. Traditionally, they have been translated as "will be" or "shall be." In the literal Greek, however, they are: "to be about to be." This double-intensified force of imminency is missed in all major English translations of the Bible. But the dye was already cast. The resurrection harvest had already begun. All that awaited was the "last day" (singular – John 6:39, 40, 44, 54; 11:24) of the "last days" (plural – Heb. 1:2).

That day came! At some point in the late summer or early fall of A.D. 70, or perhaps two or three years later in A.D. 72 or 73—

when the last stone was removed (Matt. 24:2), the field plowed over (Mic. 3:12; Jer. 26:18), and the prophesied point of "desolation" reached (Matt. 23:38)—the rest of the dead were raised. But unlike before, and in keeping with the applied harvest metaphor, no resurrection bodies were seen rising out of graves or parading around Jerusalem. Rather, their souls were taken out of the hadean realm, that spirit-realm holding place of the dead, taken to heaven, and given their judgment and "spiritual" resurrection bodies (1 Cor. 15:44). This end is history. It all took place within the spirit realm and within the time span of Jesus' "this generation" (Matt. 24:34). Moreover, this fulfillment is in perfect harmony with the imminency expectations of every New Testament writer and the early Christian community (John 16:13). This often-prophesied and imminently expected end was covenantal, and not cosmic. It occurred within history, and not at history's end—for which there is no end.

Stage #4 – The ongoing reality—"each" or "every man in his own turn/order."

From that time on, the next saint to physically die, never again went to Hades, that spirit-realm holding place of the dead, to await resurrection and judgment. Jesus who holds "the keys to death and Hades" (Rev. 1:18; 20:13-14), had emptied it out and locked it up, forever. Therefore, after Resurrection Day on the "last day," it's straight to heaven upon physical death for believers to receive their judgment and a new, "spiritual" resurrection body (1 Cor. 15:44). Heaven's door is now open wide. This fulfilled reality is in contrast to no one being in heaven during Jesus' earthly ministry (John 3:13; 13:33, 36).

Sources:

Shattering the 'Left Behind' Delusion by John Noē (out-of-print)
Unraveling the End (future book – est. 2012) by John Noē

(5)
'Bones-are-still-in-the-graves' objection.

Not so, insist the vast majority of Christian scholars. Go out to any graveyard, dig up a grave, and we can prove that this "last day" resurrection has not yet taken place. Why not? It's because the "bones are still in the graves."

This objection is simply a misunderstanding of the nature of bodily resurrection. It's assumed that since Jesus' self-same earthly and physical body arose from the grave, so will our old dead, decayed, and perhaps decomposed bodies. But is this assumption biblically accurate? Here are three reasons why it is not accurate:

1) Jesus' body was the only one promised not to see decay (Acts 2:25, 27, 31; 13:35 from Psa. 16:10; 49:9). This promise was made to no one else.
2) God does not need our old and perhaps scattered atoms and molecules from our previous physical body to give us a new "spiritual" body (1 Cor. 15: 38, 44).
3) In Paul's seed analogy in 1 Corinthians 15:37, the outer shell of a seed stays in the ground and decomposes. It does not become part of the new plant. What could be any clearer than this? Scripture never speaks of us receiving a resurrected, old earthly and physical body. Big difference.

So what will our new "spiritual" body be like? All we are told is, it "will be like his [Jesus'] glorious body" (Phil. 3:21). One other thing is also for sure. None of these resurrection verses promised a Rapture-removal of a group of believers someday off the surface of planet Earth.

For more: listen to podcasts on PRI's website (www.prophecyrefi.org) for the "Unraveling the End" MPC series on PRI's website (www.prophecyrefi.org) and listen to Lessons #12 and 13a.

Sources:

Shattering the 'Left Behind' Delusion by John Noē (out-of-print)
Unraveling the End (future book – est. 2012) by John Noē

Exposé #8

Antichrist

"The Antichrist is coming. We are looking for a man of unparalleled evil, an ultimate enemy who will deceive the world in the final days with his words and wonders. Will we know him when we see him?"

It's the advertising pitch for premillennial dispensationalist Mark Hitchcock's latest, end-times book titled, *Who Is the Antichrist?*[1]

Part and parcel of the futuristic end-times scenario popularized by the recent "Left Behind" series is a single world leader, called "the Antichrist," who wrecks havoc on all humankind for a 7- or 3 ½-year period of great tribulation. Meanwhile, all true Christians—having been raptured—are in heaven enjoying themselves and avoiding all the tribulations being put forth on earth.

This most popular postponement tradition claims that this wicked one is a future "Antichrist" figure that has yet to be revealed. Over the centuries, he has been variously identified as Attila the Hun, Napoleon, the Pope, Martin Luther, Mohammed, Hitler, Mussolini, Stalin, Franklin Roosevelt, Henry Kissinger, and Mikhail Gorbachev. Virtually every unpopular public figure has qualified. Obviously, this tradition has

---

[1] From ad in *Charisma* magazine, September 2011, 28.

proven totally inept at identifying this "Antichrist." Unfortunately, it's a tradition that has not died.

Theological Problem:

The Bible says nothing about a future-coming 7-year period of tribulation. But what does it say about "the Antichrist?" The answer is nothing in the Old Testament. Jesus never mentioned him. Nor did Peter, Paul, or any of the Gospel writers. Nor is he mentioned in the apocalyptic books of Daniel or Revelation. The only two places in the entire Bible where "antichrist" can be found are in the two short epistles of 1st and 2nd John. Here, however, we find statements that do not support the current and popular view of a future-coming world dictator.

What Scripture Says:

It's almost unbelievable how some Christians speculate that some future and final Antichrist is the one who confirms the covenant in Daniel's 70th week. What is their textual proof? There is none.

First, in Scripture, there is no such thing as a "final Antichrist." "Many antichrists" (note the plural, see 1 John 2:18) were present in the midst of 1st-century saints, and have been present ever since (1 John 2:22; 2 John 7). Moreover, they don't confirm covenants. Only God makes and confirms covenants. If anything, antichrists break them. Speculation about some future, final Antichrist is just that—pure speculation that has been read into prophecy.

"Many antichrists" ... were present in the midst of 1st-century saints, and have been present ever since.

Secondly, the idea that the beast of Revelation 13 or Paul's "man of sin in 2 Thessalonians 2 are the Antichrist is also purely assumptive. No such connection is ever made in Scripture. And we must pay close attention to what the Bible actually says and does not say. But many have not. Hence, for several centuries, Christianity has appeared foolish as the popular endsayers of their day have continually attempted to name the latest global villain as the "biblical Antichrist."

Thirdly, Jesus was the One who, through his crucifixion and resurrection, put a stop to the Jewish sacrifices. It was not some future Antichrist in some distant revived Roman Empire inside a rebuilt Jewish temple in Jerusalem. Moreover, there is no possible way a future Antichrist could fulfill even one of the six purpose statements encapsulated in this prophecy (see Dan. 9:24). Likewise, there is no need to reconstruct the same socio-political conditions of that 1st century, or revive the days of Rome, or reestablish any of the obsoleted institutions of the old Judaic system (Heb. 8:13) in order for them to be destroyed, *again*. Nor is there any need to forecast these repetitions of fulfilled end-time prophecy. It need never *again* be repeated.

**Christianity has appeared foolish
as the popular endsayers of their day
have continually attempted to name the latest global
villain as the "biblical Antichrist."**

This redundancy idea is terrible scholarship. The Bible says nothing about the Jews building a third temple in our day or in the future. Let's call this theology for what it truly is—the re-Judaizing of biblical faith (Christianity). Sadly, it has great appeal, if not a strange hypnotic power, over many who claim they are the ones who are "rightly dividing the Word of truth" (2 Tim. 2:15). If we have ever wondered how "the elect" could possibly be deceived in our day as Jesus warned (Matt. 24:24), here is another way. This delayed and deferment view does not serve the work of the Church or the purposes of God one *iota*.

Fourthly and finally, John defines who and what an "antichrist" was and is. "It is the man who denies that Jesus is the Christ . . . . Many deceivers, who do not acknowledge Jesus Christ as coming in the flesh, have gone out into the world. *Any such person is the deceiver and the antichrist*" (1 John 2:22; 2 John 7). Facts are, there were many antichrists back in that 1st century, have been many since, are many today, and will be many in the future. This is the whole teaching of Scripture on this topic of "antichrist."

Enough said. Case closed.

Sources:

The Perfect Ending for the World by John Noē
The Last Days According to Jesus by R.C. Sproul
Last Days Madness by Gary DeMar
End Times Fiction by Gary DeMar
Dictionary of Biblical Prophecy and End Times by Hays, Duvall, and
Pate

Exposé #9

The Contemporary Christ

Most people today recognize that to get to know someone, anyone, it's important we learn about their past—what they were like and what they did. But what is more important is what they are like and doing now. Why? It's because people change. The same is true if you want to know and follow Jesus as He really is today.

Theological Problem:

Every week, all around the world, a story is told and retold. For almost two thousand years, people have gathered in churches, schools, universities, seminaries, conferences, and Bible studies to hear that story. In our times, it has drawn millions more to the movies, to their TVs and radios, and onto the Internet. It has been dubbed "the greatest story ever told." It is about a man called Jesus of Nazareth—his birth, his life, his death, and his resurrection—two thousand years ago. And this story is important.

But what's more important and the big problem here is—He's not like that anymore. No longer is Jesus the sleeping baby in the manger we celebrate every Christmas, or a young man ministering in Galilee, or a dead man hanging on a cross, or even the resurrected, pre-ascended Lord. Yes, Jesus lowered himself to become a man. But now, he's not like that anymore.

What Scripture Says:

The only place we can turn to find out what Jesus is really like and doing today is to the greatly misunderstood and abused book of Revelation. Here, Jesus is unveiled in his present-day reality. And we can discover some amazing things about Him, such as: He looks different than the way we usually picture and think of Him—He rides a horse, He hosts a banquet, He comes, He fights the battle of Armageddon, He conquers some awesome creatures, He sits on a throne, He makes everything new, and He lives in a new city.

One thing is for sure, this is not the sleeping-baby-in-the-manger Jesus, the boy Jesus growing up in Egypt and Judea, or the young man Jesus ministering on a hillside in Galilee. Nor is it the crucified Jesus hanging on a cross. Here, in the Bible's last book, Jesus unveils and reveals Himself in his present-day form and global (cosmic) reality. And He's not just sitting around up in heaven waiting to come back. He's in our midst all around the world.

Elaborations:

1) A much greater Jesus
2) The historical Jesus
3) The unveiling.
4) Overcoming a major misconception.
5) Latest picture of Jesus.
6) Many countless comings.
7) He still comes.

Sources:

The Greater Jesus (future book – est. 2012) by John Noē
The Apocalypse Conspiracy by John Noē (out-of-print)

(1)
A much greater Jesus.

Make no mistake, this is the living and active Jesus of today, Who is in our world and in our midst and operates in a *much greater* manner and functions in *much broader* capacities than during his earthly ministry. Consequently, He is *much greater* than most of us can fathom and have been led to believe. He is the ascended, exalted, glorified, transformed, transfigured, transcended, apocalyptic, cosmic, crowned, and contemporary Christ of the Apocalypse, unveiled and revealed in the Bible's last book of Revelation.

And yet He is the same Jesus who walked, breathed, and left huge footprints in the sand of history and in the lives of countless millions ever since. But that story is also 2,000-year-old history! What's more important is what this Jesus is like and doing today.

No longer is Jesus the earth-bound, historical Jesus multiple millions have come to know and love. No longer is He confined within an earthly human body. Simply put, those views of Jesus are out-of-date and inadequate. He is a much greater Jesus. The Bible—which I believe every word is true—clearly and emphatically reveals this change. It's the revelation of the *contemporary Christ.*

Source:

The Greater Jesus (future book – est. 2012) by John Noē

(2)
The historical Jesus.

Over the past two-and-a-half centuries, a field of study has arisen that is termed the search for the historical Jesus. It has produced thousands of books attempting to discover more about this Jesus of Nazareth. Some of these writers accepted the Scriptures as inspired, infallible, and inerrant and proceeded from there. Others did not, and saw no reason to treat the Bible any differently than any other book. So they approached the scriptural accounts critically, preferring instead to augment or discredit them using other historical sources, human reasoning, and naturalistic speculation.

During the past 15 to 20 years many more historical-Jesus books have been written speculating upon and trying to find an alternative Jesus—i.e., the "real," "true," "other," "third" or "simply" Jesus, etc. Hence, Jesus remains a "hot topic." Some of the questions continuing to be asked are: Who really was this Jesus? What did He really say and do? How did He view Himself and his mission? Why was He crucified? Was He really resurrected from the dead? But whatever the various answers might be from different authors, one thing is sure. He's not like that anymore!

Sources:

The Greater Jesus (future book – est. 2012) by John Noē
The Jesus I Never Knew by Philip Yancey
The Quest of the Historical Jesus by Albert Schweitzer

(3)
The unveiling.

My primary goal in this book is to encourage both believers and non-believers, alike, to take a serious new look at Jesus Christ in his unveiled and revealed contemporary form. I believe this higher and greater perspective will ring true and stir you on to higher and greater heights of faith, worship, and obedience.

So if you want to see the latest and only picture of Jesus we have today—one that is sharp, clear, true, authoritative, and more revealing and challenging than any of those of the historical Jesus—there is only one place you can go. That is to the greatly misunderstood and abused book of Revelation. Unfortunately, this last book of the Bible has both fascinated and frustrated Bible readers for centuries. Its apocalyptic content and symbolic style still confuse and frighten most readers. But its first five words make it perfectly clear that this book's purpose and over-arching theme is to unveil and reveal a greater Jesus as He now is, and not to satisfy our intellectual curiosity about distant, future events or some "antichrist." It's "the revelation of Jesus Christ" (Rev. 1:1). The

Greek word translated "revelation" is *apokalypsis*. It's our word "apocalypse." The kind of imagery that comes to most people's mind in our day when they see or hear the word apocalypse is total devastation, a nuclear holocaust, or an exploding universe. That's why we have books and movies like *The Four Horsemen of the Apocalypse* and *Apocalypse Now*. But what did this word mean to John, who wrote down the Revelation, and to the Greek-speaking people for whom he wrote it nineteen centuries ago?

So if you want to see the latest and only picture of Jesus we have today—one that is sharp, clear, true, authoritative, and more revealing and challenging than any of those of the historical Jesus —there is only one place you can go.

The Greek word *apokalypsis* simply means an "unveiling" or "uncovering" both from and of Jesus Christ. Hence, Revelation unveils and uncovers Jesus of the Apocalypse in his present, ascended, and glorified form. It further details his past, present, and future activities— i.e., his involvement and interactions with humankind and spirit-realm beings. Yet most current teachings, books, and movies on the Revelation conclude that the book is primarily about Satan, his cohorts, and the supposed Antichrist and what they are supposedly going to be doing to our world at some future date. Consequently, they also miss out on this book's promised blessings in this life, here and now. No more. It is time we know Jesus as He really is today.

Source:

The Greater Jesus (future book – est. 2012) by John Noē

(4)
Overcoming a major misconception.

The fact remains, if you really want to know and follow Jesus as He is today—what He's like and what He is doing—you must come, expectantly, to the last book of the Bible. The book of Revelation is the climax, the completion, the pinnacle of God's progressive revelation to humankind. It is the only source that unveils and reveals Jesus in his present-day, pertinent, and full exalted, glorified, transformed, transfigured, and transcendent reality. This is *the Jesus of the Apocalypse, the contemporary Christ, and a much greater Jesus than most of us have been led to believe!* This is the Jesus each of us, today, needs to meet, know, and take seriously.

Make no mistake, this is the living and active Jesus of today who is in the world and in our midst and functions in a *much greater* manner and in *much broader* capacities than He did during his earthly ministry and than most of us have been led to believe. And yet, this is the same Jesus Who was born of a virgin, raised as a boy, ministered throughout Judea, and died on a cross. Without this historical Jesus we would still be lost in our sins (1 Cor. 15:17). So we must stay grounded in this Jesus who was "made a little lower than the angels" (Heb. 2:7, 9) and "made Himself nothing, taking the very nature [form] of a servant, being made in human likeness" (Phil. 2:7).

But we also must understand that this same Jesus is no longer confined in an earthly human body. Nowadays, He is both the same and a greater Jesus. Why is this so? It is because after his birth, earthly life, death, burial, resurrection, and ascension, "God exalted him to the highest place and gave him the name that is above every name that at the name of Jesus every knee should bow, in heaven and on earth and under the earth, and every tongue confess that Jesus Christ is Lord, to the glory of God the Father" (Phil. 2:8-11; also Eph. 1:20-23). "So he became as much superior to the angels as the name he has inherited is superior to theirs" (Heb. 1:4).

Consequently, we must also recognize that the divinely determined mission of Jesus—his leaving heaven, coming to earth, and going back to heaven—was a change in his bodily form and ministerial capacity. Therefore, Revelation's last revealed form of Jesus is a more complex Jesus than during his earthly ministry. Whether you agreed or disagreed that this same Jesus has changed somehow—from before creation to cradle to cross to coronation—one thing perhaps we can agree upon now is this Jesus today is a *much greater* Jesus than has been and is generally being presented, preached, and perceived in most churches.

In my opinion, the tragedy today is many people in most churches miss this point. Hence, they don't know Jesus in the greater way the Revelation unveils and reveals Him. This deficiency accounts for much of the lack of faith, power, and effectiveness in the Church today. Yet every year we joyously and magnificently present to Christians and non-Christians, alike, the image of Jesus as a baby—so tiny, so adorable, and so helpless. Frankly put, fixating on and perpetuating this 2,000-year-old image of the historical Jesus, or any image of Him during his earthly life, is, at best, a partial and outdated view.

Source:

The Greater Jesus (future book – est. 2012) by John Noē

(5)
Latest picture of Jesus.

The first chapter of the book of Revelation (the Apocalypse) unveils and reveals the latest, the most, and arguably the only physically descriptive picture of Jesus in the Bible. By inspiration, John records what he heard and saw:

I, John, your brother and companion in the suffering and kingdom and patient endurance that are ours in Jesus, was on the island of Patmos because of the word of God and the testimony of Jesus. On the Lord's Day I was in the Spirit, and I heard behind me a loud voice like a trumpet, which said: "Write on a scroll what you see and send it to the seven churches: to Ephesus, Smyrna, Pergamum, Thyatira, Sardis, Philadelphia, and Laodicea.

I turned around to see the voice that was speaking to me. And when I turned I saw seven golden lampstands, and among the lampstands was someone "like a son of man," dressed in a

robe reaching down to his feet and with a golden sash around his chest. His head and hair were white like wool, as white as snow, and his eyes were like blazing fire. His feet were like bronze glowing in a furnace, and his voice was like the sound of rushing waters. In his right hand he held seven stars, and out of his mouth came a sharp double-edged sword. His face was like the sun shining in all its brilliance.

(Revelation 1:9-16)

Yes, this is Jesus *as He is right now!* We are not told here the meaning of the sword coming out of his mouth or why his hair is white and his eyes like blazing fire, etc. Nor are we told why a crown of thorns no longer encircles his head. But one thing is sure. He is no longer the Jesus of popular thought and tradition. He is that, but He is also now much more. Here He is pictured as the ascended, exalted, glorified, transformed, transfigured, transcendent, cosmic, and crowned *Jesus of the Apocalypse, the contemporary Christ!*

Grasping the full reality of this divinely revealed image of Jesus and knowing and serving Him as He is today, and as He requires, are essential prerequisites if we hope to hear the words someday, "Well done, good and faithful servant" (Matt. 25:21, 23). Anything less is less. But where is this image of Jesus being presented, nowadays? Where is this picture of the contemporary Christ hanging on a wall? Where is this present-day perspective being taught, studied, and worshiped?

Here He is pictured as the ascended, exalted, glorified, transformed, transfigured, transcendent, cosmic, and crowned *Jesus of the Apocalypse, the contemporary Christ!*

Since the time John saw Jesus like this over nineteen hundred years ago, this Jesus has not changed. Yes, "Jesus Christ is the same yesterday and today and forever" (Heb. 13:8). That is, He is the same in his Personhood and divinity—the second Person of the Trinity. But some theologians contend that what is meant by the word "yesterday" is that Jesus has never changed from his preexistence before creation. And that assertion is partially true. But a partial truth parading as a whole truth is a lie! The testimony of Scripture is, Jesus has changed—in some major ways—from his preexistent form, into a babe, into a boy, into a man, into a dead man, into a resurrected body, and onto being the ascended, exalted, glorified, transformed, transfigured, transcendent, cosmic, and crowned Lord of the Apocalypse. Another fact these theologians tend to overlook is, more than 12,000 literal "yesterdays" transpired between Jesus' ascension and glorification in A.D. 30 (see Dan. 7:13-14) and the time of the writing of this verse in the book of Hebrews circa A.D. 65-67. Thus, we can both affirm that Jesus "is the same yesterday and today and forever" and yet He has changed.

So how did John respond after seeing and hearing Jesus this way in the Revelation? Remember, John had personally known and served Jesus during his earthly ministry, had stood at the foot of the cross, and even saw Jesus after his death in his post-resurrected form. Yet this Jesus of the Apocalypse was so different, so awesome, and so much greater than John had previously known that he reports, "When I saw him, I fell at his feet as though dead" (Rev. 1:17a).

Ask yourself, how would you react if this Jesus suddenly appeared to you face-to-face, like this, and in this form? Well, if you have the eyes of faith—i.e., spiritual eyes to see, He just did. Otherwise, these words in the first chapter of the Revelation are only ink on a page. One of the blessings of the book of Revelation offers is for Jesus to appear to you, personally, face-to-face, here and now, as He is today, through these inspired words.

Source:

The Greater Jesus (future book – est. 2012) by John Noē

(6)
Many countless comings.

Over the centuries, and as we have seen, no idea has ever gripped the human imagination more firmly than the doctrine of a Second Coming or the Return of Jesus Christ. Nor has any idea ever created more needless confusion, anxiety, or spiritual poverty among Christians and more discredit for Christ's Church in the eyes of the world. As dates have come and gone, history has continually proven false those who have tried to predict when the Second Coming will occur. Initially, this quest was considered a fringe movement or flat-out heresy. However, within the past sixty short years it has become a central tenet of American Protestantism and prime preoccupation of evangelical Christians. So we have seen a barrage of future predictions with their missed times and dates having come and gone. But with every war or global disturbance a new wave of predictive books and materials suddenly appears. In their wake, all of these writers and teachers have been left with one thing in common: they have all been wrong. Unfortunately, this fact does not seem to deter the next wave of date-setters eager to capitalize on this fear.

But the testimony of Scripture is there have been many previous comings of Jesus. They run like a thread throughout both the Old and New Testaments. And many more countless comings are promised. Clearly and convincingly, Jesus' comings cannot be limited to two or three times, or to any at all as is commonly assumed. Furthermore, Jesus has promised to continue coming in many different ways, for different purposes, at different times, in different locations, and to different people. The book of Revelation offers further support for this ongoing reality and ministry of the *contemporary Christ*.

Source:

The Greater Jesus (future book – est. 2012) by John Noē

(7)
He still comes.

What saddens and troubles me deeply is the popular idea that Jesus is off somewhere waiting to come back or to return. Yet Scripture declares He never left, is here with us right now in our midst, and still comes in many wondrous ways. But millions of Christians don't know it and most churches don't recognize his many comings. That's another reason why they don't experience Him more fully in everyday life. What a tragedy!

This is the living and active Jesus of today, the *contemporary Christ*, who is in our world and in our midst and operates in a *much greater* manner and functions in *much broader* capacities than during his earthly ministry. Consequently, He is *much greater* than most of us can fathom and have been led to believe. I assure you; this realization will not only transform your life, but most importantly, will transform you. (See again Exposé #6.)

To put it in the vernacular of today, Jesus is in the comings business. And He is still active and involved with his creation (Rev. 1:13, 20). But some of you may be wondering, how does Jesus come? Simply put, He comes in and out of the spirit realm, sometimes visibly, sometimes not. And I believe it is time for God's people to wake up to the full meaning, power, and reality of Christ's presence and many comings in and out of that spirit realm. Yet some may question if Christ's many countless comings are a second-rate option? The answer is, "No! A thousand times, no! The spirit realm is as real as anything you hold in your hands. It may even be more real, because it is eternal. And the personal and bodily presence of Jesus Himself is in the spirit realm and his many countless comings in many different ways into and out of the physical realm are a here-and-now, ongoing reality." This is precisely what continues to happen, occasionally and/or frequently, from Jesus' abiding and omnipresent presence with us, all around this world. For further support of this present-day and pertinent phenomenon, let's go to the book of Revelation.

To put it in the vernacular of today, Jesus is in the comings business. And He is still active and involved with his creation

---

Source:

The Greater Jesus (future book – est. 2012) by John Noē

Exposé #10

Book of Revelation

Three of the most perplexing questions with which I have wrestled for many years in the theological area known as eschatology (the study of last things) have been these:

1) Why don't most Christians know the pertinent truths and empowering realities the book of Revelation teaches?
2) Why is there so much confusion, controversy, and conflict among Christians and churches over this book—which reveals Jesus Christ as He is today?
3) Why can't a typical, ordinary layperson study this prophecy and trust the Holy Spirit to guide him or her into its truths?

Theological Problem:

Real estate agents have a comical but serious saying. They insist that the three most important factors in selling a property are: "Location! Location! Location!" In a similar fashion, what do you think are the three most important factors or rules for properly understanding the meaning of any piece of literature, including the Bible? The answer is: "Context! Context! Context!"

Yet the #1 reason why most people, and for centuries and today as well, have misread, misunderstood, and miss-taught the prophecy of the book of Revelation is because they have failed to place it in its divinely determined context before they try to interpret and understand it. Consequently, they lift it out of its context, stretch it like a rubber band— 1900 years and counting— plop it down out in the future, and create a pretext. A pretext allows the reader to make a text mean almost anything he or she desires. As a result the intended and true meaning is distorted and missed. Conflict and confusion then prevail between different views. And readers don't receive this book's wisdom nor promised blessings.

What Scripture Says:

The book of Revelation contextualizes itself. Therefore, by recognizing and honoring the divinely determined time and nature context this book of prophecy places upon itself, we can be better assured of grasping its true message and meaning and unlocking its wisdom and promised blessings, here and now. To do this, we must arrive at a proper understanding of these five foundational questions.

Elaborations:

1) How do we handle its strange imagery?
2) When was it most likely written?
3) How do we handle its time statements?
4) When was or will it be fulfilled?
5) What is its relevance for us today?

Sources:

The Greater Jesus (future book – est. 2012) by John Noē
The Scene Behind the Seen (future book – est. 2015-16) by John Noē
"An Exegetical Basis for a Preterist-Idealist Understanding of the Book of Revelation," article in *Journal of the Evangelical Theological Society*, Vol. 49, No. 4 (Dec. 2006) by John Noē
The Days of Vengeance by David Chilton
The Book of Revelation by Foy E. Wallace
More Than Conquerors by William Hendriksen

(1)
How do we handle its strange imagery?

The book of Revelation uses figurative language and symbols to reveal spiritual/physical events and spirit-realm realities. During his earthly ministry, Jesus used physical/material symbols to convey spirit-realm/physical-realm realities when He taught in parables. These are used because we humans have no frame of reference to enable us to understand the realities of the spirit realm. We can only relate what we don't know to what we do know.

Hence, the strange imagery of the Revelation is not God's way of keeping us confused. Rather, it represents the efforts of an infinite God to communicate with finite human beings about truth and reality in both the spiritual and physical realms. In other words, it's a behind-the-scenes peek at the reality behind the reality, the unseen world behind the seen natural world, and the great things taking place in the invisible spirit realm and how these interact with and manifest themselves in the visible physical world. Fact is, the natural world is only part of God's created reality. And the unseen world is just as real, has a powerful effect on the seen world, and plays an active role in individual lives and in human history.

The trouble lies not with the way God has chosen to convey his message but with the way we humans try to grasp it. We simply cannot grasp invisible spiritual reality in the same way as scientific or historical knowledge. Spiritual reality can only be grasped by faith, through spiritual ears (see 1 Cor. 1:18-25; 3:19; Rev. 2:7; 2:11; 2:17; 2:29; 3:6; 3:13; 3:22) and eyes (Matt.13:13-15, from Isaiah 6:9-10). Therefore, God has not complicated "the Revelation of Jesus Christ." He merely speaks in figurative language, signs, and symbols to reveal spirit-realm/physical-realm realities, but millions have tried to understand his meanings in purely physical/material terms.

We need to interpret and understand the stories and imagery of the Revelation just as we interpret and understand the parables and symbols Jesus used in the Gospel narratives—figuratively, as metaphors and similes that express both spiritual and physical realities. The parables and symbols of the Apocalypse become complicated and frightening only when we take the book's language literally, purely physically— something that God never intended for us to do. Revelation's very first verse stipulates this communication style thusly, "and he [God] sent and signified it by his angel unto his servant John" (Rev. 1:1 *KJV*). The word "signified" (Greek word, *semaino*) most literally and graphically means "sign – ified"—i.e., making known or communicating with signs and symbols. Hence, if we take the Revelation precisely for what it is, visual parables of spiritual/physical reality, any sincere believer can better understand it.

It's a behind-the-scenes peek at the reality behind the reality, the unseen world behind the seen natural world . . . .

But the physical/material mindset—the so-called scientific approach—denies or ignores the dimension of the spirit and blinds us to the spirit-world realities the Revelation reveals. Once, however, we accept that God is speaking in spirit-realm/physical-realm terms using signs and symbols, the Revelation begins to open up its treasures to us.

Source:

The Greater Jesus (future book – est. 2012) by John Noē
The Scene Behind the Seen (future book – est. 2015-16) by John Noē

(2)
When was it most likely written?

When the book of the Revelation was actually given to John on the isle of Patmos is of critical importance in unlocking its mysteries. Unfortunately, scholars have reached different conclusions after assessing the dating evidence. The majority contends for a date around A.D. 95 or 96. This date is termed the "late date." But a sizeable and growing minority feels the Revelation was written prior to Jerusalem's and the Temple's destruction in A.D. 70. This is termed the "early date." Adherence to the late date effectively rules out any contemporary and significant historical event as the soon-coming fulfillment or any relevance for its original and named recipients. But acceptance of the early date opens the possibility that it describes those events leading up to and including Jerusalem's fall and the destruction of the Temple in A.D. 70.

Notably, Philip Schaff, who wrote *History of the Christian Church* in eight volumes, and in the Preface to his Revised Edition, admits that "on two points I have changed my opinion – the second Roman captivity of Paul . . . and the date of the Apocalypse (which I now assign, with the majority of modern critics, to the year 68 or 69 instead of 95, as before)."[1]

Most interestingly, the major piece of dating evidence cited by the popular late-date theorists is an ambiguous and questionable passage written by Irenaeus, one of the early Church fathers who wrote around A.D. 180-190. But translation difficulties, precludes this passage from being used as evidence. Moreover, Irenaeus said nothing about the date of the writing of Revelation. The bigger issue with Irenaeus, however, is his credibility. He claimed that Jesus' earthly ministry lasted approximately fifteen years and that Jesus lived to be almost fifty years old. Thus, the difficulties with Irenaeus' writings in this dating matter are many and varied.

On the other hand, and in my opinion, arguments for the early date are superior, both quantitatively and qualitatively, to those advanced for the late date. For example, of the two types of dating evidence, scholars generally acknowledge internal evidence (contained inside a document) as preferable and taking precedence over external evidence (what others, like Irenaeus, have said about a document).

John A.T. Robinson in his book *Redating the New Testament* points out that Revelation, along with all New Testament books, says nothing about the destruction of Jerusalem and the Temple in A.D. 70. He terms this omission as "one of the oddest facts," and questions why this event "is never once mentioned as a past fact" by any New Testament book, even though it is "predicted" and "would appear to be the single most datable and climactic event of the period."[2]

---

[1] Philip Schaff, *History of the Christian Church*, Vol. 1, (Grand Rapids, MI.: Eerdmans, 1910 [third revision]) *vi*, also 420, 834n.

[2] John A.T. Robinson, *Redating the New Testament* (Philadelphia, PA.: Westminster Press, 1976) 13.

This omission propelled Robinson's re-dating study. His hypothesis and eventual conclusion was that "the whole of the New Testament was written before 70." He places the writing of Revelation in A.D. 68.[3] Admittedly, Robinson's argument is an argument from silence. But those who claim that Revelation was written in AD 95-96 do have major difficulties explaining this omission.

For these and many other reasons (see my article below in Sources), I agree with a growing number of reputable scholars who have seriously studied the dating issue that "a date in either AD 65 or early 66 would seem most suitable."[4] In my opinion, the weight of evidence greatly favors a pre-A.D.-70 writing. Therefore, and as Reformed theologian R.C. Sproul has suggested, "if Revelation was written before A.D. 70, then a case could be made that it describes chiefly those events leading up to Jerusalem's fall."[5]

Sources:

The Greater Jesus (future book – est. 2012) by John Noē
The Scene Behind the Seen (future book – est. 2015-16) by John Noē
"An Exegetical Basis for a Preterist-Idealist Understanding of the Book of Revelation," article in *Journal of the Evangelical Theological Society*, Vol. 49, No. 4 (Dec. 2006) by John Noē
Before Jerusalem Fell by Kenneth L. Gentry
Redating the New Testament by John A.T. Robinson
The Last Days According to Jesus by R.C. Sproul
Biblical Hermeneutics by Milton S. Terry
Biblical Apocalyptics by Milton S. Terry
Revelation by Grant R. Osborne
Revelation by Leon Morris
The Book of Revelation by Robert H. Mounce

---

[3] Ibid., 10, 352.
[4] Kenneth L. Gentry, Jr., *Before Jerusalem Fell* (Atlanta, GA.: American Vision, 1998, p336.
[5] R.C. Sproul, *The Last Days According to Jesus* (Grand Rapids, MI.: Baker Books, 1998), 132.

(3)
How do we handle its time statements?

Much of the conflict and confusion over the Revelation stems from a widespread practice of taking part or all of this prophecy out of its divinely determined time context. But disregarding or abusing context is not the prerogative of any sincere reader or honest interpreter. The book of Revelation places direct time statements on itself. Like bookends at the beginning and end (first and last chapters), these parameters establish the historical context for the soon and now past fulfillment of the whole of its prophecy:

- "what must soon [shortly] take place" (Rev. 1:1; 22:6 [*KJV*]).
- "Blessed is the one who reads the words of this prophecy . . . who hear it and take to heart [obey] what is written in it" (Rev. 1:3; 22:7 [*KJV*])
- "the time is near [at hand]" (Rev. 1:3; 22:10 [*KJV*]).
- "Do not seal up the words of the prophecy of this book" (Rev. 22:10). Note: Daniel was told to "close up and seal the words" of his book "until the time of the end" (Dan. 12:4). In the Revelation, that time was now "near" or "at hand."
- "Behold, I am coming soon [quickly]!" (Rev. 22:7, 12 [*KJV*]).
- "Yes, I am coming soon [quickly]." (Rev 22:20 [*KJV*]).

These full-content-bracketing, time statements establish the immediate historical context for the fulfillment of the whole of the prophecy. These passages tell us that a very significant event was to occur within a very short time and certainly within the lifetime of the book's original and primary recipients. These passages are stated in simple terms—so simple, in fact, that people who won't take "soon," "shortly," "at hand," "near," and "quickly" literally must read their own non-literal meanings into these declarative statements. Furthermore, these words are used hundreds of times and in a consistent literal manner throughout the New Testament. They mean what they mean in natural, everyday speech. And without a clear warrant to do so (none exists), there is no justification to assume special or unique meanings.

Thus, to look for a distant, future fulfillment (two thousand years removed from its writing) of part or all of this prophecy, as most modern-day prophecy teachers still do, is to ignore this book's plainest teachings and to engage in pretext. This common trait demands manipulation of Scripture and ensures misconception and misunderstanding. The reader who does not hold fast to the Revelation's own contextual guidelines will infallibly lose himself in a labyrinth of conjecture and wild speculations.

Hence, Revelation's prophecy only becomes difficult, if not impossible, to understand when it is lifted out of its self-declared, 1st-century time context. Sad to say, many scholars beholding to their deferment and futuristic interpretative positions, disagree. To justify their system of fulfillment, they are forced to interpret these above simple words and time-restricting phrases figuratively, or to undermine their meaning with unnatural treatments, or to ignore them entirely and jump right into fancy futuristic charts and timelines.

Bottom line is, they are trifling with words and with the Word of God. Their abusive treatments have produced an incredible amount of conflict, anxiety, and confusion. Ironically, however, one fact all nearness-evading and word-manipulating theorists recognize is that the Revelation's original recipients did not understand these simple words and phrases in the way these theorists are suggesting. 1st-century believers were expecting the occurrence and fulfillment of all these things within their lifetime. And who could blame them?

Sources:

The Greater Jesus (future book – est. 2012) by John Noē
The Scene Behind the Seen (future book – est. 2015-16) by John Noē
"An Exegetical Basis for a Preterist-Idealist Understanding of the Book of Revelation," article in *Journal of the Evangelical Theological Society*, Vol. 49, No. 4 (Dec. 2006) by John Noē
The Last Days According to Jesus by R.C. Sproul
The Days of Vengeance by David Chilton
The Book of Revelation by Foy E. Wallace
Biblical Hermeneutics by Milton S. Terry
Biblical Apocalyptics by Milton S. Terry

(4)
When was it or will it be fulfilled?

The book of Revelation does not contain end-of-the-world predictions or events, as is commonly held. Rather, it fully predicted and described, symbolically and accurately, the events leading up to and including the fall of Jerusalem in a coming of the day of the Lord, in judgment, and in the change of covenants, in A.D. 70. All this and more occurred "soon" and "shortly"—i.e., within two to seven years, depending upon the exact date of this book's writing. Any interpretation of its fulfillment that lies beyond the time frame of its original hearers and readers is, at best, suspect.

Again, first and foremost, the book of Revelation described a local series of events very near to its writing and intended for an original and primary audience. These all occurred. Mistakenly, however, many feel that these events were only local and not worldwide. But just like the birth, life, death, resurrection, and ascension of Jesus, which were also local events, the Revelation's fulfillment has universal applications and implications. Locally is just how God chose to fulfill it and his plan of redemption. These events ended, forever, biblical Judaism, its age, and the Old Covenant system (Heb. 8:13; 9:10).

The book of Revelation does not contain end-of-the-world predictions or events, as is commonly held.

Reluctantly, the late, renowned, and futuristic theologian George Eldon Ladd conceded that "there must be an element of truth in this approach, for surely the Revelation was intended to speak to its own generation."[6] Mistakenly, however, he and many others feel that if this prophecy is totally fulfilled, this makes it meaningless to modern-day Christians. But as we are about to see, Revelation's past fulfillment does not exhaust its meaning, relevance, and symbolism. In fact, just the opposite is true. Past fulfillment makes this prophecy *more meaningful*, not less. Why? It's because the Revelation is more than a tract for its own times. How can we know this? It's not some doctrine I have

---

[6] Ladd, *A Theology of the New Testament*, 672.

dreamed up, which leads us to our fifth foundational key for unlearning many popular misconceptions and unlocking the mysteries of this vital book.

Sources:

The Greater Jesus (future book – est. 2012) by John Noē
The Scene Behind the Seen (future book – est. 2015-16) by John Noē
"An Exegetical Basis for a Preterist-Idealist Understanding of the Book of Revelation," article in *Journal of the Evangelical Theological Society*, Vol. 49, No. 4 (Dec. 2006) by John Noē
The Last Days According to Jesus by R.C. Sproul
The Days of Vengeance by David Chilton
The Book of Revelation by Foy E. Wallace
Biblical Hermeneutics by Milton S. Terry
Biblical Apocalyptics by Milton S. Terry

(5)
What is its relevance for us today?

In the middle of the unfolding apocalyptic drama of the breaking of the seals, the sounding of the trumpets, and pouring out of the vials, is a drastic instruction given to John that is downplayed by most commentators. In Revelation chapter ten, the angel of the Lord instructs John to *eat the scroll* (Rev. 10:9b). This is the same sealed scroll handed to the Lamb for Him to open in Revelation chapter five. Why was John told to perform such a graphic and grotesque act? (Have you eaten any good books lately?)

Let's not forget that this instruction is contained in a book filled with signs and symbols. The reason is, as we shall further see, God did not intend the prophetic message in this scroll (the book of Revelation) to be limited to one particular time period and one particular people—i.e., for John's original audience, the seven churches and the Christians of that 1st century alone. Fact is, the physical act of eating and ingesting something always transforms it. And so the whole of the prophecy of the book of Revelation is transformed.

Immediately after John ate the scroll, he was commanded to regurgitate it, if you will; but this time it is directed to a different audience. The angel told him, "You must prophesy again about many peoples, nations, languages, and kings" (Rev. 10:11). When you couple this statement with the angel's later instructions to John, "do not seal up the words of the prophecy of this book, because the time is at hand" (Rev. 22:10), it should soon become clear that the Revelation's prophecy was not exhausted in its A.D. 70 fulfillment. Its relevance was broadened from its primary fulfillment audience and focus to a different audience and focus.

Below are six additional insights supporting a universal application and timeless relevance of this prophecy beyond its A.D. 70 fulfillment. This is what theologians call a *sensus plenior*—i.e. "a fuller sense . . . . the possibility of more significance to . . . [a] passage than was consciously apparent to the original author . . . ."[7]

Again, and *first and foremost*, the *whole* of this prophecy, from first to last, was written to encourage its original audience. They were under severe persecution and in need of relief. This is the Revelation's primary focus. The *whole* of it, therefore, is rooted, time-restricted, and fulfilled in one, immediate, specific, and real coming of Jesus Christ in judgment in A.D. 70. That contemporary and historical setting was Revelation's one and only fulfillment. And, this historical fulfillment must play a controlling role as we explore a *sensus plenior*.

Its relevance was broadened from its primary fulfillment audience and focus to a different audience and focus.

Secondly, John's prophesying "again about many peoples, nations, languages and kings" (Rev 10:9-11), is clearly a different and broader group of recipients of this prophecy than John's original area and audience of the seven churches (Rev 1:4, 11). Traditionally, however, commentators have tried to minimize the meaning of this dramatic symbolism of John's eating the scroll and prophesying again. They

---

[7] Virkler, *Hermeneutics,* 25.

contend it only meant a personal application for John. Suggested applications (in *italics*), along with my comments, include:

- *John must yet receive the rest of the prophecy (chapters 11-22)*. But John was not going anywhere. He was there for the duration. This explanation is not only highly reductionistic, in comparison with the dramatic symbolism used, it is superfluous and weak.
- *John would later travel throughout the area of the seven churches sharing this prophecy verbally (a book tour of sorts)*. But it was not necessary for John to travel about doing this. That was the purpose of sending the letters. They were to be read aloud in the seven churches.
- *This was a commissioning for John*. But John had already been commissioned on at least two previous occasions (see Rev. 1:10-20 and 4:1-2), and also in Revelation 1:19. Therefore, another commissioning would be unnecessary and overly redundant.

Thirdly, similar expressions are found five other times in Revelation 5:9; 7:9; 13:7; 14:6; and 17:15 (also see Rev. 22:9 and Dan. 4:1; 7:14). In Revelation 5:9, for example, this expression universalizes the application of Jesus' sacrifice: "And they sang a new song; 'You [Jesus] are worthy to take the scroll and to open its seals, because you were slain, and with your blood you purchased men [and women] for God from every tribe and language and people and nation." That includes me, and hopefully you as well.

Fourthly, if this expression's use in Revelation 10:11 is consistent with this book's other five uses, and we employ the interpretative principle of letting "Scripture interpret Scripture," then it must carry the same universalized and timeless meaning here. This widening of application is the textual rationale for applying the *whole* prophecy beyond its A.D. 70 fulfillment. Hence, the words of this climactic prophecy refer and pertain to all peoples and nations throughout the world. We must also specially note that in Revelation 10:11, "kings" replaced "'tribes' as the fourth element in the quartet. In Revelation 1:6 and 5:10, believers are called "kings." Thus, the Apocalypse is concerned with the whole of humankind from both a corporate and an individual sense. This universal and timeless application, beyond its fulfillment, is the most natural way to understand a consistent use of this terminology.

Fifthly, the Revelation's fulfillment (its realities, blessings, judgments, principles, and portrayals, which cannot be limited to a one-time, historic, and static eschatological fulfillment for its own day, which it was, or to someday still out in the future) serves in a typological and controlling manner. Thus, the fulfillment of Revelation's imagery and visions now serves as a type for repeating patterns of Christ's ongoing involvement and activity in history and in individual lives. In other words, John's prophecy now transcends its fulfillment time and context into new historical and personal applications, globally. Post A.D. 70, this prophecy is not only timeless but also multifaceted.

This ongoing relevancy and timeless, universal applications are part of the Revelation's uniqueness and further differentiate it from Jesus' Olivet Discourse in Matthew 24, Mark 13, and Luke 21, which cover the same fulfillment time frame and events. However, the Revelation's ongoing aspects resist predictability because John's prophesying "again" was general and not time-sensitive or place-specific. The whole book echoes this relevancy theme that it is for all who live and die for Christ from that time on (Rev. 14:12-13).

Hence, the Revelation is still an open book and meant to be forever kept open from the time of its writing forward. Its exciting message proclaims the ongoing involvement of Jesus Christ in the struggles of the spirit realm and the physical/material realm, for all ages. Such a reformed application can help us better understand the rise and fall of empires, the history of nations, the lives of people, the comings and goings of groups, institutions, and other corporate bodies. They, indeed, are controlled by God and Christ (also see Dan. 2:21). Moreover, this textual understanding of Revelation's ongoing relevance and timeless applications secures its meaningfulness from the time of its fulfillment onward for all periods of Church and world history.

The Revelation also warns, "If anyone adds anything to them, God will add to him the plagues described in this book. And if anyone takes away from this book of prophecy, God will take away from him his share in the tree of life and in the holy city, which are described in this book" (Rev. 22:18-19). Let me urge you to constantly make sure that no message you believe or present adds to or takes away from the content and the spirit of the Apocalypse. These two dire warnings and consequences are just as relevant for us today as they were for the Revelation's original audience. If not, they are toothless. In my opinion, any modern-day interpretation that relegates the relevance of all or any portion of this prophecy solely to the past or solely to the future is at risk of violating these warnings and opening ones self to their consequences.

Hence, the Revelation is still an open book and meant to be forever kept open from the time of its writing forward.

This ongoing relevancy also perfectly corresponds with God's redemptive grace and purpose. While totally local in fulfillment, all are universal in goal, scope, and application. Seen in this manner, the Revelation is truly a prophecy of "the eternal gospel to proclaim to those who live on the earth – to every nation, tribe, language and people" (Rev. 14:6).

Sixthly, there is no suggestion of a termination of these applications. The popular terminology of a "final" or "last judgment," a "final blessing," a "final coming," a "final day of the Lord," or a "final Antichrist" is non-scriptural and unscriptural. Therefore, in the prophecy of the book of Revelation, we moderns have real, ongoing blessings, warnings, comings, judgments, and interactions of Christ with which to be personally involved and concerned (Rev. 1:3; 22:7, 14-19). Yet there is no "antichrist" contained therein. That notion has been imported into this book. Rather, "many antichrists," who fit the descriptions found *only* in 1 John 2:18, 22; 4:3; 2 John 7, still roam the earth today, as they did in the past and will continue in the future. (See again, Exposé #8.)

Make no mistake; this realization of the Revelation's ongoing relevancy is not a lesser reality or a second-rate option in comparison with solely past or mostly futuristic fulfillment views. In effect, it is more significant than any single view. Through the Revelation, God is equipping believers of all generations with an understanding of how the world of the spirit operates. This revelation is the highest form of knowledge and wisdom revealed to humankind and is just as pertinent today as it was in the past and will be in the future. It is the knowledge of how the kingdom of God functions and how we can enter and, effectively and victoriously, live in it in this present world. Thus, nowadays, the entire vision of the Revelation is past, present, and future. It is the timeless unveiling of Jesus Christ as He is now, and not a timetable of yet-future events. To see this is to understand the Revelation as it was intended and to receive one of its blessings; not to see this is to miss its richest meaning, for in this greater Jesus Christ "are hidden all the treasures of wisdom and knowledge" (Col. 2:3).

Make no mistake; this realization of the Revelation's ongoing relevancy is not a lesser reality or a second-rate option in comparison with solely past or mostly futuristic fulfillment views.

Our recognition of *both* the total fulfillment and total relevancy of "the revelation of Jesus Christ" (Rev. 1:1) in our lives, here and now, should create a greater sense of responsibility, a greater motivation for obedience, and a greater desire to worship than the traditional deferment views—past or future. God through Christ continues to act in history and in the lives of his saints in an apocalyptically revealed manner.

Sources:

The Greater Jesus (future book – est. 2012) by John Noē
The Scene Behind the Seen (future book – est. 2015-16) by John Noē
"An Exegetical Basis for a Preterist-Idealist Understanding of the Book of Revelation," article in *Journal of the Evangelical Theological Society*, Vol. 49, No. 4 (Dec. 2006) by John Noē
More Than Conquerors by William Hendriksen

Exposé #11

Battle of Armageddon

Armageddon? Is it past or future? Are millions possibly being led astray, again? The front cover of *Publishers Weekly*, January 13, 2003, featured this headline:

'ARMAGEDDON
UNLEASHING EVERYWHERE APRIL 8, 2003'

On the inside cover it continued with this headline: '**NO ONE WILL ESCAPE ARMAGEDDON.**' Fortunately, this alarming announcement was not about a real and so-called final "battle of Armageddon" at the supposed end of the world. At the time, this article was dramatically announcing the upcoming release of Tim LaHaye and Jerry Jenkins' tenth blockbuster title in their wildly popular *Left Behind* series. Provocatively, it was titled *Armageddon*.

Even though this book was another work of fiction, LaHaye contends that his works of fiction are conduits of "God's end-times truths" and they contain "prophetic knowledge that God expects His children to have."[1] The *Left Behind* series has proven to be the best vehicle to achieve his goal. Its reported 65 million copies (to date, 2011) are designed to reach people in a way his "non-fiction" books cannot. And

---

[1] From advertisement – "Introducing the LaHaye Prophecy Study Group," *Christianity Today*, February 2003, 13.

they are doing just that—literally influencing and convincing multiple millions toward LaHaye's view.

Theological Problem:

The *Left Behind* series' books are based upon an eschatological view that is not held by all Christians, and for good reasons. A case in point is this *Armageddon* book. To illustrate just how far off-target LaHaye and Jenkins are, they claim this battle will be fought in a valley. But as we shall soon see, it was to be fought on a mountain—the exact opposite from a valley.

What Scripture Says:

Below are ten biblical and historical reasons why the theology behind LaHaye and Jenkins' *Armageddon* story line is *flawed*.

Elaborations:

1) Reasons #1-3
2) Reasons #4-7
3) Reasons #8-9
4) Reason #10
5) In sum

Sources:

The Greater Jesus (future book – est. 2012) by John Noē
The Scene Behind the Seen (future book – est. 2015-16) by John Noē
"An Exegetical Basis for a Preterist-Idealist Understanding of the Book of Revelation," article in *Journal of the Evangelical Theological Society*, Vol. 49, No. 4 (Dec. 2006) by John Noē
The Perfect Ending for the World by John Noē
The Last Days According to Jesus by R.C. Sproul
The Days of Vengeance by David Chilton

The Book of Revelation by Foy E. Wallace

(1)
Reasons #1-3

1. The name of the battle is *not* "Armageddon" or "the battle of Armageddon." It's "the battle on the great day of God Almighty" (Rev. 16:14). Armageddon is the location of this battle. Big difference, as we shall see!

2. The location is *not* in Israel's largest valley, 50 miles north of Jerusalem, as is commonly thought and taught. Yet this 20-mile long and 14-mile wide valley (presently known as the Valley of Jezreel or the Plain of Megiddo) remains one of the popular stops on most tours of Israel. According to Scripture, the location of this battle "in Hebrew is called Har-Magedon or Har-Megiddo" (Rev. 16:16). But "har" is the Hebrew word for mountain. A mountain is the exact opposite in meaning from a valley. Admittedly, the ancient town of Megiddo was situated on a small mound and adjacent to this valley on the west. But it was only a few hundred feet high. And since in Hebrew the 'h' is silent, the Greek rending became "Armageddon."

3. This battle is part of the whole prophecy of the book of Revelation. According to Revelation itself, its whole prophecy contains realities and events that *all* "would shortly take place" (Rev. 1:1; 22:6), were "at hand" (Rev. 1:3; 22:10), and were obeyable, heedable, keepable (Rev. 1:3; 22:7) in the lives of this book's original recipients in that 1st-century time frame. (See again, Exposé #10.)

Sources:

The Greater Jesus (future book – est. 2012) by John Noē
The Scene Behind the Seen (future book – est. 2015-16) by John Noē

(2)
Reasons #4-7

4. Likewise, the whole of this prophecy was not to be sealed up (Rev. 22:10). But LaHaye and Jenkins have, in essence, sealed it up for over nineteen centuries and counting via their postponement interpretation. Now, however, they want to unseal it by claiming that these events will finally and soon occur in our day and time.

5. A strong case can be made that the book of Revelation was written prior to the destruction of Jerusalem and the Temple in A.D. 70.

6. Har-Magedon or Har-Megiddo, where this great end-time battle takes place, is a composite name and, most likely, symbolic. It is contained in a book filled with signs and symbols. Therefore, it is not unreasonable to conclude that it, too, is symbolic of a real battle. *Bauer, Arndt, Gingrich and Danker*, the foremost Greek-English lexicon, rightly recognizes that "Armageddon is a mystic place-name" and "has been identified with Megiddo and Jerusalem." Yet it laments that "its interpretation is beset with difficulties that have not yet been surmounted." Or have they? Read on.

7. The most likely case is that Revelation's "Har" is and was Jerusalem. Geographically, Jerusalem sits on top of a mountain. To get there from any direction one must go "up to Jerusalem" (2 Sam. 19:34; 1 Ki. 12:28; 2 Ki. 18:17; 2 Chron. 2:16; Ezra 1:3; 7:7; Zech. 14:17; Matt. 20:17, 18; Mark 10:32, 33; Luke 18:31; 19:28; John 2:13; 5:1; Acts 11:2; 15:2; 21:12, 15; 24:11; 25:9; Gal. 1:17, 18). Jerusalem is also called God's "holy mountain" (Psa. 43:3) and the "chief among the mountains" (Isa. 2:2-3; also 14:13; Exod. 15:17; Joel 2:32; 3:16-17).

Sources:

The Greater Jesus (future book – est. 2012) by John Noē
The Scene Behind the Seen (future book – est. 2015-16) by John Noē

(3)
Reasons #8-9

8. Based on other Scriptures, one can also make a case for "Magedon" or "Megiddo" pointing to Jerusalem. During the time of Jesus and Revelation's subsequent writing, large crowds of devout Jews would gather three times a year to celebrate their religious feasts in this central city. Other related Hebrew terms support this identification:

   - *Har Mo'edh*, the mount of assembly
   - *Ar himdah*, God's city of desire
   - *Har migdo*, His fruitful mountain (Mount Zion)
   - *megiddow*, rendezvous – from *gadad*, to crowd, assemble, gather.

9. "Magedon" or "Megiddo" may also be comparative imagery. A great slaughter once took place in the valley of *Megiddo* (2 Ki. 9:27; Zech. 12:11). Throughout ancient history, this valley was also a favorite corridor for invading armies and the scene of numerous famous battles (Jud. 4-7; 1 Sam. 29-31; 2 Sam. 4; 1 Ki. 9:15; 2 Ki. 9-10; 22; 2 Chron. 35). So much blood was shed in this valley of Jezreel or Megiddo that it became a synonym for slaughter, violence, bloodshed, and a battlefield, as well as a symbol for God's judgment (Hos. 1:4-5). In our day, Armageddon has also become synonymous with and a symbol for the ultimate in warfare and conflict.

   In a similar fashion, the word "Waterloo" has garnered a symbolic use. In 1815, this town in Belgium was the battleground and scene of Napoleon's final defeat. Today, we have a saying that some one or some thing has met their "Waterloo." We don't mean they have met that city in Europe. We mean, by way of comparative imagery, that they have met a decisive or crushing defeat, or their demise. I suggest Revelation could have employed the word "Magedon" or "Megiddo" in a similar manner.

Sources:

The Greater Jesus (future book – est. 2012) by John Noē
The Scene Behind the Seen (future book – est. 2015-16) by John Noē

(4)
Reason #10

10. History records that a great slaughter took place on a mountain in Palestine within the lifetime of the original recipients of the book of Revelation. In A.D. 70 the Roman armies of Titus totally destroyed Jerusalem and the Temple. According to Eusebius, 1.1 million Jews were killed. Even more perished in the Galilean fighting, died of starvation or disease, and/or were taken into captivity.

This event was certainly a judgment of God. I submit that it was more than that. First, it was a day-of-the-Lord judgment of God and in keeping with Jehovah God's many comings "on the clouds" in day-of-the-Lord judgments in Old Testament times:

- Isaiah 13:10, 13—judgment of Babylon (539 B.C.)
- Isaiah 34:4—judgment of Edom (late 6th century B.C.)
- Ezekiel 32:7—judgment of Egypt (568 B.C.)
- Nahum 1:5—judgment of Nineveh (612 B.C.)
- Joel 2:10—judgment of Judah (586 B.C.)
- Amos 8:9—judgment of the northern kingdom (722 B.C.)

Secondly, since the New Testament states that all judgment has been given by the Father to the Son (John 5:22), I submit that this A.D. 70 coming in judgment was "the great day of God Almighty" (Rev. 16:14). It was also Jesus' coming "on the clouds" (Matt. 24:30; 26:64; Rev. 1:7) and "in the Father's glory" (Matt. 16:27; Mark 8:38; Luke 9:26), as Jehovah God had come many times before (see, again, above bullets).

Consequently, in speaking of his coming again, Jesus, who is God, used exactly the same *language* of the Prophets (cosmic-darkening and collapsing, earth-shaking), described it exactly in the same *way* ("on the clouds"), for exactly the same *purpose* (judgment), to accomplish exactly the same *thing* (destruction of a nation), and employed exactly the same *instrumentality* (foreign armies). And it all happened within the generation Jesus said it would happen (Matt. 23:36; 24:34).

Sources:

The Greater Jesus (future book – est. 2012) by John Noē
The Scene Behind the Seen (future book – est. 2015-16) by John Noē

(5)
In sum

This decisive battle of the "last days" period, in which they were living back then and there (Heb. 1:2), was totally relevant to, took place during, and was fulfilled within the lifetime of Revelation's original readers. Hence, Revelation's "Armageddon" took place on the mountain of Jerusalem. Historically, its fulfillment is behind us, and not ahead of us. It is past, and not future. But its ongoing applications (not fulfillments), post A.D. 70 and from an idealist standpoint, are beyond the scope of this brief exposé.

A strong case also can be made that all of the literal and symbolic end-time details portrayed in the book of Revelation were precisely fulfilled during these same events and in keeping with the time-restricted context this last book of the Bible imposed upon itself.

Revelation's "Armageddon" took place on the mountain of Jerusalem. . . . its fulfillment is behind us, and not ahead of us.

Of course, there is more, much more. But the biblical facts seem to indicate that LaHaye and Jenkins are over nineteen centuries off in their timing and topographically (valley vs. mountain) far off-target in their location of this "battle on the great day of God Almighty." They, and others, have erroneously termed it "the battle of Armageddon."

I further suggest that it is time for God's people to "wake up, O sleeper . . ." (Eph. 5:14) —i.e., those who love biblical truth, and not fiction or fantasy. We must stop abdicating this area of our faith to the likes of LaHaye and Jenkins and others of their ilk. Everyday, millions are being adversely affected and many more deeply entrenched by their biblically flawed view. But as Jesus said, "then you will know the truth, and the truth will set you free" (John 8:32). First, however, truth must get a hearing. If it doesn't, truth can get left behind.

Sources:

The Greater Jesus (future book – est. 2012) by John Noē
The Scene Behind the Seen (future book – est. 2015-16) by John Noē

Exposé #12

⟶

Israel

Perhaps no more volatile or politically charged issue has exploded onto the front page of the world scene and into the Church than that of the contemporary role, or non-role, of the modern-day nation of Israel in fulfillment of end-time Bible prophecy.

Ever since its rebirth in 1948, an end-time obsession has characterized popular Christianity. Prophecy charts, rapture movies, best-selling books, and Antichrist speculations abound. Apparently, the stage is set. Israel is ground zero. How do Israeli Jews feel about their upcoming prophetic role and the pending Battle of Armageddon? Their wooing of Christians and prophecy popularizers has paid off handsomely.

Theological Problem:

America is passionately pro-Israel. And more than anything else, this end-time obsession has shaped our stance. It has also conditioned an almost uncritical support for Israel's existence and actions in world affairs. But while Zionist Christians are longing for a rebuilt temple in Jerusalem and anticipating the soon-arrival of other disastrous end-time events, they do not believe peace in the Middle East is possible, or even desirable. Meanwhile, other Christians claim that God is finished with the Jews and that the Bible should not be used to advance or detract from the position of any of the three main religious groups whose origins are in the Holy Land.

What Scripture Says:

While both of these views are understandable, I believe that confusion over eschatology should not be a catalyst in this conflict. In an attempt to prove that point, this exposé will address the top 5 of 13 popular eschatological misconceptions and provide scriptural responses.

Elaborations:

1) Misconception #1
2) Misconception #2
3) Misconception #3
4) Misconception #4
5) Misconception #5

Sources:

The Israel Illusion (future book – est. 2013-14) by John Noē
Dictionary of Biblical Prophecy and End Times by Hays, Duvall, and Pate
Major Bible Prophecies by John F. Walvoord
Dispensational: Today, Yesterday, and Tomorrow by Crenshaw and Gunn III
Issues in Dispensationalism by Willis, Master, and Ryrie, editors

(1)
Misconception #1

1948 marked the fulfillment of all 'return-to-the-land' biblical prophecies and signaled the beginning of the end!

One huge problem: the immediate historical settings for the literal fulfillment of all "return-to-the-land" prophecies were one of two returns of the Jews from either Assyrian or Babylonian exile/captivity in the 8th and 6th/5th centuries B.C., respectively. Why? Because all return prophecies were given prior to or during those exile periods:

> *Pre-exilic return prophecies* – Isa. 11:11-12; 14:1-2; 27:12-13; Jer. 16:15; 23:3,7-8; 29:10,14; 32:28, 37-44; 50:4-5; Amos 9:11, 14-15; Zeph. 3:19-20.

> *Mid-exilic return prophecies* – Dan. 9:25; Isa. 43:5-7; 49:8; Ezek. 11:16-18; 20:41-42; 34:12-13; 36:8, 24; 37:12, 21-23; 39:28; Zech. 2:6; 8:7-8; 9:12; 10:8-12]

Objection – "Then wasn't the Jews pouring into Israel from all over the world, prior to and circa 1948, *another* return fulfillment?"

No, it wasn't! God's promised and covenantal blessings for both dwelling in the Promised Land and returning to it after being scattered were contingent upon Israel's faith and obedience to the Law. A return in unbelief was never promised or prophesied, nor would it qualify as return fulfillment. As far back as Abraham, God issued his command for keeping covenant (Gen. 17:9). In the Mosaic covenant, He made dwelling in the land and returning to it conditional (Deut. 4:25-31; 28:15-68; 30:1-5; 31:16-17; also Jer. 29:10-14; 50:4-5; Ezek. 5:8-12). God's conditions of faith and covenant obedience were met prior to return from Assyrian and Babylonian exiles. The return of the Jews to Palestine in unbelief and unrepentance, during the 1800s through 1948 and afterwards, does not fulfill these spiritual requirements.

Hence, 1948 did not signal the beginning of the end or the start of God's prophetic time clock ticking into a countdown, "last days" mode. After all, the time period termed the "last days" was biblically affixed to the 1st century (Heb. 1:2; 1 Pet. 1:5, 20; 1 John 2:18). (See again, Exposé #5.)

Source:

The Israel Illusion (future book – est. 2013-14) by John Noē

(2)
Misconception #2

The 1948 re-establishment of the modern-day nation of Israel was the greatest prophetic sign ever fulfilled and a miraculous 'act of God.'

Farthest thing from it. One only has to read the history of Zionism (the Jewish nationalistic movement, 1800's thru 1948) and you'll discover how truly ungodly it was. It's a sad history of political maneuvering and racial hatred. As a result, the costs have been huge and the conflicts unending. What passed as a national rebirth for Jews uprooted in the process hundreds of thousands of Arab residents from their homes.

Tragically, support for a Jewish homeland in Palestine was fueled by massive anti-Semitic prejudices, hatreds, and persecutions in Europe, Russia and northern Africa. This produced a century-long series of secular, political, and financial manipulations designed to get the Jews "back in their land"—and "out of ours." Of course, these blatant acts of men were allowed by God. But the fact was that Jews were not wanted in those nations at that time. Meanwhile, many Christian associations in the West welcomed the movement as a step toward fulfillment of a newly-popularized, "literal view" of end-times prophecy (dispensational premillennialism) and as hastening the return of Christ.

Paradoxically, most Jews had no desire to leave their countries and return to a desolate Palestine. But Jewish reluctance gradually broke down in the face of accelerating hatred and persecutions. Returning Jews were even forced to buy land at highly inflated prices. Gradually, world opinion became outraged over British mishandling of the emerging Palestinian displacement problem. Devout Muslims in the area vowed to destroy the proposed Jewish state. But after much Holocaust guilt and political maneuvering and a final and close vote in the United Nations, the modern nation of Israel was formally created.

Many sincere Christians in America pointed to Israel's 1948 statehood as proof the Jews were still "God's Chosen People," and as a literal validation of their brand of biblical faith. Sadly, while hoping for peace, most Zionists ignored or were blind to the fact that others, including Palestinian Christians, already occupied the land. These inhabitants were viewed as obstacles to be forcibly removed from their homes and villages that they had occupied for hundreds of years. What a mistake this has been. Still 20th- and 21st-century prophecy writers, after 1948, have provided plenty of end-times' rationale for this anti-Arab or anti-Palestinian bias.

Paradoxically, most Jews had no desire to leave their countries and return to a desolate Palestine.

Thus, the century-long, hatred-serving, and humanly fabricated re-establishment of Israel in 1948 bears no resemblance to any biblical "act of God" and had nothing whatsoever to do with divine fulfillment of prophecy. Compare, for example, this history of human manipulation with the sudden, unexpected, and absolutely unplanned fall of the Berlin Wall and collapse of Soviet communism in 1989. Not a shot was fired. Surely, this was an incredible and obviously miraculous "act of God" in our lifetime. But the modern-day state of Israel, as it exists today, is a secular nation, basically anti-God, and certainly anti-Christ. It is of no biblical, prophetic, end-time significance —farthest thing from it.

Source:

The Israel Illusion (future book – est. 2013-14) by John Noē

(3)
Misconception #3

God has TWO separate and distinct peoples, TWO programs of redemption, and TWO different destinies—one for the nation of Israel and one for the Church.

Since when? From the beginning, there has only been a *oneness*— *one* Garden of Eden, *one* tree of life, *one* Noah's ark, *one* ark of the covenant, *one* Tabernacle, *one* Temple, *one* priesthood, *one* hope, *one* faith, *one* Spirit, *one* baptism, *one* body depicted by *one* olive tree into which believing Gentiles were grafted and unbelieving Jews broken off, but can be re-grafted in. There is only *one* everlasting New Covenant promised to Israel, *one* "time of the end," *one* salvation that is of the Jews, and *one* nation or people of God. This *oneness* has been consistently maintained throughout God's dispensations. This *oneness* has never been divided or disconnected.

The relatively modern theory of a separation or distinction between Israel and the Church was introduced into Church history in the 1830's by John Nelson Darby. Darby placed the ethnic Jews at the heart of his dispensational prophetic system. He taught that when the Jews rejected Christ, God set them aside for awhile and inserted the Church Age. Hence, Darby and his followers surmised that God has *two* different programs and *two* different destinies for *two* different peoples. But Darby's dichotomizing notion is without scriptural warrant. Even worse, it would be "crucifying the Son of God all over again" (Heb. 6:6).

God's *one* plan was that his Christ would appear "*once* and for all at the end of the ages to do away with sin by the sacrifice of himself" (Heb. 9:26). That *once* was sufficient. In this manner, believing Jews and Gentiles are united together as equal heirs of God's blessings and equal partakers of God's promises in *one* body through the *one* Messiah. This union of Jew-Gentile *oneness* was the goal of God's *one*, completed program of redemption. That's why "in Christ" the distinction between Jew and Gentile has been utterly done away and *one*, New Covenant people formed (Rom. 10:12; Gal. 3:26-29; Eph. 2:14-22; 3:6; 4:4; Col. 3:15; John 17:21; 1 Cor. 12:12-13). Jew-Gentile unity was the bottom line.

The relatively modern theory of a separation or distinction between Israel and the Church was introduced into Church history in the 1830's by John Nelson Darby.

Let's not put ethnic division back. There is no such thing as an exempted group of people. Nor are Christianity and the Church Age a "plan B." Christianity is God's *one* and *only* plan. God's grand purpose was not to draw more boundaries or put up another wall of partition between Jews and Gentiles, but to make all *one* in Christ (Eph. 1:10).

Jews must come to God in exactly the same way as the Gentiles do. This Christological unity and *oneness* continuity is the fulfillment of the Abrahamic promise from Genesis to Revelation that "all peoples of earth will be blessed through you" (Gen. 12:3b; also see: 18:18; 22:18; Gal. 3:8; Rev. 21 & 22). It's the mystery Paul made known (Eph. 3:3-6). Thus, biblical faith became truly universal in the 1st century. All physical Jews and Gentiles are invited to become citizens of that *one* nation and *one* people of God via God's *one* and only way of salvation (1 Pet. 2:9).

God's *one* inclusive plan of redemption does not await a future millennium or tribulation period. Nor is Christianity merely a "fill-in religion," a "great gap," or a "parenthesis" between two ends for a national or ethnic Israel. There is no room in Scripture for *two* separate peoples, programs, destinies, or even *two* separate applications. The idea of a "Church/Israel dichotomy" is a popular but unbiblical invention. Unfortunately, it's so deeply implanted in some hearts that God's *oneness* may be hard to swallow.

Let's not put ethnic division back. . . . Nor are Christianity and the Church Age a "plan B." Christianity is God's *one* and *only* plan.

Let's understand that "Christ has become a servant of the Jews on behalf of God's truth, to confirm the promises made to the patriarchs so that the Gentiles may glorify God for his mercy" (Rom. 15:8-9). This understanding saves us from the error that Christianity is separate from the Jewish promises. We'd all be well-advised in this instance to follow the admonition "What God has joined together, let man not separate [put assunder]" (Matt. 19:6 *NIV* [*KJV*]).

Source:

The Israel Illusion (future book – est. 2013-14) by John Noē

(4)
Misconception #4

The Jews are still 'God's Chosen People.'

ALL of them never were! Here are three historic reasons why:

Reason #1.) Not all of Abraham's physical descendants were included under the *unconditional* but by faith Abrahamic covenant. Nor were they all children of the promise. God made his covenant with a person, Abraham, and not with one nation. But it was always by faith that Abraham and his descendants were justified before God, and not by national origin (Gen. 15:6; Rom. 4:3-22; Jas. 2:23).

God further specified that "In Isaac [not Ishmael] shall thy seed be called" (Gen. 21:12). Of Abraham's two sons, Isaac's birth was supernaturally determined by the Spirit and required the patient faith of Abraham and Sarah. Ishmael's birth was different. It was conceived by human possibility in the flesh. Faith was thus the decisive factor differentiating the manner of these two births. But from Isaac's twin sons God chose Jacob and rejected Esau. Both were the direct grandsons of Abraham and of equal physical lineage and natural descendancy status. They had the same mother. But by God's sovereign right and election, Jacob's descendants, not Esau's, carried forth the Abrahamic seed promise as those "called" [in the sense of "invited"] of God. In this manner, God set forth the by faith precedent for future covenants.

Reason #2.) Four hundred years later, God further clarified his seed promise to Abraham when He made a *conditional* covenant with Moses and the Jewish people. Faith again, not natural descendancy, would continue to be the determining factor of inclusion or exclusion for those "called" as "God's Chosen People."

Under this nationalistic, Mosaic covenant, God set the ethnic nation of Israel apart from the other nations, and brought them into a conditional covenant relationship with Him. It required them to be holy (Lev. 20:24, 26) and provided either blessings or cursings (Exod. 19:5; Deut. 28). Membership was mostly restricted to Jews, but could be gained or lost. Gentiles gained inclusion via the proselyte laws—circumcision, ritual cleansing, repentance, obedience to the Torah, and renouncement of natural parentage and heritage. On the other hand, ethnic Jews who committed certain high sins and refused to repent could be excommunicated. They were then treated as pagans. Many ethnic Jews refused to be part of "God's Chosen People." Through their unbelief, hardening, idolatry, or refusal to keep the Law, they lost their identity, citizenship, and covenant privileges. Once again, faith, not natural descendancy, was the basis of inclusion, and disobedience the basis of exclusion.

Reason #3.) With the birth coming of Christ, the long-promised New Covenant broke into human history (Jer. 31:31-37; Ezek.16:60; 36:26, 27). The two designations for one identical people, "the Israel of God" and "God's Chosen People," were then covenantally redefined (Gal. 3:16, 26-29; 4:21-31; 6:15, 16; Acts 2:16-21; 1 Pet. 2:9, 10). The basis of inclusion or exclusion changed (John 3:1-8; Luke 19:9) and expanded to the whole world (Matt. 21:43).

Jesus summed up this by-faith inclusiveness and the dichotomous division within the Jewish people of his day quite succinctly, saying:

"Many are called, but few are chosen" (Matt. 22:14).
"You belong to your father, the devil" (John 8:44a; Rev. 2:9; 3:9).
"Do not presume to say to yourselves, 'We have Abraham as our father,' for I tell you God is able from these stones to raise up children to Abraham" (Matt. 3:9).

Surely, these words of Jesus shocked his hearers. But long before Jesus, Isaiah had prophesied of this contrast between these two Jewish groups and their different destinies (Isa. 65:7-16). Likewise, God through the prophet Hosea prophesied about many Jews, "Ye are not my people" (Hos. 1:9-10; 2:23). They were only Jews outwardly, but not inwardly (Matt. 3:9; John 8:37, 39; Rom. 2:28, 29). The Apostle Paul confirmed, "For they are not all Israel, which are of Israel" (Rom. 9:6). Thus, it should be evident that either a Jew or a Gentile could be a member of Israel physically, nationally, culturally, and religiously without being a member of the true Israel, spiritually. *Inclusion was never grounded in physical/biological descendancy.*

So even though God chose Israel out of all the nations (Amos 3:2) to be a people for Himself, a witness to the nations, the channel for his revelation, and through whom the Messiah would come, the whole nation of Israel never was "God's Chosen People." It was only the faithful remnant (Rom. 9:27; 11:5; Isa. 10:20-22). That's why today, neither the modern-day nation nor all ethnic Jews worldwide should be so considered. Who counts as the true Israel, the children of the promise, was not and is not determined by a blood-line or a race-line, but always by a faith-line which transcends the natural descendancy realm. In Old Covenant times, only the righteous remnant in the midst of the greater Israel was "God's Chosen People" and the true Israel of God. Nowadays, Abraham's real descendants ("seed") are believers in Jesus Christ, whether they are racially Jews or Gentiles. We are all on equal footing. This is the promised and ultimate fulfillment of biblical prophecy. And, consequently, there is no other stage of fulfillment needed or to come.

Source:

The Israel Illusion (future book – est. 2013-14) by John Noē

(5)
Misconception #5

Israel has a biblical entitlement and permanent right to possess all their land in the Middle East, and this transcends all else.

Not any more. That changed in the 1st century A.D. when the covenant upon which this land right was based became "obsolete" (Heb. 8:13). New Testament Christians need to accept this obsolescence. But we should also note that unbelieving Jews never had a claim upon Old Covenant benefits, including the land promise. Only those who exercised faith and obedient received its benefits.

Furthermore, the Promised Land of Canaan was a temporary type and shadow as were all the physical components peculiar to the Mosaic Law system. They all pointed to the "coming good things" of the New Covenant age (Heb. 8:5; 9:9, 11, 23, 24; 10:1). These types and shadows were "not the realities themselves" (Heb. 10:1; also 8:5; 9:10; Col. 2:16, 17; John 5:39). When the New Covenant fully superseded the old in A.D.

70, the Jews were physically removed from that geographic patch of land and their covenant-determined "right" to it ceased and became moot.

This same fulfillment destiny holds true for every element and physical institution of the Old Covenant, Judaic system: the Temple, the city, the priesthood, sacrifices, ceremonies, feast days, circumcision, everything, as well as the physical, Promised Land itself. Of course, the God-given land promised to Abraham and his descendants was an "everlasting possession/inheritance" and unconditional (Gen. 12:7; 13:15; 15:7, 18; 17:8; 48:4; Rom. 4:13-17). Only in Solomon's empire were its farthest boundaries ever physically realized —from the River of Egypt to the River Euphrates (1 Ki. 4:12, 24; 2 Chron. 9:26; Jos. 21:43-45). But from a purely logistical standpoint today, it's questionable whether this patch of real estate is capable of physically holding all the 12-15 million or so Jews (depending on how one defines a Jew) —let alone "all families of the earth" who were and are to receive this Abrahamic land promise and blessing, unconditionally (Gen. 12:3).

Re-applying this Middle East land promise is a classic example of a common materialistic error—making the type be the fulfillment of itself. What's missed is that the land promise, as well as the total Abrahamic inheritance, was fulfilled and established in a greater, higher, better, and expanded way in Christ (Heb. 9:15; Rom. 4:13,16; Gal. 3:29). This is why Jesus "de-territorialized" or universalized Psalm 37:11 from "But the meek will inherit the land . . ." to "Blessed are the meek, for they will inherit the earth" (Matt. 5:5; also see Psa. 2:8; 46:10; 67:2-7; Amos 9:15; Luke 24:47; Dan. 7:14). The true fulfillment of the land promise is only realized in the New Covenant reality of the new Israel, and not in the old, type and shadow system. It's part of the essence of the New Covenant in which Jews and Gentiles are fused into one body by the work of Christ (Eph. 2:14; 3:6). No longer do God's people all over the world need to dwell in a special and restricted territory—in "the whole land of Canaan" (Gen. 17:8) which meant so much to Old Testament Israel. Instead, we are to dwell in its ultimate and unrestricted fulfillment "in Christ." This is the "better country – a heavenly one" for which Abraham longed. Even he did not see the literal, earthly, real estate as the fulfillment of the promise (Heb. 11:16).

Again, the land promise has been "de-territorialized" just as Jesus said it would be (John 4:20-24). That's also why no other return-to-the-land prophecy or promise was given in the Bible after the Jews returned to Palestine from Babylonian captivity. Likewise, this ultimate fulfillment and expansion into better substance explains why God's people never again would be "uprooted from the land" (Amos 9:15). Even though the Jewish nation was removed from their "type" and "shadow" earthly land by the Roman armies circa A.D. 70, God's people in Christ can never be removed from this land's antitype.

No other return-to-the-land prophecy or promise was given in the Bible after the Jews returned to Palestine from Babylonian captivity.

Seen under the light of this past fulfillment, the modern-day nation of Israel, which was created by the United Nations, has *no more* and *no less* special entitlement or divine right to their land than do any other nations whose boundaries were similarly drawn by human agency. The Bible long ago told all peoples everywhere that all land is the Lord's (Lev. 25:23; Psa. 24:1). This certainly includes the land of every nation in the volatile Middle East. Thus, there is no biblical reason why Arabs and others are not equally entitled to and cannot live in the land of Palestine along with the Jews, just like they did in ancient times. God loves and cares about all these people.
Source:

The Israel Illusion (future book – est. 2013-14) by John Noē

Exposé #13

---→

Conflicting End-time Views

"One of the most divisive elements in recent Christian history . . . . few doctrines untie and separate Christians as much as eschatology."[1]

Theological Problem:

The field of eschatology is a complex maze of confusing and conflicting end-time views in which no consensus has ever existed. This lack of consensus has led to major disarray and division in the Church. Premillennialists say the amillennialists are wrong. Amillennialists say the premillennialists are wrong. Postmillennialists say they are right and everybody else is wrong. Few scholars are familiar with and even fewer lay people are aware that there is another comprehensive view—the preterist view.

Even more troubling, this field of theology has been plagued by the traditions of men and unscriptural false paradigms. These imperfections have forced their proponents to overrule sound hermeneutical and exegetical principles to reinterpret Scripture according to their view. Consequently, three major dichotomizing hermeneutics and many

---

[1] Kenneth S. Kantzer, ed., "Our Future Hope: Eschatology and Its Role in the Church," *Christianity Today*, 6 February 1987, 1- (I).

unsound conclusions have resulted in a stalemate that has plagued Christianity throughout its history.

What Scripture Says:

According to God Himself, the *timely and precise* fulfillment of prophecy is how we humans can know who the one true God truly is (see Isa. 44:6-8; also 41:21-24; 42:8-9; 45:20-22; 46:9-11; 48:3-6; Rev. 19:10b).

This fulfillment was also the once-for-all-delivered and completed foundation of our faith upon which we are to build—that was precisely foretold by the prophets (Amos 3:7), expected by the apostles (John 16:13), and *time-restricted* by Jesus Christ Himself (Matt. 24:34; Rev. 1:1, 3 ~ 22:6, 10): *". . . contend for the faith that was once for all delivered to the saints"*(Jude 3).

Originally, this topic and material was presented in a 13-week seminar series at Madison Park Church of God in Anderson, Indiana. Its purpose was to present, study, and analyze the four major eschatological views of the historic, evangelical, and conservative Church, to determine their principal strengths and weaknesses and synthesize their strengths into one meaningful, coherent, and consistent view that is more Christ-honoring, Scripture-authenticating, and faith-validating than any one view in and of itself.

Elaborations:

1) 7 reasons why your end-time view is so vital.
2) Fourfold premise.
3) Preterist view.
4) Dispensational premillennial view.
5) Amillennial view.
6) Postmillennial view.
7) Synthesis of views.
8) Comments from others.

Sources:

"Unraveling the End" MPC series by John Noē – listen to podcasts on PRI's website (www.prophecyrefi.org).
Unraveling the End (future book – est. 2012) by John Noē
Dictionary of Biblical Prophecy and End Times by Hays, Duvall, and Pate
Publication of John Noē's Ph.D. dissertation – est. 2012

(1)
7 reasons why your end-time view is so vital.

1. *__How much of the Bible is involved?__* "It has been argued that no less than *two thirds* of the content of the New Testament is concerned directly or indirectly with eschatology."[2] Some experts estimate that 25 to 30 percent of the whole Bible is so concerned. So, we are not dealing with a fringe issue.

   Fact is, your view or non-view of eschatology dramatically affects your understanding, misunderstanding, or lack of understanding of many other important aspects of the Christian faith. For instance, it impacts on points 2 through 7.

2. *__How much salvation do we currently have?__* The whole of the Bible is concerned with man's problem and God's solution.

   The final outworking of that redemptive solution for those alive and those dead is what salvation and eschatology are both all about. But depending upon your end-time view, your answer to this question will vary from "some" to "most" to "all."

3. *__How much of the kingdom do we currently have?__* According to your eschatological view, your answer will vary from: "none," to "some," to "most," to "all," to "all minus—some major parts."

---

[2] R.C. Sproul, "A Journey Back in Time," *Tabletalk,* January 1999, 5.

Fact is, the kingdom of God was the *central teaching* of our Lord and at the *heart* of his earthly ministry. It was also the *very essence* of New Testament Christianity. Today, however, the kingdom is no longer the central teaching of his Church, at the heart of its ministry, nor Christianity's very essence—an automatic "red flag." *What has happened? What has changed?*

4. ***What do you do with the modern-day nation of Israel?*** Many believe that Israel has a biblical entitlement to possess the land promised them by God. What say you? Do they or don't they? Your answer depends on your eschatological view.

    They further believe that if we don't support Israel, we'll be biblically *cursed,* individually and nationally (Gen. 12:3; Zech. 2:8-9). Will we or won't we? Others believe that biblical Israel has been *replaced* by the Church. Most simply don't know what to think, believe, or do. Or, they don't care.

5. ***It's the focal point of the liberal-skeptic attack on the Bible and Deity of Christ***. "In seminary I was exposed daily to critical theories espoused by my professors regarding the Scriptures. What stands out in my memory of those days is the heavy emphasis on biblical texts regarding the return of Christ, which were constantly cited as examples of errors in the New Testament and proof that the text had been edited to accommodate the crisis in the early church caused by the so-called parousia-delay of Jesus. . . ."[3]

    It is called the "battle for the Bible." Fact is, liberals and critics, alike, have hit Christianity at its weakest point—the embarrassing statements of Jesus to supposedly "return" within the lifetime of his contemporaries and the "failed," Holy-Spirit-guided expectations of the New Testament writers that He would (John 16:13).

    Consequently, in America over the past 75 to 100 years, we Christians have lost half of our people as seminary after seminary,

---

[3] Sproul, *The Last Days According to Jesus*, 14-15.

denomination after denomination, church after church, and believer after believer have departed from the conservative faith.

6. ***It makes a difference in your worldview***. Our forefathers in the faith came to this country under a particular, and a historically optimistic, eschatological view to expand the kingdom of God.

   They believed the world would become a better and better place as it became more Christianized, and as each Christian took responsibility to do his or her part to help make this happen. Hence, they came and founded the great institutions of our country—the government, the schools, the universities—under Judeo-Christian principles—and Christianity became the moral influencer in America.

   But 50 to 75 years ago all this began to change. Now, we've almost given it all away, and without a fight. And we didn't get pushed out by a more powerful force. We simply withdrew. Into the vacuum gladly came the ungodly forces. *Why did this happen? What can we now do about it?*

7. ***It makes a difference in your life and family***. If you have bought into the popular ideas that the Christ will soon return and the world is going to end, these beliefs affect how you and your family think, pray, work, save, plan, invest, and commit or don't commit to do things in the present—especially things that have long-term payouts.

   As someone once put it, "Your view of the future determines your philosophy of life." And *"if there's no faith in the future, there is no power in the present."*

   Eschatological ideas and beliefs do have consequences. And for most evangelicals, their worldview is this: "We are living in the 'last days.' So, why fuss, why fight, we're on the next flight?"

Source:

Unraveling the End (future book – est. 2012) by John Noē

(2)
Fourfold premise.

The solution of synthesis presented in this series is based on my completed Ph.D. dissertation, which was subtitled, "An Evaluation (and Synthesis) of the Four Major Evangelical Views of the Return of Christ." My premise was simple, straightforward, and fourfold:

1. **God is not the author of our confusion in eschatology (1 Cor. 14:33, *KJV*). We are.** I assumed that it was not and is not God's character or nature to have included in his Word any content that would create the amount of confusion, conflict, divisiveness, and/or ambivalence we see among Christians in this area of eschatology. Personal interpretations have "muddied the waters" for everyone.

   I further assumed that we are the ones who have misconstrued the whole thing, and that this impasse could be resolved—scripturally.

2. **Each of the four views centers on the return of Christ as the central, pivotal and controlling end-time event.** So get this one right and the others events will fall readily into place.

3. **Each view has principal strengths and weaknesses that can be identified through a scripturally disciplined approach grounded upon what the text actually says and does not say.** Eschatology is an area filled with problems caused by both additions and subtractions to the text.

   These are necessitated by the traditions of men and will not stand up to an honest and sincere test of Scripture. Yet more often than not, we are unaware of the weaknesses inherent in our own view, until someone points them out to us. They are blind spots. *And unlearning is the hardest form of learning.* I also knew I'd have to be both objective and gracious in exposing these weaknesses for each view.

4. **The solution would be a solution of synthesis—discarding the weakness, keeping the strengths, and synthesizing the strengths into one meaningful, coherent, and consistent view that is more**

Christ-honoring, Scripture-authenticating, and faith-validating than any one view in and of itself.

Since each view has grasped a portion of the biblical truth regarding the end times, I proposed a synthesis treatment that would meet all hermeneutical and exegetical demands and not contradict itself. This approach was significant because no one had ever done this before— i.e., to the degree and scope I was proposing—and none of the four views themselves meets this criterion.

Next, are recaps of the strengths and weaknesses for each view.

Source:

"Unraveling the End" MPC series by John Noē – listen to podcasts on PRI's website (www.prophecyrefi.org).
Unraveling the End (future book – est. 2012) by John Noē
Publication of John Noē's Ph.D. dissertation – est. 2012)

(3)
Preterist view

Strengths:
- Fully accepts the natural reading and understanding of eschatological timeframes and NT time and imminency statements, including those bracketing the entire prophecy of Revelation.
- Supports the 1st-century Holy-Spirit-guided expectations as the correct ones.
- Balances literal and figurative language for nature of fulfillment.
- Uses biblical precedent to explain the nature of fulfillment.
- Harmonizes time convergence of OT time prophecies with NT time statements and Holy-Spirit-led expectations.
- Recognizes that eschatology is connected to Israel and pertains to the end of the Jewish age.
- Affirms that God has always had only one, continuous, by-faith people.

- Posits a positive worldview, long-term outlook.
- Acknowledges that God's material creation is without end.
- Answers the liberal/skeptic attack on the Bible and on Christ, effectively.

Weaknesses:
- Positing A.D. 70 as the time of Christ's "Second Coming" and "Return."
- A finality paradigm which limits the comings of Jesus to only two.
- Thus, A.D. 70 was Christ's final coming.
- Overly spiritualizes Christ's return, resurrection, and his kingdom.
- Enormous exegetical and historical burden for documenting fulfillment.
- Lack of attention in writings to the nature of post-A.D.-70 reality and implications for Christian living.
- Gross cessationism abounds—some preterists advocate the annihilation of Satan, his kingdom, and demons. Many advocate the cessation of the operation of angels, ministries of the Holy Spirit, and the miraculous gifts in A.D. 70.

(4)
Dispensational premillennial view

Strengths:
- Strong interest in end-time prophecy.
- Emphasis on the dynamic role of Christ in the present and future affairs of humankind.
- Recognizes that eschatology is connected to Israel and pertains to the end of the Jewish age.
- Realization that, at least, one coming of Christ is not visible.

Weaknesses:
- Positing the time of Christ's "Second Coming" and "Return" as being very soon.
- Interrupting divine time frames without clear textual justification.
- Arbitrary use of gaps of time.

- Bifurcating passages of Scripture, including the book of Revelation.
- Interpreting by exception and specialized meanings—i.e., ignoring or changing the meaning of commonly used and normally understood words in the time statements.
- Postulating postponement of the kingdom of God.
- Postulating delay theory.
- Advocating a future 7-year period of tribulation.
- Inventing the "Rapture" idea in direct contradiction of Scripture.
- Identifying Daniel's 70th week with Jesus' Olivet Discourse.
- Advocating separate redemptive plans for Israel and the Church.
- Denigrating the Church as unforeseen and a parenthesis in God's redemptive plan.
- Advocating a future restoration of the old and inferior Judaic order.
- A dichotomizing hermeneutic based upon a false paradigm—i.e., the Israel-Church distinctive.
- Incomplete salvation and resurrection reality.
- Positing a negative worldview and short-term outlook for our present time.

(5)
Amillennial view

Strengths:
- Idealist interpretation of the book of Revelation.
- Emphasis on the literal/unseen realities behind symbolic fulfillment.
- Recognition that the "last days" existed in the 1st century.
- The present reality of the kingdom of Christ.
- Rejection of the idea of a future kingdom.
- Attempts to honor both literal and figurative language.

Weaknesses:
- Positing the time of Christ's "Second Coming" and "Return" as being unknowable.
- Advocating ambiguity and uncertainty re the understanding of eschatological prophecies.
- Insistence that the time of fulfillment cannot be known.

- Little interest in end-time prophecy.
- Reliance on delay theory.
- Adherence to an unscriptural "end-of-time" paradigm.
- Use of a dichotomizing hermeneutic based upon that paradigm.
- Bifurcating passages of Scripture, including the book of Revelation.
- Advocating a final return, final consummation (how many are there?).
- Incomplete salvation and resurrection reality.
- Numerous partial-preterist inconsistencies from failure to fully honor the time statements.
- Belief that the Jewish age, the Old Covenant order, and the law were completely fulfilled and removed, and that all Old Testament promises/prophecies were fulfilled, accomplished, and completed at the Cross.
- The New Covenant began and was fully in force at Pentecost—i.e. the full establishment of the kingdom/Church/New Covenant order was given, perfected, and fulfilled.
- The Church as the replacement of Israel.
- Claim that eschatology pertains to the end of the Christian age, or to a split fulfillment in time and disposition (Jewish age/Christian age) with a gap of thousands of years in between.
- Advocating a current intermediate state of disembodied existence in heaven.
- Advocating a future evil-less, utopian, and eternal state on earth for believers and not in heaven.
- Equating the "age to come" to being heaven or yet-future.
- A mixed positive-negative worldview.

(6)
Postmillennial view

__Strengths:__
- Strong kingdom-society orientation.
- Positive emphasis and motivation for human effort to expand God's kingdom on earth as it is in heaven.
- Positive worldview, long-term outlook.

- Recognition of many comings of Christ.
- Many valid preterist understandings.

Weaknesses:
- Positing the time of Christ's "Second Coming" and "Return" as being far, far away.
- Insistence the world must be "Christianized" to a significant degree before Christ can return.
- Adherence to an unscriptural "end-of-time" paradigm.
- Use of a dichotomizing hermeneutic based on that paradigm.
- Claim that eschatology pertains to the end of the Christian age.
- Postulating two or more *parousia* returns of Christ.
- Postulating a final coming and last judgment, after which there will be no more.
- Numerous partial-preterist inconsistencies from failure to fully honor the time statements.
- Bifurcating passages of Scripture, including the book of Revelation.
- Reliance on delay theory.
- Insistence that the time of fulfillment cannot be known.
- Incomplete salvation and resurrection reality.
- Advocating a future evil-less, utopian, and eternal state on earth.
- Over-dependence on creedal authority.
- The "age to come" is yet-future

(7)
Synthesis of views

First and foremost, the central, pivotal, and controlling end-time event contained in each of the four views—the "second coming" or "return" of Christ—is taken off the table of synthesis. It is a weakness to be discarded for the following reasons:

- "The words 'return' and 'second coming' are not properly speaking Biblical words in that the two words do not represent any equivalent Greek words."[4]
- These two non-scriptural expressions are also un-scriptural concepts that will not stand up to an honest and sincere test of Scripture.
- They are to be replaced by the many comings of Jesus and the biblical fact that He never left as He said (Matt. 28:20).[5]
- Hence, these two traditional expressions and concepts are inappropriate and that's why the Bible (properly translated) never uses them.

Secondly, the superiority of the **preterist view** over the other three views is simple and profound but it's not sufficient in and of itself. It is the only view that fully accepts and honors the natural reading and understanding of Jesus' time-restrictive words and the intensifying imminency declarations of the New Testament writers. No other view can legitimately make this claim. It also documents how Jesus came "on the clouds" in age-ending judgment exactly *as* and *when* He said He would and exactly *as* and *when* every New Testament writer and the early Church expected—as they were led into all truth and shown the things that were to come by the Holy Spirit (John 16:13; 14:26). It emphasizes the harmony of this precise past fulfillment with the literal, exact, chronological, and sequential fulfillment of Daniel's two specific and two general time prophecies—no interruptive gaps, no exegetical devices. These prophecies frame the end times and establish its historical setting and defining characteristic (Dan. 12:7).

The "second coming" or "return" of Christ —is taken off the table of synthesis. It is a weakness to be discarded.

[4] Ladd, *The Blessed Hope*, 69.
[5] See "Unraveling the End" MPC series podcasts on PRI's website (www.prophecyrefi.org) and listen to Lesson #7, #8 and #11.)

Thus, everything happened "at just the *right* time" (Rom. 5:6) and "in its *proper* time" (1 Tim. 2:6). This amazing harmony and perfection of timely past fulfillment is God's stamp or fingerprint of divinity, or divine perfection—not only in Bible times— but also in the end times.

While superior, however, the **preterist view** was found to be insufficient in and of itself. Two of it major identified weaknesses are, the preterist insistence that: 1) the destruction of Jerusalem and the Temple was the "final coming" of Christ. 2) The prophecy of the book of Revelation was exhausted in the events of A.D. 70. Therefore, the strengths of the other three views must also be incorporated with strengths of the preterist view.

From the **amillennial view** was kept the idealist interpretation of the book of Revelation with its ongoing, timeless, and countless applications in human history. But these now follow, rather than precede, Christ's historic and literal coming in judgment and consummation in A.D. 70.

From the **postmillennial view** was incorporated but reapplied its strong kingdom-society orientation, positive worldview, long-term outlook, and many comings of Christ—past, present, and future.

From the **dispensational premillennial view** was retained its strong interest in prophecy and the current dynamic role of Christ in the present and future affairs of humankind (although this must now be reapplied per this synthesis).

Discarded were the identified weaknesses from each of the four views that did not stand up to an honest and objective test of Scripture.

In sum, this series has presented a new groundwork—or break-through initiative—for eschatological reform, consensus, and unity. Others can now build on these findings as we more readily come together to build a fuller and deeper understanding of our "once for all delivered faith" (Jude 3) and God's once-again demonstrated attribute of divine perfection in *foretelling* and *fulfilling* his plan of redemption.

Sources:

"Unraveling the End" MPC series by John Noē – listen to podcasts on PRI's website (www.prophecyrefi.org).
Unraveling the End (future book – est. 2012) by John Noē
Publication of John Noē's Ph.D. dissertation – est. 2012)

(8)
Comments from others

<u>**From seminar participants:**</u>

"I am enthralled with Divine Perfection—it is so encouraging and invigorating."

"The question for me now is how do I demonstrate the beauty of this in my thinking and life?"

"I probably will have to go over this study more than three times!"

"The best Bible study I have ever had!"

"This has filled in the gaps that have been open for so long."

"Very thorough, highly scholarly, top drawer presentation. Wouldn't trade it for anything!"

"I will never *JUST* read the Bible again."

"My faith is deepened. God blesses when we seek truth."

"I now read and understand the Bible in a whole new light."

"An eye-opener to me of our awesome Lord in his exactness of prophecy. I'm floored!"

"It has changed my whole outlook."

"Personally, I express profound appreciation to our Pastoral staff for making this watershed experience a reality."
—Rev. Dr. Ben Ruth, Facilitator

From podcast listeners:

"As a former Jehovah's Witness Elder that has spent the last 5 years spinning in circles, listening to your exposition on Synthesis in 13 parts over the last day and a half has been absolute Manna from Heaven. Since leaving the Jehovah Witness organization, I have explored everything you describe, the latest been Preterism, after Pre-Trib at Calvary Chapel, Baptist, Church of England, and Non-denominational.

I was a Witness for 20 years, that was hard enough, but coming out of there and going back to the maze of ideas has been worse.

The United Kingdom is crying out for this message. I live in Cardiff . . . and you can be sure that within the circles I operate in, the views and audios you present will become centre-stage for at least the next 6 months, and let's see how many will join with me in running with this."

David Brown – Cardiff, Wales, UK

"It makes ever so much more sense. . . ."

Cindy Eggert – America

"I really enjoyed the series on your website, "Unraveling the End." I just listened to it, now I am going to listen again and take notes. I think you have really hit the nail on the head. There were a few things that you said that finally 'turned on the light' . . . . I really like it when you challenge my beliefs . . . . As you believe, let us see what the Scripture teaches on this subject, if I am wrong, I will have to change!"

Michael Riemer – Philippines

Sources:

"Unraveling the End" MPC series by John Noē – listen to podcasts on PRI's website (www.prophecyrefi.org).
Unraveling the End (future book – est. 2012) by John Noē

Exposé #14

Doing the Works of Jesus

The increasing presence of the kingdom was not only being realized in Jesus' Person and his words, but would be further manifested and modeled by his works (John 14:10; Acts 1:1), as Jesus obediently performed the "will of him who sent me" (John 6:38). Dramatically and dynamically, He demonstrated the kingdom's internal and external, spiritual and physical characteristics by:

- the life He led
- by his relationship with the Father
- by his dependence upon the Father
- by forgiving sins
- by healing the sick
- by casting out demons
- by taking authority over nature
- by performing miracles
- by releasing the oppressed
- by taking care of physical needs.

Jesus regarded *all these* as essential and intrinsic elements of his kingdom. Thus, his kingdom affected the whole person. It produced both spiritual transformations and physical blessings or consequences. But one of Jesus' most prominent works was the casting out or exorcism of demons, which He interpreted as clear proof that "the kingdom of God has come upon you" (Matt. 12:28; Luke 11:20; Matt. 8:16-17; Mark 1:32-34).

Theological Problem:

Using oath language, Jesus also made this dramatic and radical statement: "Verily, verily, I say unto you, He that believeth on me, the works that I do shall you do also; and greater works than these shall he do; because I go unto my Father" (John 14:12 *KJV*).

So if we claim to believe in Jesus and are not doing the works He did, why shouldn't we be considered in the ranks of the unbeliever? (The "greater works" will be covered next.)

What Scripture Says:

Jesus made this same radical demand of his first disciples when He called together the Twelve, and later the seventy, empowered them, and sent them out. As his representatives, they were to proclaim the same gospel of the kingdom and perform its same mighty works exactly as He had been doing. He "gave them authority" to:

- Preach this message: 'The kingdom of heaven is at hand.'
- Heal the sick.
- Raise the dead.
- Cleanse those who have leprosy.
- Drive out demons.
                    (Matt. 10:1, 7-8; Luke 9:1-2, 6; 10:1-17)

Additionally, in his Great Commission, Jesus not only commissioned his first followers to "baptize" and "make disciples of all nations," but He also commanded them (and us today) to "teach them to obey *everything* I have commanded you to do" (*emphasis mine,* Matt. 28:19-20). Jesus' "everything" certainly included the preaching of the kingdom *and* the performance of its miraculous, merciful, and fruit-producing works. But this understanding is in sharp contrast with the contemporary teaching that "witnessing" only involves telling the message of Christ and salvation. Practically speaking, the tendency of many scholars and pastors is to ignore, downplay, or try to explain away the full meaning of Jesus' Great Commission.

Darrell L. Guder laments this great-omission tendency this way:

> In spite of Jesus' admonition at the end of Matthew's Gospel . . . to "teach the nations all that I have commanded you," our reductionism with regard to Jesus' concrete teaching . . . has been massive.[1]

Lastly, and completing a scriptural "threefold witness" (see Matt. 18:16 from Duet. 19:15; 17:6; also 2 Cor. 13:1; 1 Tim. 5:19; Heb. 10:28) are these two verses in 1 John:

> "But if anyone obeys his word, God's love is truly made complete in him. This is how we know we are in him [in Jesus]. Whoever claims to live in him [Jesus] must walk as Jesus did" (1 John 2:5-6).

"Walk as Jesus did" is an idiomatic expression that means "do what Jesus had been doing—i.e., the works of Jesus.

The bottom line here is this. While many of us profess faith in Jesus, we hesitate or simply do not want to do what He had and has plainly commanded them and us to do. Perhaps, the Great Commission is *much greater* than most of us have been led to believe. Dallas Willard poignantly bemoans that, most Christians "do not really understand what discipleship to him . . .is, and it [the Kingdom Among Us] therefore remains only a distant, if beautiful, ideal."[2]

Elaborations:

1) What is true biblical Christianity?
2) Do you find this offensive?
3) Settling for a 'lower calling?'
4) Onto the greater works.

---

[1] Guder, *The Continuing Conversion of the Church*, 195.
[2] Willard, *The Divine Conspiracy*, 291.

Sources:

A Once-Mighty Faith (future book – est. 2013) by John Noē
The Continuing Conversion of the Church by Darrell L. Guder
The Divine Conspiracy by Dallas Willard
The Great Omission by Dallas Willard
Pagan Christianity by Frank Viola and George Barna

(1)
What is true biblical Christianity?

The Apostle Paul encouraged the Corinthians, and us today as well, to "stand firm. Let nothing move you. Always give yourselves fully to the work of the Lord, because you know that your labor in the Lord is not in vain" (1 Cor. 15:58). But what is "the work of the Lord?" Is it not the works Jesus had been doing (John 14:12)?

Yet the kingdom Jesus Christ taught, modeled, trained, conferred, and commanded his followers to seek, enter, and expand was so offensive to the religious people of his day, He was killed because of it. So is this same-natured kingdom normative for us today? Is it still true biblical Christianity? Was this mainstay of Jesus' teaching and ministry part of "the faith that was once for all entrusted/delivered to the saints" (Jude 3), or not?

For our society at large, church is mostly a meeting place, a social gathering spot to interact with nice people. And/or, it is a place to worship and learn about things that happened almost two thousand years ago. And most of us have been conditioned to be content to live with a Christianity without a mighty kingdom. No wonder the world and our culture is largely passing us by.

What a yawning gulf exists between the versions or brands of Christianity most Christians and churches today model, preach, teach, and practice from the type we find in the New Testament! Instead, we have settled for a more comfortable Christianity that is principally based on Jesus' birth, life, death, and resurrection. But where is the kingdom in that, doing his works, and our being "fellow workers for the kingdom of God" (Col. 4:11)?

What has happened? What has changed?

Frankly, today we are witnessing the decline of many institutional churches and the rise of the so-called post-Christian era. Some wonder what can be done? If things are going to change, I suggest we have to restore the preaching, teaching, and practices of the kingdom Jesus taught, modeled, conferred, and commanded. Isn't that our model? Or, do we have no model?

What is true biblical Christianity—our brand or Jesus' brand?

Source:

A Once-Mighty Faith (future book – est. 2013) by John Noē

(2)
Do you find this offensive?

Like Jesus' first disciples, we, too, are faced with a choice. Will we follow Jesus in the way He modeled and commands, or not? Remember, Jesus said that "he that believeth on me, the works that I do shall he do also" (John 14:12 *KJV*). So do you find this emphatic statement and his same-natured kingdom offensive?

Let me illustrate this offensiveness in a very practical way. How would you feel if twelve or seventy unlearned people, whom you don't know and from out in the countryside, suddenly showed up, uninvited, at your church. Then, they started proclaiming out loud that the kingdom of God is "at hand," casting out evil spirits from some of your staff, and trying to heal diseases and sicknesses of some of your members?

Or, let us put the shoe on the other foot. How successful do you think you would be in enlisting twelve or seventy people from your church to go out into local neighborhoods next Sunday after church services and minister the same miraculous works of Jesus to unbelievers? I suspect that not many modern-day, American Christians would want anything to do with this brand or type of the kingdom or Christianity. It goes so against the grain of our sensitivities, intellectualism, and desires for control. Most Christians I know would resist, just as many 1st-century Jews defamed and dismissed Jesus and his kingdom.

Guder notes that "The favored way to accomplish this over the centuries has been to diminish the historical particularity of Jesus by reducing him and his message to a set of ideas, an intellectual system, often connected with a codified ethic, and managed thematically within the church's rites and celebrations." This watering down makes our brand of Christianity "more compatible to our world and palatable for ourselves." Sorry to say, and as Guder further adds, "the real and sinful purpose of reductionism is to back away from the call of Jesus . . . . to reduce the gospel, to bring it under control, to render it intellectually respectful, or to make it serve another agenda than God's purposes."[3]

Fact is, Jesus' kingdom was and still is offensive, and frightening! Yet obedience and a faithful witness to this same-natured kingdom and its King by Jesus' first followers in that 1st century, along with the empowerment of the Holy Spirit, proved world-transforming. Luke records that "*In this way* [not in some other way] the word of the Lord spread widely and grew in power" (Acts 19:20; also see 5:12-14 – *emphasis added*). Consequently, they were accused by their opponents of "turning the world upside down" (Acts 17:6). Today, it seems the other way around—the world is/has turned the Church upside down.

Source:

A Once-Mighty Faith (future book – est. 2013) by John Noē

(3)
Settling for a 'lower calling?'

So today, we have countless Christians who believe they are going to heaven and little else really matters. This attitude can only be described as brazen, if not defiant. And leadership allows it. But each and every Christian is called to have the same attitude as Christ (Phil. 2:5). And He is still our model. As Peter declared, Jesus left "an example, that you should follow in his steps" (1 Pet. 2:21). Paul certainly so followed and proclaimed himself as the example of the Christian life, "Follow my

---

[3] Guder, *The Continuing Conversion of the Church*, 101-2.

example, as I follow the example of Christ" (1 Cor. 11:1). And what example was Paul emulating? He recaps his ministry at the end of his life this way:

> Therefore I glory in Christ Jesus in my service to God. I will not venture to speak of anything except what Christ has accomplished through me in leading the Gentiles to obey God by what I have said and done—by the power of signs and miracles, through the power of the Spirit (Rom. 15:17-19a).

Likewise, there is no reason for us today to be confused about or misunderstand the nature of his kingdom. Again, it is a much higher high calling than most of us have been led to believe (Phil. 3:14; 2 Thess. 1:11; Heb. 3:1; 2 Pet. 1:10-11). And we all have become too comfortable and conditioned to a much "lower calling." But if you and I are sincerely seeking to be Christ-like, shouldn't we be seeking opportunities to minister to others as Jesus and the 1st-century Church did and advance his kingdom in the process?

The kingdom of God as presented, modeled, and conferred by Jesus Christ demanded and still demands a serious response. It also requires action, action not only in the form of preaching and teaching but also with living demonstrations of its presence and power. The kingdom is our faith in action. It is a demonstration of whose we are, Whom we serve, and the oneness that binds us together with Jesus, Paul, and the early Church. Of course, there is a natural resistance to this in all of us. But this form of the Christian life was modeled for us for good reason. The Apostle Paul, in his letter to the Thessalonians, pinpoints this reason:

> Brothers loved by God, we know that he has chosen you, because our gospel came to you not simply with words, but also with power, with the Holy Spirit and with deep conviction. You know how we lived among you for your sake. You became imitators of us and of the Lord [their role models]; in spite of severe suffering, you welcomed the message with the joy given by the Holy Spirit. And so you became a *model* to all the believers in Macedonia and Achaia—your faith has become known everywhere . . . . (1 Thess. 1:4-8 – *emphasis added*, also see Titus 2:7).

So, what kind of models are we Christians being today? Have we not been called to serve the same King and kingdom in our lives as did Paul and these Thessalonians? Are we not to become "imitators" of them and their ministry practice? Or does this passage only speak to their time? In other words, is the kingdom they preached and presented still present, relevant, and *same-natured* today? Or, is it not? Remember, and as we saw in Exposé #2, there is no other kingdom or form of yet-to-come.

In sum, Jesus set the example for all that claim to be his. Our task is to take up the cross, follow Him, and carry on his work (Matt. 16:24)—and "boldly and without hindrance" proclaim and demonstrate the kingdom of God *and* of the Lord Jesus Christ (Acts 28:31).

Source:

A Once-Mighty Faith (future book – est. 2013) by John Noē

(4)
Onto the greater works.

If you are offended by the modern-day presence of Jesus' *same-natured* kingdom and his declaration that those of us who believe in Him will be doing the same works He did, then wait until we get to the "greater works," which we are also suppose to be doing (John 14:12). They, too, have been the subject of much speculation, disagreement, and reductionism. Ironically, most of us would rather skip the works of Jesus and go directly to what we think are the "greater works." But, as someone once said, this would be like building a second story on a vacant lot.

What these "greater works" really are, however, has not been left up to our imaginations or whims. They are fully and clearly revealed in God's Word. As Jesus said, "There is nothing concealed that will not be disclosed, or hidden that will not be made known (Matt. 10:26; also Luke 8:17; 12:2).

Sources:

A Once-Mighty Faith (future book – est. 2013) by John Noē

Exposé #15

Doing Greater Works than Jesus

Once again and using oath language, Jesus made this dramatic and radical statement: "Verily, verily, I say unto you, He that believeth on me, the works that I do shall you do also; and *greater works* than these shall he do; because I go unto my Father" (John 14:12 *KJV emphasis mine*).

Theological Problem:

Some think it's arrogant or even blasphemous to expect or even think today that we can or even should be doing the same or greater works and miracles than Jesus did, even though we do have access to precisely the same power that Jesus used to do all his works. After all, what could be greater than dying on the cross for our sins?

What Scripture Says:

But Jesus is the one who made this statement—not me, not Paul or Peter, and not some pastor or radical right-winger. What's more, this statement contains common and ordinary words used frequently in the New Testament and in those times:

"Greater" = *meizon* (*midé zone*): larger (lit. or fig.), greater, more.

"Works" = *ergon* (from *ergo*, to work): deed, doing, labor, work.

Elaborations:

1) Speculations.
2) My working definition.
3) Scriptural Support – Old Testament.
4) Scriptural Support – New Testament.
5) Concluding thoughts.

Sources:

A Once-Mighty Faith (future book – est. 2013) by John Noē
Dominion by C. Peter Wagner
He Shall Have Dominion by Kenneth L. Gentry, Jr.
An Eschatology of Victory by J. Marcellus Kik
Postmillennialism: An Eschatology of Hope by Keith A. Mathison
Abandonment Theology / America A Call to Greatness by John Chalfant
The Transformation of American Religion by Alan Wolfe
When Nations Die by Jim Nelson Black
The Myth of a Christian Nation by Gregory A. Boyd
To Change the World by James Davison Hunter

(1)
Speculations.

"Interpreters have been at a loss in what way to understand this."[1]

---

[1] *Barnes' Notes Commentary.*

Below is a brief overview of the many different ideas that have been voiced about what these "greater works" Jesus spoke about might be— i.e., greater . . .

In Effect / Extent
- Cannot refer to miracles themselves (their quality) but to greater in their effects or extent.
- More extensive results—i.e., larger numbers.
- The conversion of more sinners and souls in many more nations.
- Christian TV, satellites, radio, Internet, books, etc.

In Kind
- Not in degree but in kind . . .
- Christ had healed with the hem of his garment . . .
- But the very shadow of Peter and handkerchiefs and aprons of Paul healed.
- By the words of Peter, Ananias and Sapphria were struck dead.
- By Paul's words, Elymas the sorcerer was struck blind.

In Location
- Christ only preached in one country and in that language; but the apostles preached in most of the known world and in all the languages.

In More Power
- They would have more power to do the "works" than they had when He first sent them out. (The reasons are "because I go unto my Father" and the sending the Holy Spirit.)
- Hence, these "greater works" would not be done in independence from Christ; but with Him in the form of answered prayer and the sent Holy Spirit operating in and through them and us (Eph. 3:20).

In Time
- Christ only did miracles for three and a half years in one country, but his followers would do so for many ages in many countries.

In Manpower
- We will do more than Jesus because He was only one man and there are more of us.
- In millions of relationships . . . and change the face of humanity.

In Faith
- John 6:28-29: they would have "to believe in the one he has sent." Hence, the greater works is faith.
- Did Jesus have "faith?" (check Heb. 11:1).
- Jesus said He could only do what He <u>saw</u> the Father doing (John 5:19-20).
- Jesus didn't need faith. He had personal experience and previous knowledge of the Father and the workings of the Godhead having been with them before the beginning and before his incarnation.

In Quality
- The works of Jesus' followers are of a greater quality, since they belong to the era of God's promises fulfilled—i.e., the gift of God's Spirit and the forgiveness of sins both come about because of Jesus' work on the Cross.
- Luke 7:28 is offered in support: "All believers in the new era are greater than he was, because their works are empowered by the Spirit."[2]
- But weren't Jesus works also empowered by the Spirit?

Source:

A Once-Mighty Faith (future book – est. 2013) by John Noē

---

[2] Darrell Bock, "Dribbling Circles Around Jesus," *Christianity Today*, June 06, 56.

(2)
My working definition.

Admittedly, this topic calls for *some* speculation on my part; but not pure speculation. Here's my working definition:

The "Greater Works" are: "The works Jesus did *not* do during his earthly ministry, but works God's people have been instructed *to do* throughout Scripture—from the beginning of the Bible in the Old Testament to the end in the New Testament):

- Jesus did not take on Rome or try to take it back for God, but we are to (?)
- He didn't make disciples of all nations—i.e., change not only lives, but also laws, institutions, and relationships. But we're commanded to do all of that (?)
- Jesus was "only sent to the lost sheep of the house of Israel" (Matt. 15:24). But we are to leave Judea and Samaria and go into "all the world" (Acts 1:8).
- He didn't take back all the territory Satan (and his forces – human and superhuman) had seized, but we're instructed to do it (?)
- He didn't reign and rule over governments, peoples, and nations, but we are to do it (?)
- He did not engage in politics, take on political powers and structures, nor attempt to fix, steer, or assault the tyranny of the Roman government. Rather, He allowed Himself to be crucified by them. So was Jesus non- or apolitical?

"Those who claim that Jesus was apolitical and interested in only what goes on in individual's hearts/souls have a difficult time explaining how he could have ended up antagonizing the political powers enough to get himself crucified. . . . (others – activists) have a difficult time explaining why he taught his disciples to love their enemies and not to resist an evil person . . . . Jesus calls us to follow him in renouncing the world's reliance on power that originated in violent coercion and to rely instead on a witness that consists of proclaiming and living out the good news of the gospel."[3]

- Jesus did not set out to reform society, but we are to do that (?)

"He did not attempt to reform culture; He ignored it and everything concerned with material civilization. Therefore his people rejected him."[4]

- He did not work to build a government or take a stretch of land, but Israel did and we are to, sometimes (?)
- He refused to use the means of this world – either the clash of arms or the processes of politics to further his ends. (Are we?)
- He refused to be made "King;" but we were made to be "kings and priests" (Rev. 1:6; 5:10).
- He did not exert this kind of open power, but we are to (?)
- The early Church had no hope of reforming the state or bringing it into conformity to the kingdom of God, but we are to (?)
- Jesus said "no" to the devil's offer to give Him "all the kingdoms of the world and their splendor" (Matt. 4:8), but the bishops of the Christian Church in the 4th century said, "yes." Thus, Christendom was born. What do we do with that?
- He did not build a great church (?)
- He did not give us any mandate to fix the cultural order (Oh?)

Bottom line is Jesus was anything but victorious, culturally. He was despised, rejected, spit upon, beaten, and put to death like a common criminal. Clearly, his victory was the victory of the Cross—yielding and submission to the powers that be. And yet, there are these "greater works"—something Jesus either did not do at all or not do much of . . . that his followers are called to do. Perhaps, Jesus' "greater works" are some or all of the above. But I think there might be more to it. And that something more may not be something new but old. Furthermore, it is

---

[3] Craig A. Carter, *Rethinking Christ and Culture* (Grand Rapids, MI.: Brazos Press, 2006), 208.
[4] H. Richard Niebuhr, *Christ and Culture* (New York, NY.: Harper Torchbooks, 1951), 3.

presented throughout the Bible from Genesis to Revelation and follows naturally, logically, and directly from the *Lordship* of Christ.

But before we go there, let's specially note that Jesus did not change the world. What He did was provide the means for his followers to change the world by doing the works He did and even greater works. Remember that Jesus came into human history to establish two great works:

1) The everlasting kingdom.
2) Salvation.

Both were announced and accomplished in that order. It all took place in a small postage-stamp-sized patch of land in the Middle East during a short 74-some-year period of time. Believers since then and we today are to continue his mission by doing his works and greater works. And we know what his works are. He modeled them for us. His "greater works"—in my opinion—can further be characterized in this manner. We are to <u>implement</u> / <u>advance</u> / <u>expand</u> / <u>extent</u> / <u>promote</u> / <u>put into practice</u> these two great works of the victory of God through Christ in and over the whole world not only to transform human lives and activities but to transform all of society—lives, laws, institutions, and relationships.

- Thus, societal transformations are the "greater works" and part of our grand destiny as believers in and followers of Jesus Christ.
- This duty is also the strength of the historic postmillennial view of the advancement of the kingdom of God's throughout the world and into all areas of society.
- This is how we are biblically called to live out the radical difference that Jesus made available.
- Jesus is going to do this alright, but do it through his Holy-Spirit empowered people.
- Yes, it's about activism vs. pietism and not "reclaiming for Christ" but about "transforming through Christ."

It starts with us as individuals. We have to be able to reign and rule over our own lives before we can reign and rule in and over the world—in every aspect and area of our earthly existence. That means having our flesh and our minds under the control of the Spirit, reaching our full potential in Christ, and being the best we can be at whatever God has directed us to do. Sadly, most believers shrink from living at this level of responsibility, influence, and blessings. They are quite ready to leave all behind for the so-called Antichrist and Beast to occupy.

Will this theology go against the grain and traditions of many Christians? Of course, it will. Therefore, not everyone will agree with me, initially, at least. But there is abundant support throughout Scripture. So, let's go to the Bible and make a case for this above understanding of the "greater works."

Sources:

A Once-Mighty Faith (future book – est. 2013) by John Noē
Rethinking Christ and Culture by Craig A. Carter
Christ and Culture by H. Richard Niebuhr
The Transformation of American Religion by Alan Wolfe

(3)
Scriptural support – Old Testament.

The Bible is full of verses and admonitions to transform society. It's a theme frequently found throughout both the Old and New Testaments. But it is also widely ignored and even denied in off-target Christian theology and Church circles for being part of, if not, the solution to the problems of this world. Thus, many Christians have been conditioned to feel the world must get progressively worse and worse before Jesus returns to save it, all by Himself, someday.

Gen. 1:28-30 – Starting from the very beginning – "Be fruitful, and multiply, and replenish the earth, and subdue it; and have dominion over the fish of the sea, and over the fowl of the air, and over every living thing that moveth upon the earth." (*KJV*) –and on through verse 30.
- Its our threefold purpose as God's image bearers (vs. 27):
  1) To protect what has been given.
  2) To extend the glory of God to the ends of the earth.
  3) To extend his image to all of creation.

- It is termed—the "dominion mandate," or "Genesis mandate," or the "theocratic mandate," or "cultural mandate."
  - To be stewards over every aspect of God's earthly creation.
  - As God's image-bearer, we are to serve as his divine representatives in the physical world.
  - As we shall further see, this mandate has never been rescinded.
  - It has only been expanded.

<u>Gen. 9:1-7f</u> – God repeats this mandate after the Fall to Noah and his sons.
- To be stewards over all creation.
- This is the beginning of a "given, lost, regain/redeem it" theme.
- Hence, this mandate was not lost or rescinded at the Fall.

<u>Gen. 12:3b</u> – "and all the peoples (families *KJV*) of the earth will be blessed through you."
- This blessing was not to be a privatized or horded – which the Old Covenant Jews did.
- In Gal. 3:29 we are told that if we belong to Christ, then we "are Abraham's seed and heirs according to the promise." Therefore, we are called to be a blessing to "all the peoples of the earth."
- Isn't this also what the Lord's Prayer is all about—worldwide dominion—"Thy kingdom come; *Thy will be done on earth as it is in heaven*" (Matt. 6:10)?
- A synonym for *dominion* is *kingdom.*
- Kingdom is also a political metaphor that insists that everything and everyone is under the rule of God.
- The "King-dom" is where the King is in dominion.
- So how extensive is his dominion/kingdom?

<u>Psa. 24:1</u> – "The earth is the Lord's, and everything in it, the world, and all who live in it."

<u>Psa. 50: 10, 12</u> – Is like Psa. 24:1.

<u>Psa. 72:8</u> – "His dominion shall be also from sea to sea and from the river unto the ends of the land."

<u>Psa. 103:19</u> – The universe is a theocracy.

<u>Psa. 115:16</u> – "The highest heavens belong to the Lord, but the earth he has given to man."

<u>Psa. 8:4-6</u> (*KJV*) – "What is man, that thou art mindful of him? And the son of man, that thou visitest him? For thou hast made him a little lower than the angels, and hast crowned him with glory and honour. Thou madest him to have dominion over the works of they hands; thou hast put all things under his feet."

> - "Man was commissioned to manage God's very creation! That which He spoke into existence and proclaimed to be good, He entrusted into the hands of human beings for care and stewardship. Man, being created in God's image, was thoroughly equipped for the task because the capacity for rulership is also one of the central aspects of what it means to be made in the likeness of God. . . . We are the only creatures given stewardship, and a position of tremendous honor."[5]

<u>Ezek. 22:30</u> – "I looked for a man among them who would build up the wall and stand before me in the gap on behalf of the land so I would not have to destroy it, but I found none."
- Check out the context for this in verses 25, 27, and 29.

<u>Hag. 2:8</u> – re: economics (silver and gold).

<u>Exodus 20:5</u> – "Thou shalt not bow down thyself to them [other gods, such as secularism or humanism], nor serve them: for I the Lord thy God am a jealous God, visiting the iniquity of the fathers upon the children unto the third and fourth generation."
- Is America bowing down to "other gods" today?
- Remember, God judges the compromisers along with their country.

<u>Deut. 30:16</u> – "For I command you today to love the Lord your God, to walk in his ways, and to keep his commands, decrees and laws; then you

---

[5] Overman, *Assumptions That Affect Our Lives*, 59.

will live and increase, and the Lord your God will bless you in the land you are entering to possess."
- Doesn't this command include the "dominion mandate?"

2 Chron. 7:14 – "If my people, who are called by my name, will humble themselves and pray and seek my face and turn from their wicked ways, then will I hear from heaven and will forgive their sin and will heal their land."
- This is the biblical model for "healing the land."
- But what "wicked ways" must they/we "turn from?"
- How about abrogation of our dominion-mandated duties, etc.?

Eccl. 12:13 – "Here is the conclusion of the matter: Fear God and keep his commandments, for this is the whole duty of man."
- What about the "dominion mandate?"

Jer. 1:6-10 – "'Ah, sovereign LORD,' I said, 'I do not know how to speak; I am only a child.' But the Lord said to me, 'Do not say, 'I am only a child.' You must go to everyone I send you to and say whatever I command you. Do not be afraid of them, for I am with you and will rescue you,' declares the LORD. Then the LORD reached out his hand and touched my mouth and said to me, 'Now, I have put my words in your mouth. See, today I appoint you over nations and kingdoms to uproot and tear down, to destroy and overthrow, to build and to plant.'"
- Is this not a continuation of the "dominion mandate?"

Amos 5:24 – "Let justice roll down like waters, and righteousness as a mighty stream."
- There is a lot in the Old Testament about "justice." It's "the great theme of the justice of God."[6]

Psa. 82:3 and Prov. 21:3 – "doing justice."
- Reflecting the justice / righteousness of God.
- Also see Psa. 45:6; 11:5-7.

---

[6] N.T. Wright, *Evil and the Justice of God* (Downers Grove, IL.: IVP Books, 2006), 117.

<u>Isa. 1: 16-17</u> – "Stop doing wrong, learn to do right! Seek justice, encourage the oppressed. Defend the cause of the fatherless, plead the case of the widow."

- Unbiblical laws need to be abolished or our societies will suffer for the sin they allow. This is termed "biblical law."

<u>Psa. 2: 8-12</u> – "Ask of me, and I will make the nations your inheritance, the ends of the earth your possession. You will rule them with an iron scepter; you will dash them to pieces like pottery. Therefore, you kings, be wise; be warned, you rulers of the earth. Serve the Lord with fear and rejoice with trembling. Kiss the son, lest he be angry and you be destroyed in your way, for his wrath can flare up in a moment. Blessed are all who take refuge in him."

- This messianic psalm for ruling the nations is part of and an expansion of the original "dominion mandate" and we are Christ's agents in doing this works and the "greater works."

<u>Psa. 94:16</u> – "Who will stand up for me against the workers of iniquity?"

<u>Micah 6:8</u> – "And what does the Lord require of you: To act justly and to love mercy and to walk humbly with your God."

- The message from the prophets of the OT was a combination of both forth-telling and foretelling, with forth telling being the major component.
- And forth telling involved calling out wrongs, idolatry, and injustices in the current culture and a prediction of hard times ahead should Israel not change its ways.

<u>Zech. 7:9-12</u> – "This is what the LORD Almighty says: 'Administer true justice; show mercy and compassion to one another. Do not oppress the widow or the fatherless, the alien or the poor. In your hearts do not think evil of each other.' But they refused to pay attention; stubbornly they turned their backs and stopped up their ears. They made their hearts as hard as flint and would not listen to the law or to the words that the LORD Almighty had sent by his Spirit through the earlier prophets. So the LORD Almighty was very angry."

<u>Isa. 9:6-7</u> – "For to us a child is born, to us a son is given, and the government will be on his shoulders. And he will be called Wonderful Counselor, Mighty God, Everlasting Father, Prince of Peace. Of the increase of his government and peace there will be no end. He will reign on David's throne and over his kingdom, establishing and upholding it with justice and righteousness from that time on and forever."
- From what "time on and forever?"—"for to us a child is born."
- This is the messianic prophecy of the coming everlasting kingdom and Jesus' expansion of the "dominion mandate."

<u>Dan. 7:13-14</u> – ". . . . And there was given him dominion, and glory, and a kingdom, that all people, nations, and languages, should serve him: his dominion is an everlasting dominion, which shall not pass away, and his kingdom that which shall not be destroyed." (*KJV*)
<u>Dan. 7:18, 27</u> – But at some point in history "the saints of the Most High" were to "receive" this kingdom and this dominion and "possess it forever" as it was to be "handed over to the saints" by Christ, which is exactly what He did during his earthly ministry (see Luke 22:29-30).

Source:

A Once-Mighty Faith (future book – est. 2013) by John Noē

(4)
Scriptural support – New Testament.

<u>Luke 1:33</u> – The fulfillment of Isaiah 9:6-7 and the expansion of the "dominion mandate"—with the birth of the Messiah, Jesus Christ, and "his kingdom will never end"—has now arrived in human history.

<u>Mark 1:15</u> – "the time is fulfilled . . . the kingdom of God is at hand." What time?
- The time Daniel prophesied when "a huge mountain" [the kingdom] would fill "the whole earth" (Dan. 2:35, 44; 7:19-25).

<u>John 3:16-17</u> – "For God so loved the world . . . . *but to save the world through him*."

- In one of the most quoted passages of the Bible, have we missed this point?
- That Jesus Christ came to save the whole world—and not just a sinner, here and there?
- He wants to save the *world* (*kosmos*)—lives, laws, institutions, and relationships! How do we *only* get salvation of souls from a postmortem hell out of this?

Luke 4:18-19 – the Messiah's job description and another restatement of the "dominion mandate.

- "The Spirit of the Lord is on me, because he has anointed me to preach good news to the poor. He has sent me to proclaim freedom for the prisoners and recovery of sight for the blind, to release the oppressed, to proclaim the year of the Lord's favor."
- Again, how do we *only* get the salvation of souls from going to hell out of this?

Matt. 5-7 – Known as *The Beatitudes*, it's a "road map" to being "in Christ" and to doing his "works" and the "greater works."

How do we *only* get the salvation of souls from going to hell out of this?

So much throughout the New Testament confirms the extension and expansion of the "dominion mandate" from the Old Testament and provides a massive and persuasive foundation for doing the "works" and "greater works," as I have defined and presented them above. But the ultimate revelation in God's Word of progressive revelation is found in the Bible's last book of Revelation. Here, you will find the final and pinnacle supports for the "dominion mandate" and doing the works of Jesus and even greater works. I suggest you read them for yourself. And remember, the whole of this prophecy was fulfilled in the 1st century and has been just as relevant and applicable ever since (see again Exposé #10). Here are the references for you to check out and without comment: Rev. 1:5-6; 2:2, 5, 26-27; 3:15; 5:9-10; 11:15-18; 12:10-11; 21:24-26; 22:2.

Source:

A Once-Mighty Faith (future book – est. 2013) by John Noē

**(5)
Concluding thoughts.**

Jesus' teachings are so radical and challenging that it is easier and more comfortable to focus on a quiet, private, and personal relationship with Him than it is to follow his teachings that call for a public prophetic witness—i.e., being a "state-of-the-art" Christian by doing both his "works" and "greater works" (John 14:12). So for too many Christians, they passively pass their days on earth looking forward to our citizenship in heaven.

Yet the Bible is full of politics (Mark 6:14-29; Acts 17:7) and we see God placing people strategically in the political realm (Joseph, Daniel, Nehemiah, Esther, Deborah). This testimony of Scripture means we cannot divide life down the middle, putting God on one side and politics, social involvement, and/or other things on the other side. Yet politics, for one, is a major arena that affects everyone and all aspects of life. It can become the most terrible of all institutions if left unchecked vs. being subject to God and his human and "dominion-mandated" stewards.

Sadly, much of the Church is preoccupied with itself and greatly ignoring (or only giving lip service to) the needs of the community. But there is an old evangelical saying, "If He's not Lord of all, He's not Lord at all." This means we must recognize, realize, and honor that salvation covers the whole of human existence. It's a "comprehensive salvation." Moreover, we should not be out to "Christianize America"—but rather to advance Christ's kingdom throughout the whole world! What else does the Great Commission really mean but that?

... being a "state-of-the-art" Christian by doing both his "works" and "greater works" (John 14:12).

This advancing, however, does not mean we take up the sword to force Christ's kingdom on others. That methodology has been tried before—the Crusades, the Inquisition, and the witch-hunts, or shooting abortion providers. That is not the way of Christ.

But it would take many more pages than can be allotted here to cover all this as well as the numerous objections off-target leaders and theologians have contrived to justify their and our shirking away from this level of Christian involvement and responsibility in society. So I'm going to save that material for my future book, *A Once-Mighty Faith: Whatever happened to the central teaching of Jesus?*

I'll close this exposé with these two relevant quotations:

"The Christian ideal has not been tried and found wanting;
it has been found difficult and left untried."[7]

"This takes a reformation of our thinking."[8]

Source:

A Once-Mighty Faith (future book – est. 2013) by John Noē

---

[7] G.K. Chesterton, *What's Wrong with the World* (San Francisco, CA.: Ignatius Press, 1994), chap. 5.
[8] Cindy Jacobs, *The Reformation Manifesto* (Minneapolis, MN.: Bethany House, 2008), 168.

Exposé #16

Origin of Evil

T he existence of evil in our world is and has been one of if not the strongest argument against the existence of God. For centuries, Jewish and Christian scholars, as well as those from other religions and even secular philosophers, have struggled with the so-called problem of evil.

Theological Problem:

Many feel that the existence of evil is incompatible with an omnipotent and omnibenevolent God. Hence, theologians and philosophers alike have termed this conundrum the "awkward trilemma" or "inconsistent triad." That is: 1) God is good and loves us, 2) God is all powerful, and 3) evil exists and its amount is staggering.

Ever since the emergence of monotheism—Jewish-Christian-Islamic tradition—scholars have wrestled with how to incorporate all three statements into one coherent concept of God. But as futurist, Robert B. Mellert notes, "attempts to accomplish this task" have always met "with questionable success."[1] Therefore, these scholars have tried everything they can think of to either distance God from evil or diminished one of the above three "triad" components. All of which, as we shall see, is highly problematic.

---

[1] Robert B. Mellert, "The Future of God," *The Futurist* (October 1999): 31.

What Scripture Says:

Shockingly for some, Scripture, clearly and plainly, presents evil as
part of God's plan for this world. Moreover, it also teaches that God is
the origin of evil.

- "In the beginning God created the heavens and the earth" (Gen.
  1:1f) . . . .
- "God saw all that he had made, and it was very good" (Gen.
  1:31).
- Part of his original, pre-Fall, and "very good" creation was the
  garden of Eden (Gen. 2:8).
- "In the middle of the garden" was *evil*, in the form of "the tree of
  the knowledge of good and *evil*" (Gen. 2:9), as well as the
  opportunity to partake of it (Gen. 2:17), and the tempter himself,
  Satan (Gen. 3:1f).
- Moreover, God proclaims that "I form the light, and create
  darkness; I make peace, and *create evil*: I the LORD have do all
  these things. Drop down, ye heavens, from above, and let the
  skies pour down righteousness: let the earth open, and let them
  bring forth salvation, and let righteousness spring up together; I
  the LORD have created it" (Isa. 45:7-8 *KJV – italic mine*).
- "For everything God *created* is *good*, and nothing is to be
  rejected . . . ." (1 Tim. 4:4).

This literal, biblical fact of the presence of evil in God's original
creation and his continuing acts of creating evil are the crucial points
totally missed, ignored, or denied by almost every writer in my literature
review, and in most, if not all, of the greater body of writings on this
subject. Christian Overman provides an insightful and emblematic
example as he insists on the following:

> Things are not the way God originally made them to be. God's good
> creation has been abused, misused, and warped. . . . the earth and all it
> contains has suffered since the day of the first sin. . . . These are the
> harsh realities of a fallen world.[2]

---

[2] Overman, *Assumptions That Affect Our Lives*, 118.

But evil and sin are two different things. And God is *not* the origin of sin. Big difference. Sorry to say, numerous theologians have come up with all sorts of other explanations.

Elaborations:

1) My Literature Review
2) Side-stepping Solutions—Conservative
3) Side-stepping Solutions—Liberal
4) No Consensus
5) Theodicy
6) Eschatology
7) The Purpose of Evil

Sources:

Origin and Purpose of Evil (future book – est. 2014-15) by John Noē

(1)
My Literature Review

During my doctoral program a few years ago and as part of my second course on systematic theology, I wrote a paper on "The Origin of Evil." The course required that I perform a comprehensive survey of articles related to this topic in two theological journals and one major Christian magazine. I picked the following:

- *Journal of Evangelical Theological Society* – conservative (a 23-year period).
- *Encounter* – the journal of Christian Theological Seminary—liberal (a 19-year period).
- *Christianity Today* magazine – conservative (a 32-year period).

The purpose of my paper was to demonstrate that the failure to biblically account for the origin of evil accounts for much of the equivocating, mumbo-jumbo language, confusion, conflict, compromise, and ambiguity in the literature. In this brief exposé I will only share a few excerpts as examples from the articles I uncovered. Every article, however, that I found could be classified either as an attempt to:

1) Protect, relieve, or exonerate God of the responsibility for evil—insisting "God did not originate evil – this would be incompatible with his holiness." Therefore, He only "allows,' "permits," or "tolerates" it.

2) Tamper with or compromise one of the trilemma components:

    • Impose limitations on one of God's two divine attributes—God is not wholly good, because He allows these bad things to happen and will not eliminate evil.
    • Or, God is not totally omnipotent, preferring the concept of a good God Who cannot intervene.
    • Or, (the 3rd component) maintain that evil does not exist—it's only an abstraction and not real.

Source:

Origin and Purpose of Evil (future book – est. 2014-2015) by John Noē

(2)
Side-stepping Solutions—Conservatives

In sparse writings, most conservative scholars have tried to either absolve God of involvement or at least distance Him from the moral responsibility of evil's existence and prevalence. They cite various verses such as:

    • "God is light; in him there is no is no darkness. . . (1 John 1:5),
    • "For God cannot be tempted by evil, nor does he tempt anyone" (Jas. 1:13),
    • Your eyes are too pure to look on evil; you cannot tolerate wrong" (Hab. 1:13).

James Montgomery Boice, for instance, in his systematic theology textbook asks, "How can evil be compatible with the concept of a good God who is actively ruling this world?"[3] But Boice, like so many others, never addressed the issue of the origin of evil. Instead, he merely concedes that "God uses [evil] in accomplishing his good purposes in the world" and correctly cites several biblical examples.[4]

He summarizes that "Evil is still evil, but God is greater than the evil."[5] And he tries to distance God from creating evil by conceding, "Why God permits evil to exist even temporarily as he obviously does is also beyond our full comprehension."[6]

So Boice ends up blaming evil on us humans and our rebellion against God and his perfectly created world—"But one thing we can say is that evil is our fault, whatever reasons God may have for tolerating it."[7]

Like so many other conservative evangelicals, Boice is saying that God designed a perfect world for us to live in and to enjoy Him forever, but something went wrong. That is the essence, the totality, and the shallowness of his treatment. Again, he never addressed the origin of evil.

God designed a perfect world for us to live in and to enjoy Him forever, but something went wrong.

The much revered Dr. Billy Graham blames the origin of evil on Satan. In his syndicated column answering a reader's question, "Where does evil come from?" Dr. Graham replies:

> Evil is real . . . . Although there is much we can't understand about evil this side of heaven, the Bible does make it clear that evil comes from

---

[3] James Montgomery Boice, *Foundations of the Christian Faith* (Downers Grove, IL: InterVarsity Press, 1986), 176.
[4] Ibid, 181.
[5] Ibid, 182.
[6] Ibid, 195.
[7] Ibid, 195.

Satan, not from God. Evil came into the world because Satan rebelled against God and his will.[8]

Then does this make Satan a second creator? In two other columns Graham writes:

> This present world is not the way God wants it to be. All creation, including humanity, has been scarred by sin, and that is why we have suffering and evil in our world. Even the physical creation is not what God intended it to be. But one day God will change all that.[9]
> Some day, all evil will be destroyed, and God, not Satan, will be victorious. . . . some day the final battle will be fought between good and evil . . . between God and Satan. . . . Christ will come to establish his kingdom of perfect justice and love.[10]

With all due respect to Drs. Boice and Graham, and many other conservative evangelicals, I believe they are biblically incorrect on this issue of evil and its origin, as well as Graham on the kingdom (see again Exposé #2).

Source:

Origin and Purpose of Evil (future book – est. 2014-2015) by John Noē

(3)
Side-stepping Solutions—Liberals

Liberal scholars, on the other hand, have much more to say about both suffering and the problem of evil than do conservatives.

One answers the fundamental question of "why did God let this happen or that happen?" in writing: It's because "God does not have the

---

[8] Billy Graham, "My Answer," *The Indianapolis Star* (Indianapolis, IN), 7 August 2000, B-6.

[9] Billy Graham, "My Answer," *The Indianapolis Star* (Indianapolis, IN), 11 October 2000, B-2.

[10] Billy Graham, "My Answer," *The Indianapolis Star* (Indianapolis, IN), 31 March 2010, C-15

power to insure that this happens in every situation." He notes that while God doesn't choose, will, or want bad things to happen, some things are out of his control. He "is not able to prevent them. . . . They just happen." He also cites the "misuse of human freedom" and "existence of laws of nature." Not surprisingly in this liberal approach, prayer, too, is only of limited, self-talking value, and we must be willing to "forgive the imperfections in God."[11]

Another, in attempting to address the question of, "How are God's power and goodness to be understood in the face of tragedy?" attacks God's omnipotence. In order to explain "why suffering was so pervasive and evil so powerful in a world that God has created and governs," she calls for "a reconstructed doctrine of omnipotence based upon a new meaning for power is both desirable and possible."

She suggests that this should be "along the lines of . . . feminist-process proposal—i.e. changing the kind of power we attribute to God from that of "God as king" to that of "God as mother." She does admit, however, that "there are problems with this image. . . and I do not cherish any illusion of having conclusively settled the problems surrounding divine power."[12]

A third liberal attempts to resolve the problem of evil by Self-limiting God. He says that God lets us be because He emptied and limited Himself (*kenosis*), just as Christ did. Hence, God's divine omnipotence is redefined to mean He chose to limit Himself because his love for us, which is his "defining characteristic," and this overrides all else. His explanation further contends that evil "ultimately results from the freedom given by God in the creative process." Thus, evil becomes a by-product of that freedom. And the more freedom, of course, the more evil; the more evil, the more suffering—and all this from a loving God.

He summarizes that while "God is responsible for . . . evil because he created the kind of world in which, for example, wars and tornadoes can occur . . . . Kenotic love refuses to intervene." So, "the origin of evil is due to God's self-limitation of divine power and the freedom of all creatures."

---

[11] Book review essay: *When Bad Things Happen to Good People* by Harold S. Kushner, reviewer Rufus Burrow, Jr. in *Encounter* (Vol. 55: 69-76 Winter 1994.
[12] "What Do We Mean When We Affirm That God Is 'All-Powerful'?" by Anna Case-Winters in *Encounter* (Vol. 57: 215-230 Summer 1996.

A good question to ask at this point is why pray if God never intervenes? This liberal answers, it will "show us ways of coping and sustains us in our efforts to cope . . . rather than to enlist God's direct, magical intervention in the situation." In other words, we serve a "laissez-faire" and "deistic God . . . . [a] God totally non-involved in the course of history."[13]

Of course, the application of *kenosis* to the totality of God's nature and behavior is without biblical support. Interestingly, eschatological aspects of a future resolution to the problem of evil (as conservatives advocate) are rarely, if ever, mentioned in liberal articles on this subject. Some liberals even scold evangelicals for coming up with a "comfortable notion of God as our warm protector" and thinking that God will someday "make all things right . . . When this, our world, shall be no more."[14]

Another liberal simply throws up his hands and concludes that "there is no completely satisfying answer." In the "Believe it or not" category – and to the contrary – another liberal believes that God did not create *ex nihilo*, but the creation was "the result of a dynamic victory of God over the forces of chaos." For this "scholar," the evil forces pre-dated creation, still survive, and must be subdued. They are the source of evil.[15]

Finally, in Rabbi Kushner's popular book, *When Bad Things Happen to Good People*, Kushner, also assumed that God did not create the world from nothing, but created it from chaos. And these "pockets of chaos remain." They are the source of the random and arbitrary occurrences of much human suffering—people struck with cancer, earthquakes, airplane crashes, etc. Human lawlessness is another source. Of course, Kushner feels that these occurrences pain God. But God is unable to prevent all of them. The forces of chaos are too powerful for a good God. Once again, Kushner's conclusions "lack any kind of scriptural support." But if

---

[13] "A Kenotic God and the Problem of Evil" by Warren McWilliams in *Encounter* (Vol. 42: 15-17 Winter 1981.

[14] "Master of the Universe, Why?" by Frederick Sontag in *Encounter* (Vol. 50: 141-149 Spring 1989.

[15] Book review: *Creation and the Persistence of Evil: The Jewish Drama of Divine Omnipotence* by John D. Levenson's, reviewer J. Gerald Janzen in *Encounter* (Vol. 50: 101-103 Winter 1989.

Kushner is right, "Why bother with a God who will not or cannot help us?"[16]

Once again, what is rarely if ever addressed in these theories on the problem of evil is the question of the origin of evil.

Source:

Origin and Purpose of Evil (future book – est. 2014-2015) by John Noē

(4)
No Consensus

The obvious result of my literature review was that no consensus exists among scholars for the problem of, the purpose of, or the origin of evil. Rather, I found a vast array of confusing and conflicting human opinions. This lack of consensus seems to characterize this whole subject area. My major and consistent criticism of all the above articles, the books reviewed, and the book reviews lies in the question, "What does the Bible really teach about God and the origin of evil?"

But if we truly do subscribe to the concept of an omnipotent and omniscience God and the inspiration and inerrancy of his Word, then we must also submit to the realization that God through Christ is the Creator and Sustainer of *everything* in the universe—i.e. He is the first cause behind everything that exists (Isa. 42:5; 45:7; Job 41:11; John 1:3; Rom. 11:36; 13:1; Col. 1:16-17; Heb. 1:3; 2:10; Rev. 4:11). Evil cannot be excluded from these passages. Still many Christians presume that God could not have created anything evil. They believe, like Augustine, that it exists because some angels and then human beings chose to rebel against God. Or, it resulted from human mismanagement or misuse of freedom. Or, it was a non-existent entity and outside of God's original program until sin entered. Or, it pre-existed creation.

---

[16] From a book review: "'My God Is Not Cruel': The Theodicy of Harold S. Kushner," reviewer Michael J. Latzer in *Encounter* (Vol. 57: 139-147 Spring 1996.

"What does the Bible really teach about God
and the origin of evil?"

Clearly, God is good and "in him there is no is no darkness" (1 John 1:5). But there is no scriptural reason why God could not have created something that is "incompatible" with his own nature. After all, He is separate from his creation. And just as clearly, the Bible says, He created evil, at least in the form of a tree. Who can deny it? Both good and evil were structurally present in the original, pre-Fall, "very-good" creation.

But there is greater proof. God specifically tells us that He both created and creates evil:

> *I form the light, and create darkness; I make peace,*
> *and create evil: I the Lord do all these things.* (Isa. 45:7 *KJV*)

The Hebrew word *ra* (Strong's #7451) is translated as "evil" here in the *KJV*, as "disaster" in the *NIV*, and as "calamity" in the *NAS*. It means "bad, evil, adversity, affliction, calamity, distress," etc. It's derived from the verb *raa* (Strong's #7489), which means "to spoil." The noun *ra* is used numerous times throughout the Old Testament in this consistent manner.

For example, Isaiah further writes (*KJV*): "Therefore shall *evil* come upon thee" (Isa. 47:11), "and keepth his hand from doing any *evil* (Isa. 56:2), "righteousness is taken away from the *evil*" (Isa. 57:1), "Their feet run to *evil*" (Isa. 59:7), "he that departeth from *evil*" (Isa. 59:15), and "hear, but did *evil* before mine eyes" (Isa. 65:12; also 66:4).

For instance, Jeremiah records these collaborative, evil-disaster-sending statements from God Himself:

- "I will send the sword, famine and plague against them until they are destroyed from the land I gave to them and their fathers" (Jer. 24:10).
- "'But you did not listen to me,' declares the LORD, 'and you have provoked me with what you hands have made, and you have brought harm to yourselves'" (Jer. 25:7).
- "This is what the LORD, the God of Israel, said to me: 'Take from my hand this cup filled with the wine of my wrath and

make all the nations to whom I send you drink it. When they drink it, they will stagger and go mad because of the sword I will send among them'" (Jer. 25:15-16).

- "Perhaps they will listen and each will turn from his *evil* way. Then I will relent and not bring on the disaster I was planning because of the evil they have done" (Jer. 26:3).
- Also see: Jeremiah 21:5-6 and 10.
- And less one think that this was just the wrathful God of the Old Testament, see: Matt. 18:21-35; 23:35; Acts 5:1-11; 1 Cor. 11:29-34; Rev. 22:18-19, for instance.

Failure to recognize this truth of creation and God's ongoing role in it has not only undermined the authority of the Bible and the unity of the creation account but it has also created many unnecessary speculations and problems of understanding. Like it or not, we simply must square our discussions of evil with the fact that the origin of evil is God! He intended it. He created it. He sustains it. He creates it. Apparently, evil was part of his creative purpose and is "good" (1 Tim. 4:4).

Is it any wonder then why we have so much confusion and conflict regarding the so-called problem of evil? In actuality, it is not a problem at all. Nor does it impugn upon God's existence, his power, or his goodness. Again, it was part of his original creation. This identification of the origin of evil and recognition of God's responsibility for creating and sustaining a world and conditions in which it can operate will greatly impact and rearrange our understanding in two major and related subject areas: theodicy and eschatology.

Source:

Origin and Purpose of Evil (future book – est. 2014-2015) by John Noē

(5)
Theodicy

Theodicy – (*theos* god + *dike* justice). Theodicy is an effort to justify God in the face of evil; or as dictionaries define it: "a vindication of the justice and holiness of God in establishing a world in which evil exists."

However, I strongly suggest that the proper identification of the origin of evil breaks the impasse of the classical "triad" or "trilemma" used by traditionalists—God is good, God is all-powerful, evil exists.

Unfortunately, most theodicies have functioned to obscure the fact that God is the origin of evil. Consequently, they have taken the approach of defending God's honor, trying to vindicate Him, or exonerating Him of any responsibility for evil. Others have depreciated his goodness or power attributes, while trying to sooth those suffering. Most never attempt to find a divine purpose(s) for evil. Unfortunately, this shifting of responsibility away from God, even partially, leads to passivity, resignation, and cynicism in the face of evil.

Admittedly, and on this side of heaven, we will never be able to account for all suffering and evil with a single model. But a biblically consistent and coherent theodicy must not seek to divert responsibility from God. Of course, some suffering is avoidable. But some isn't. Therefore, we must recognize that we are called to resist it, to overcome it, and to reduce and eliminate it wherever possible. But we must also understand that sometimes God creates and sends evil and suffering into our lives and world.

Source:

Origin and Purpose of Evil (future book – est. 2014-2015) by John Noē

(6)
Eschatology

The existence of evil is pointed to as evidence against the preterist (past-fulfillment) position and the consummation of "all things" circa A.D. 70 to which I adhere as part of my eschatological synthesis position (see again Exposés #1 and 13). The traditional assumption and emphasis of Christian eschatology and classic objection generally goes like this. "At the 'restoration of all things' (Acts 3:21 *NAS*), God will finally deal with evil and make an end to it in order to restore this world back to its original, pristine, pre-Fall perfection"—i.e., an evil-less, new or re-creation, called a "paradise restored."

That is—someday all evil will be removed from planet Earth and a utopian, physical paradise, once again, set up. Billy Graham explains his belief in this future reality this way: "Our world will never be perfect – not until Jesus comes back to destroy all evil and injustice, and usher in his rule of perfect justice and peace."[17]

The traditional assumption . . . God will finally deal with evil and make an end to it in order to restore this world back to its original, pristine, pre-Fall perfection."

Conversely, Gordon J. Spykman in his systematic theology textbook made a very apropos eschatological statement in this regard, "If we get the 'first things' wrong, 'last things' will also turn out wrong . . . ."[18] How true, because we indeed have gotten first things wrong. The assumption of a an evil-less new or re-creation in a "paradise restored," has been shown to be an invalid assumption, regardless of where one places the time of consummation, since evil was a part of that "very good" creation from the beginning. God Himself put it there during the creation week.

Sadly, therefore, the hope of many Christians is a misguided hope. They are looking for an evil-less earthly world someday that is different from what God created and now sustains. Supposedly, all this will be part of God's ultimate triumph. But does this utopian belief line up with the Bible? Indeed, this old order has already passed away (Heb. 9:10; Matt. 23:38) and yet these "evil" realities are still present in our world. Furthermore, in the last chapter of the Bible's last book of Revelation and in the "new heaven and a new earth" and "the Holy City, the new Jerusalem" that comes "down out of heaven" to earth (Rev. 21:1-2) evil is still present. It lies just outside the gates of the new Jerusalem on earth: "Outside are the dogs, those who practice magic arts, the sexually

---

[17] Billy Graham, "My Answer," *The Indianapolis Star* (Indianapolis, IN), 17 November 2011, E-4.
[18] Gordon J. Spykman, *Reformational Theology: A New Paradigm for Doing Dogmatics* (Grand Rapids, MI: Eerdmans, 1992), 152.

immoral, the murderers, the idolaters and everyone who loves and practices falsehood" (Rev. 22:15). Also, the nations enter this city for "healing" (Rev. 22:2b). What do they need to be healed of if all evil is gone?

Source:

Origin and Purpose of Evil (future book – est. 2014-2015) by John Noē

(7)
The Purpose of Evil

So if God truly was and is the origin of evil, why? If He is all-good and all-powerful, as many of us Christians believe, why didn't He just create a world without any evil, suffering, risk, or danger in the first place? Fact is, He is the Creator of all things and He did not create this type of world. This realization inevitably forces one to seriously reconsider that there may be a divine purpose or purposes for evil.

Perhaps, God did create the perfect world for our advantage, and not for our convenience. Perhaps, evil really is "very good" and necessary in some manner. Indeed, with the realization that God is responsible for evil, the long trail of failures to find an adequate theism and theodicy may now be resolvable. Therefore, our challenge must become to make better sense of our God-created, good-and-evil world. This challenge and the addressing of this greater issue, however, is beyond our scope here and deserves a book all of its own.

Perhaps, God did create the perfect world for our advantage, and not for our convenience.

Source:

Origin and Purpose of Evil (future book – est. 2014-2015) by John Noē

Exposé #17

Eternal Rewards and Punishment
for Believers

F or a believer in Christ, life on earth does not go unrewarded or unpunished. This is true both in this life and in the afterlife. Not only do a believer's righteous acts (see Rev. 19: 8), here and now, bring rewards in this life, but perhaps even more and greater rewards in the afterlife and for all eternity. However, there is also punishment and loss that goes along with this. It's termed "The Doctrine of Eternal Rewards and Punishment." Over one hundred verses of Scripture address this postmortem reality.

WARNING: This exposé may not be a message some believers in Christ want to hear.

Theological Problem:

Rarely, if ever, is the doctrine of eternal rewards, loss, and punishments for believers taught or preached in most churches. Therefore, "there are countless 'Christians' who believe they have a ticket to heaven, and nothing else really matters."[1]

---

[1] *Whistleblower* magazine, April, 2005, 22.

So why is this biblical teaching rarely if ever taught? Here's a short, recent, and true story that might shed some light on this huge omission and problem.

The senior pastor's sermon that Sunday was on the topic of "Universal Judgment." Confidently, he assured the large congregation that "if they are believers in Jesus Christ, they have nothing to fear, nothing to worry about, concerning judgment, because Christ has taken care of it for us."

In a follow-up conversation, I asked this pastor if he was familiar with the doctrine of eternal rewards, loss, and even punishment for believers in heaven. He said he wasn't interested. I mentioned that many verses speak of this and I'd be happy to send them to him. He responded that there are many more verses that speak of God's grace and love and of setting people free. He would focus on those and not the others, thank you.

No doubt, this pastor is both a victim as well as a perpetrator of a led-astray, dumbed-down, and off-target version of Christianity.

What Scripture Says:

Someday, each and every one of us—believers and unbelievers alike—will face, go into, and dwell forever in the postmortem experience. It's the afterlife destiny of every person who has ever lived, is now living, or will live on planet Earth. Individually, everyone of us will "stand before God's judgment seat . . . . [and] give an account of himself to God" (Rom. 14:10b, 12b). For believers, there and then, we "receive what is due him for the things done while in the body, whether good or bad" (2 Cor. 5:10). Jesus further elaborated about this experience, thusly: "But I tell you that men will have to give account on the day of judgment for every careless word they have spoken. For by your words you will be acquitted, and by your words you will be condemned" (Matt. 12:36-37). No believer is exempt not even females, despite this use of masculine language.[2]

---

[2] Whether this is happening currently every day as people die (I think so) or is a future event yet to happen will not be addressed herein.

Twice, and on the positive side, this encouraging tidbit also has been revealed. "However, as it is written: 'No eye has seen, no ear has heard, no mind has conceived what God has prepared for those who love him' – but God has revealed it to us by his Spirit" (1 Cor. 2:9-10; from Isa. 64:4).

Elaborations:

1) Basis of your judgment
2) Rewards
3) Loss
4) How will you spend eternity?
5) Closing quotes

Sources:

Hell Yes / Hell No by John Noē
The Perfect Ending for the World by John Noē
In Light of Eternity by Randy Alcorn

(1)
Basis of your judgment

Certainly, the Bible does not teach salvation by works. Salvation is a gift and comes by faith alone (Eph. 2:8-9). But once saved, and if this happens in this life, you then have the opportunity to do "good works" (Eph. 2:10). Those "good works" are the basis for storing up heavenly rewards (Matt.6:19-21). It is also true that we are not saved *without* works (Phil. 2:12-13; Jas. 2:17-20), that rewards and punishments for believers are based on works for or against God, and works are also the basis of punishment for both believers and non-believers.

Source:

Hell Yes / Hell No by John Noē

(2)
Rewards

Let's look at a few of many scriptures that speak of rewards:

"God 'will give to each person according to what he has done'" (Rom. 2:6; Psa. 62:12; Prov. 24:12).

"For we must all appear before the judgment seat of Christ, that each one may receive what is due him for the things done while in the body, whether good or bad" (2 Cor. 5:10).

"So do not throw away your confidence; it will be richly rewarded. You need to persevere so that when you have done the will of God, you will receive what he has promised" (Heb. 10:35-36).

"And without faith it is impossible to please God, because anyone who comes to him must believe that he exists and that he rewards those who earnestly seek him" (Heb. 11:6).

"Then all the churches will know that I am he who searches hearts and minds, and I will repay each of you according to your deeds (Rev. 2:23b).

"'Blessed are the dead who die in the Lord from now on.' 'Yes,' says the Spirit, 'they will rest from their labor, for their deeds will follow them'" (Rev. 14:13b).

"The dead were judged according to what they had done as recorded in the books" (Rev. 20:12b).

"My reward is with me, and I will give to everyone according to what he has done" (Rev. 22:12b).

As we can see from these scriptures and as Randy Alcorn writes, "Works do *not* affect our redemption. Works *do* affect our reward. Just as there are eternal consequences to our faith, so there are eternal consequences to our works." He defines our "reward-earning works" as those works that "are empowered by the Holy Spirit (Colossians 1:29)." Next, he adds this interesting insight that "*Eternal* rewards are guaranteed; *temporal* rewards are not. . . . Scripture does not guarantee I will always receive rewards on earth." But "in the end, our righteous God promises to make all things right."[3]

Alcorn also warns his readers and confesses that "when it comes to my bad works and my failure to do good works, it gets tricky. . . . Once lost or squandered, opportunity doesn't reappear. . . . many times as I've failed him . . . . The question is, will you seek to do more rewardable works for him now, while you still can? Anticipating this future joy should fuel our present ministry efforts. . . . God is watching. He's keeping track. In heaven he'll reward us for our acts of faithfulness to him. . . ."[4]

Likewise, Tony Evans makes some poignant points:

> God paid a high price for you and me. We cost Him the life of His Son. Not only that, but He has entrusted us with the stewardship of His kingdom. He has given us the privilege of ruling with Him in His kingdom. Are we going to turn around and give God sloppy work, our left-over time, talents, and treasure? . . . the fundamental question that Christ will ask every believer at His judgment seat is this: 'Did you finish? Did you complete the task of living for Me that I gave you when I saved you? Were you faithful to Me?[5]

How each of us fares on that day of judgment when this evaluation is made will determine how we spend eternity.

Sources:

Hell Yes / Hell No by John Noē
In Light of Eternity by Randy Alcorn
What a Way to Live! by Tony Evans

---

[3] Randy Alcorn, *In the Light of Eternity* (Colorado Springs, CO.: Waterbrook Press, 1999), 117-118.
[4] Ibid., 118-120, 122.
[5] Tony Evans, *What a Way to Live!* (Nashville, TN.: Word Publishing, 1997), 169, 182.

(3)
Loss

On the negative side, this judgment event will not only involve blessings and rewards, but also loss and possible punishment:

> *"If any man builds on this foundation using gold, silver, costly stones, wood, hay or straw, this work will be shown for what it is, because the Day will bring it to light. It will be revealed with fire, and the fire will test the quality of each man's work. If what he has built survives, he will receive his reward. If it is burned up, he will suffer loss; he himself will be saved, but only as one escaping through the flames."* (1 Cor. 3:11-15)

So we have this sticky little issue, or not-so-little, depending on your perspective. But most believers who have confessed Christ as their Savior in this life have been told, taught, and think they will completely avoid God's wrath and punishments and upon physical death go instantly into the blissful paradise of heaven. Maybe some will.

But biblically, it has been revealed that the souls of many, if not all, believers may not be ready to receive and enjoy the blessings of heaven immediately after they die. Plenty of scriptures warn that we all will be held accountable for what we have done and/or not done in this life and some unpleasant afterlife consequences are possible after we face and undergo "the judgment" (Heb. 9:27; Rom. 14:10-12; 2 Cor. 5:10).

How all this transpires for each person—saved and unsaved—has not been revealed. But this universal reality and the administration of this process has been the subject of many debates over the centuries. Below are several additional verses from the New Testament that many ignore or lightly brush aside, which seem to teach this truth:

> *"Everyone will be salted with fire"* (Mark 9:49).

> *"That servant who knows his master's will and does not get ready or does not do what his master wants will be beaten with many blows. But the one who does not know and does things deserving punishment will be beaten with few blows. . . .* (Luke 12:47-48a).

"Then he will say to those on his left, 'Depart from me, you who are cursed, into the eternal fire prepared for the devil and his angels. For I was hungry and you gave me nothing to eat, I was thirsty and you gave me nothing to drink, I was a stranger and you did not invite me in, I needed clothes and you did not clothe me, I was sick and in prison and you did not look after me.' They also will answer, 'Lord, when did we see you hungry or thirsty or a stranger or needing clothes or sick or in prison, and did not help you?' He will reply, 'I tell you the truth, whatever you did not do for one of the least of these, you did not do for me'" (Matt. 25:41-45).

And arguably one of the most troubling and "scariest passages . . . in the entire Bible:"[6] *"Many will say to me on that day, 'Lord, Lord, did we not prophesy in your name, and in your name drive out demons and perform many miracles?' Then I will tell them plainly, 'I never knew you. Away from me, you evildoers!'"* (Matt. 7:22-23).

"for our God is a consuming fire" (Heb. 12:29; Deut. 4:24; Isa. 33:14).

So, really, is a believer in Christ in this life immune from all, some, or none of these negative consequences in the afterlife, or not? Baker certainly recognizes this possibility or reality that everyone may "stand in the fiery presence of God and suffer the purifying flames of God's love. This burning love might feel like burning wrath to the one who experiences it." And since everyone is a sinner, even those of us already saved by grace, this fire may just be God's "love that burns away the sin, purifying the sinner so that true reconciliation and restoration can take place."[7]

But I also think we believers can rest assured that this divine use of fire is good for us because everything God does is good, right, and just. And this postmortem experience, whatever it might entail, will likewise

---

[6] Francis Chan and Preston Sprinkle, *Erasing Hell* (Colorado Springs, CO.: David C. Cook, 2011), 118.

[7] Baker, *Razing Hell*, 122.

be good, right, and just for each of us because He is the loving Father of all and we are all made in his image and likeness. We can also rest assured that God in his omniscience knows what will work best in each case to bring about his desired result.

Source:

Hell Yes / Hell No by John Noē

(4)
How will you spend eternity?

These comments from Brian D. McLaren speak frankly and directly to this area of dumbed-downedness:

> What could be more serious than standing in front of your Creator—the Creator of the universe—and finding out that you had wasted your life, squandered your inheritance, caused others pain and sorrow, worked against the good plans and desires of God? What could be more serious than that? To have to face the real, eternal, unavoidable, absolute, naked truth about yourself, what you've done, what you've become? . . . . Nothing could be more serious than that . . . . We cannot select out comfortable passages and ignore those that make us uneasy.[8]

Yet McLaren reminds his readers that he is "not denying salvation by grace . . . . I'm just advocating judgment by works," and that "being judged isn't the same as being condemned and that being saved means a lot more than not being judged."[9]

In sum, a hierarchical heaven is where some, many, most, or all will spend eternity. And heaven is gift, not a reward. But how we spend eternity there will be determined by our good works on this earth during this life. These works earn rewards. Hence, how we live this life determines our next life—our status, privileges, provisions, levels of

---

[8] McLaren, *The Last Word and the Word after That*, 79, 80, 96.
[9] Ibid., 138.

reward, treasure, glory, authority, joy, enjoyment, and also "rewards lost due to disobedience on earth."[10]

And contrary to what most Christians have been told and taught, "all men [and women] are *not* equal before God; the facts of heaven and hell (sic), election and reprobation, make clear that they are not equal."[11] Hence, these differing degrees of reward will be determined according to:

- The knowledge, time, talents and resources given us. (Matt. 25:14-30; Luke 19:11-27)
- How we use them for God's glory to expand his kingdom. (2 Thess. 1:4-5; 1 Pet. 4:13; Phil. 3:10-11).

Yes, we have a great and unlimited heavenly future awaiting us. But since there will be different rewards, different positions, and different experiences in heaven that are currently being determined in *this* life, doesn't this future destiny give this life even greater meaning? You might be wondering how could someone in heaven be happy with a "lesser" amount than they could have received or with less than someone else receives? The answer is, I don't know. And, yes, this is a threatening, controversial, and surprising message for some people. But once again, would you rather hear it now while you can do something about it? Or would you rather wait until later when you can't and have it come as a complete surprise?

So what's going to be your degree of glory, level of blessings, rewards, station, position, responsibilities, joy, and/or punishment in this eternal afterlife in God's hierarchical heaven?

Sources:

Hell Yes / Hell No by John Noē
The Last Word and the Word after That by Brian D. McLaren
In Light of Eternity by Randy Alcorn

---

[10] Alcorn, *In Light of Eternity*, 123.

[11] Rousa John Rushdoony, *The Institutes of Biblical Law* (n.l.: The Presbyterian and Reformed Publishing Company, 1973), 509-510.

(5)
Closing quotes

"No wonder Scripture makes clear that the one central business of this life is to prepare for the next. . . . Your life on earth is a dot. From that dot extends a line that goes on for all eternity. Right now you're living *in* the dot. But what are you living *for*? Are you living for the dot or for the line? Are you living for earth or for heaven? Are you living for the short today or the long tomorrow?"[12]

—Randy Alcorn, *In Light of Eternity*

"There is a long list of martyrs . . . . The famous Lutheran martyr Dietrich Bonhoeffer . . . In his last letters from prison, Bonhoeffer reveals how his Christian faith gave him the resources to give up everything for the sake of others. . . . had a joy and hope in God that made it possible for him to do what he did."[13]

—Timothy Keller, *The Reason for God*.

"Let me tell you, if you are too busy to serve Christ, you are too busy to be great in His kingdom. If you are too busy to serve now, you are too busy to be recognized then."[14]

—Tony Evans, *What a Way to Live!*

"Not that I have already obtained all this, or have already been made perfect, but I press on to take hold of that for which Christ Jesus took hold of me. Brothers, I do not consider myself yet to have taken hold of it. But one thing I do: Forgetting what is behind and straining toward what is ahead, I press on toward the goal to win the prize for which God has called me heavenward in Christ Jesus."

(Philippians 3:12-14)

"I have fought the good fight, I have finished the race, I have kept the faith. Now there is in store for me the crown of righteousness, which the

---

[12] Alcorn, *In Light of Eternity*, 142-143.
[13] Timothy Keller, *The Reason for God* (New York, NY.: Dutton, 2008), 66.
[14] Evans, *What a Way to Live!*, 192.

Lord, the righteous judge, will award to me on that day – not only to me, but also to all who have longed for his appearing."

(2 Timothy 4:7)

"Therefore, since we are surrounded by such a great cloud of witnesses, let us throw off everything that hinders and the sin that so easily entangles, and let us run with perseverance the race marked out for us."

(Hebrews 12:1)

Dear reader, let's you and I do this! Let's get our eyes on this prize, fight the good fight of faith, and finish the race . . . unto our "crowning day" when hopefully we will hear these words, "Well done, good and faithful servant! You have been faithful with a few things; I will put you in charge of many things. Come and share your master's happiness!" (Matt. 25:21, 23). So, what do you say now? Hell yes? Hell no?

For more, see Appendix A in *Hell Yes / Hell No*. It provides a more extensive scriptural recap of God's Incentive Plan, a Hierarchical View of Heaven, and "The Doctrine of Eternal Rewards and Punishment for Believers."

Source:

Hell Yes / Hell No by John Noē

Exposé #18

Your Worldview

Your worldview is a paradigm. The word paradigm comes from the Greek *pardeigma* (*para*, side by side + *deiknynai*, to show, point out). A paradigm is a model, a pattern, a frame of reference, or simply a way of thinking for understanding and interpreting external reality. It's the way we "see" the world, not visually but by perception. It is the mental framework by which we construe reality, process information, make decisions, and determine actions. For individuals, it brings order and meaning to our experiences. It's also at the very heart of any culture.

In practice, a person may not live what he or she professes, but that person will always live in accordance with his or her paradigm. In other words, we live out what we truly believe and think. Consequently, when our paradigm shifts, many things will change.

Theological Problem:

Jesus' paradigm or worldview was the kingdom of God. What's your worldview? That's why the kingdom was his central teaching and at the heart of his ministry. He also commanded his followers to "seek first the kingdom and his righteousness (justice)" (Matt. 6:33). What are you seeking, first?

Today's sad reality is the kingdom of God is no longer the worldview of most of Christ's church, its central teaching, nor at the heart of its ministry. *What has happened? What has changed?*

What Scripture Says:

Below are five foundational verses that, in my opinion, should significantly inform our worldview if we truly want to be true to Scripture. The proper understanding of and obedience to these five verses will also cause our worldview to radically depart from the current worldview of most of Christ's Church. What do you think?

1. *"I felt I had to write and urge you to contend for the faith that was once for all entrusted/delivered to the saints"* (Jude 3).

    The construction "once for all" here means exactly the same as it means in Romans 6:10 when applied to Jesus' death; in Hebrews 9:12 with Jesus entering the Most Holy Place to pour out his blood; in Hebrews 9:26 with Jesus' appearance and sacrifice of Himself; in Hebrews 10:10 with us being made holy by the sacrifice of his body; and in 1 Peter 3:18 with Christ dying for our sins. All these are part of that "once-for-all-delivered" faith. And all four are totally done deals. That means, no more remains to be done or delivered. But most of the Church today is contending for a faith that was only partially delivered. Thus, they are waiting for Jesus to come back some day and finish the job. (See again Exposés #1, 5, 6, 7, 10, 11, 13.)

2. *"'The time is fulfilled,' he said. 'The kingdom of God is at hand. Repent and believe the good news!'"* (Mark 1:15).

    This was the fulfillment of Daniel's time-restricted prophecies for the coming of the everlasting kingdom (Dan. 2:44 and 7:14, 18, 22, 27). No other kingdom or form of this kingdom is promise or prophesied in Scripture. But most of Christ's Church is still looking for Jesus to come back and either establish his kingdom or consummate the one he supposedly only initiated. (See again Exposés #2 and 3.)

3. *"Verily, verily, I say unto you, He that believeth on me, the works that I do shall he do also; and greater works than these shall he do; because I go unto my Father"* (John 14:12 *KJV*).

    Most of Christ's Church today is in functional avoidance, if not doctrinal denial, of this verse. (See again Exposés #14 and 15.)

4. *"You have made them to be a kingdom and priests to serve our God, and they will reign on the earth"* (Rev. 5:10)

    Most of Christ's Church today is in functional avoidance, if not doctrinal denial, of this verse, as well. The preferred avoidance tactic is to futurize it—"Oh, someday we will, after Christ returns and removes all evil." But then what would be left to reign and rule over? (See again Exposés #2, 10, 14, 15.)

5. *"The kingdom of the world has become the kingdom of our Lord and of his Christ, and he will reign for ever and ever"* (Rev. 11:15b)

    It's the message of 7th trumpet and part of the Handel's "Messiah" with its famous "Hallelujah Chorus." But do we believe this? No! We futurize it, too. (See again Exposés #2 and 10.)

What a big difference this totally biblical and further reformed worldview would make for how Christianity is preached, practiced, and perceived—and received! What do you think?

Elaborations:

1) Kingdom Edited Out.

Sources:

The Perfect Ending for the World by John Noē
A Once-Mighty Faith (future book – est. 2013) by John Noē
The Greater Jesus (future book – est. 2012) by John Noē

(1)
Kingdom Edited Out

Another telling sign of our current led-astray, dumbed-down, and off-target versions of the Christian faith is: the kingdom of God also has been edited out of most, if not all, of today's biblical-worldview or Christian-worldview presentations.

Yet in 1890-1891 James Orr, a leading theologian of his day, presented a series of lectures in Edinburgh, Scotland entitled *The Christian View of God and the World.* Orr listed nine specific areas covered by "the Christian view of the world." His eighth area was described thusly:

(8) the founding of the Kingdom of God on earth, which includes the spiritual salvation of individuals and a new order of society ("the result of the action of the spiritual forces set in motion through Christ"); . . . [1]

In contrast, and in the most widely acclaimed, modern-day book on this subject, *Understanding the Times: The Religious Worldviews of Our Day and the Search for Truth,* author David A. Noebel compares and contrasts his conception of a Christian worldview with those of secular humanism and Marxism/Leninism. Paradoxically, Noebel lists Orr's nine specific areas including #8 about the "Kingdom of God on earth" and its purpose of establishing "a new order of society." But without explanation, Noebel drops the kingdom from his own biblical worldview presentation. Most likely, the reason for this exclusion is his eschatological position, which has no present kingdom in the world

---

[1] James Orr, *The Christian View of God and the World* (Edinburgh: Andrew Elliot, 1897), 32-34.

today. In this book's "Revised 2nd Edition" several years later (2006), Orr's whole worldview and kingdom component was totally edited out.[2]

Below are some other prominent examples of Christian worldview books in which there is no kingdom addressed or mentioned. I compiled this list in preparation for a theological paper presentation at the 49th Annual Meeting of the Midwest Region of the Evangelical Theological Society in 2004. It was titled, "Restoring the Kingdom-of-God Worldview to the Church and the World:"

- David K. Naugle, *Worldview: The History of a Concept* (Grand Rapids, MI.: Eerdmans, 2002.
- David S. Dockery & Gregory Alan Thornbury, eds. *Shaping a Christian Worldview* (Nashville, TN.: Broadman & Holman, 2002.
- J. P. Moreland & William Lane Craig, *Philosophical Foundations for a Christian Worldview* (Downers Grove, IL.: InterVarsity Press, 2003.
- N. Allan Moseley, *Thinking against the Grain: Developing a Biblical Worldview in a Culture of Myths* (Grand Rapids, MI.: Kregel, 2003.
- Ronald H. Nash, *Worldviews in Conflict* (Grand Rapids, MI.: Zondervan, 1992.

Dr. Naugle (above) also spoke at this meeting. He and I met and talked. During our conversation I asked him why the kingdom, which was the central teaching of Jesus, at the heart of his ministry, and the very essence of his worldview was not included in his (Dr. Naugle's) book's worldview presentation. To his credit, he admitted this omission was a major deficiency and promised he would correct this error in a future revision. I do not know if he has followed up on that promise.

Lastly, as we saw in Exposé #3, in 2003 Christian researcher George Barna in a poll about who does or doesn't have a biblical worldview— had no kingdom in his definition of a biblical worldview. In other words,

---

[2] David A. Noebel, *Understanding the Times* (Eugene OR.: Harvest House Publishers, 1991, 1995), 11.

Barna edited out or simply failed to include the central teaching and worldview of our Lord Jesus Christ.[3]

Is it any wonder we are in such a led-astray, dumbed-down, off-target mess?

Sources:

The Perfect Ending for the World by John Noē
A Once-Mighty Faith (future book – est. 2013) by John Noē

---

[3] Barna Research Online, "A Biblical Worldview Has a Radical Effect on a Person's Life" (www.barna.org/cgi-bin/PagePressRelease.asp., 1 December 2003), 1-2.

Conclusion

Bull's-eye Theology

Something significant is now possible. Like arrows flying straight to a target, I believe this book's 18 exposés are hitting dead center, right in the theological bull's-eye, and staking out the pragmatic basis and scope for the next reformation of Christianity.

Please be assured, once again, that I'm not down on Christianity—just the opposite. I'm down on what we have done to it. Indeed, as we have seen, we Christians have become our own worst enemy. But if Christianity has been as successful as it has been for the past 19 centuries and counting, how much more successful might it be if we would get our faith right, on-target, and into the bull's eye?

Indeed, as we have seen, we Christians have become our own worse enemy.

Call it "bull's-eye theology" if you will, or whatever. But where am I wrong or off target on any or all of this? I have no desire to be in error in any way. Nor do I have a career position to protect at all costs in some dumbed-downed denomination or led-astray church—thank God! If this were so, I could not and would not have written this book. I am simply an ardent student of God's Word and a passionate seeker of truth who has a high view of the ancient Scriptures but a low view of what we moderns have done to them—and to the practice of our faith in the process. At the least, would you now agree with me on these three propositions?

1) The vast majority of we Christians today have been led astray, dumbed down, and pulled off target by our own leaders.

2) Most of today's versions of Christianity have significantly compromised our faith and are substantially substandard compared to the faith preached, practiced, and perceived as well as modeled, conferred, and consummated in the 1st century—exactly as specified and expected.

3) The theology supporting this book's 18 exposé areas will indeed standup to an honest and sincere test of Scripture.

If you do agree that's all the conclusion this book really needs. Now it's . . .

Onto the Next Reformation

Much more could have been presented and other topics included. But I wanted to keep these 18 exposés concise and this book at medium length. More extensive treatments in depth and breadth are available in my two already published books and those to be published in the future.

Now, and with your help, it's onto pioneering the next reformation of Christianity. Each one of us who is convinced of the truths contained herein needs to be involved. Be assured, you will be blessed. And it's upon this sure foundation that the next reformation will go forth—so help us God. So how can you get involved, you ask? Help us get this word out—to people you know, people in your church, in other churches, family, friends, contacts you have on the Internet, and any other ways you can think of.

But remember from page 33 that reformation is not easy business and can be messy. It always has resisters and attackers. This next reformation will be no exception. Some will keep on preaching and teaching things not found in the Bible simply because they are committed to it, have built their ministries upon it, and would be embarrassed or find it awkward or career-threatening to "change horses in the middle of the stream"—so to speak. Others will come against me and fellow co-reformers. But for many of you, who seek after truth and long for a firmer foundation upon which a genuine biblical faith can be built, it will be right on-target, a proverbial breath of fresh air, and, perhaps, a godsend. This is the further reformed faith that must be re-established in the Church and taken to the world—so help us God.

And it's upon this sure foundation that the next reformation will go forth—so help us God.

So how many of you will join with us? We have a great deal of further reforming to do. And if there ever was a time for us Christians to move out of our traditional traps and trenches, it is now. Christianity must be re-targeted and further reformed toward equipping Christ's followers to expand his everlasting kingdom and contend for our "once-for-all-delivered" faith (Jude 3) not only in our own personal lives but throughout all spheres of today's world. Would you now agree? If so, will you join with us? Will you?

More extensive treatments in depth and breadth are available in my two already published books and those to be published in the future.

More Books from John Noē

(Available on Amazon.com)

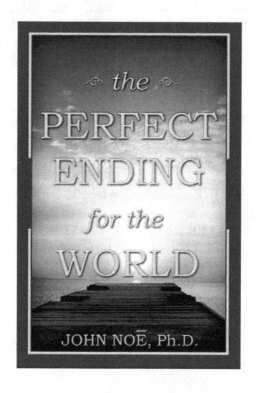

*What are millions worldwide
looking for today?
That's right! The perfect ending!
Here it is . . .*

Why All 'End-of-the-World' Prophets Will <u>Always</u> Be Wrong!

The perennial prophets of doom have failed to recognize that our world is without end and "the end" the Bible consistently proclaims *for* the world is behind us and not ahead of us; is past and not future. This is the perfect ending! It's also the climax of the rest of the greatest story ever foretold. In this book you'll discover:

~ WHY THE WORLD WILL NEVER END.
~ HOW THE PERFECT ENDING FOR THE
   WORLD CAME RIGHT ON TIME.
~ DIVINE PERFECTION IN GOD'S END-TIME PLAN.
~ A NEW & GREATER PARADIGM OF THOUGHT AND
   FAITH.
~ OUR GREATER RESPONSIBILITIES HEREIN.
~ WHY THE FUTURE IS BRIGHT AND PROMISING.
~ THE BASIS FOR THE NEXT REFORMATION OF
   CHRISTIANITY.

"Noē's book just could be the spark that ignites the next reformation of Christianity." – Dr. James Earl Massey, Former Sr. Editor, *Christianity Today* Dean Emeritus, School of Theology, Anderson University & Distinguished Professor-at-Large

"Your treatment of the 'end of the world' is the best treatment of this idea . . . . Your book could really open the eyes of a lot of people." – Walter C. Hibbard, Former Chairman, Great Christian Books

"Noē . . . argues, with no little energy, against traditional views . . . [it] does have an internal logic that makes for exegetically interesting reading." – Mark Galli, Book Review Editor, *Christianity Today*

<u>Description for – *'Hell Yes / Hell No: What really is the extent of God's grace . . . and wrath?'* –</u>

This compelling and controversial book strikes at the heart of Christian theology and Christianity itself. It presents a balanced and scholarly re-exploration of "one of Christianity's most offensive doctrines"—Hell and the greater issue of the extent of God's grace (mercy, love, compassion, justice) and wrath in the eternal, afterlife destiny for all people. Inside, conflicting views are reevaluated, their strengths and weaknesses reassessed, and all the demands of Scripture are reconciled into one coherent and consistent synthesized view. The author further suggests that our limited earthly view has been the problem, re-discovers the ultimate mystery of God's expressed desire, will, and purpose, and transcends troubling traditions as never before. The bottom line is, God's plan of salvation and condemnation may be far different and greater than we've been led to believe. In a clear and straightforward manner, this book lays out the historical and scriptural evidence as never before.

Can We Really Be So Sure Anymore?

Battle lines are drawn. Sides are fixed. Arguments are exhausted. The majority proclaim, "Hell yes!" But growing numbers are protesting, "Hell no!" After nineteen centuries of church history, no effective resolution or scriptural reconciliation has been offered—until now!

So what really is the true Christian doctrine on this matter of hell and the greater issue of the extent of God's grace (mercy, love, compassion, justice) and wrath in the eternal, afterlife destiny for all people? The answer goes to the heart of Christian theology and Christianity itself. Has our limited earthly view been the problem? Could God's plan of salvation be far different than we've been led to believe?

In this book you'll discover:

- A balanced scholarly re-exploration of the mystery of God's desire, will, and purpose in the eternal afterlife destiny for all people.
- Re-evaluation of conflicting views.
- Re-assessment of the strengths and weaknesses of pro and con arguments.
- Synthesis of the strengths into one coherent and consistent view that meets all scriptural demands.
- Reconciliation of the greatest debate of 'all.'
- Transcending troubling traditions as never before!

(Available on Amazon.com)

Revised edition – PEAK PERFORMANCE PRINICIPLES FOR HIGH ACHIEVERS *is a dynamic story of how one man transformed himself, sedentary and out-of-shape in his mid-thirties, into a dynamic leader – and how you can too.*

John R. Noē is using his mountain-climbing adventures as an allegory for the challenge of goal setting and the thrill of high achievement. He shows you how to choose accurate goals, how to reach them, how to remain committed to the accomplishment of a goal whether earthly or spiritual, and—in short—how to become a high achiever. To help you succeed, Noē offers a unique philosophy of reaching "beyond self-motivation" to the spiritual motivation that comes from God.

In this revised edition, Noē adds further insights and updates his reader on how these principles have fared in his life since the book's original writing in 1984—which was named one of Amway Corporation's "top ten recommended books."

Noē shows you how to learn the six essential attitudes of a high achiever:

1. High Achievers make no small plans.
2. Are willing to do what they fear.
3. Are willing to prepare.
4. To risk failure.
5. To be taught.
6. And must have heart.

"After reading this marvelous book I realized how little I have accomplished with my life . . . compared to what I could have done. But, it's not too late."

> Og Mandino, Author of:
> *The Greatest Salesman in the World*

"So many Christians are going through life settling for mediocre, settling for second best, and choosing the path of least resistance. Not Dr. John R. Noē, author of this old (1984) and new (2006) book, *Peak Performance Principles for High Achievers – Revised Edition*. He reminds us that the first mountain we need to conquer is that of ourselves and that God wants us to accomplish great things for His glory."

> Dr. D. James Kennedy, Ph.D.
> Senior Minister
> Coral Ridge Presbyterian Church

What's Next?

More pioneering and next-reformation titles are in development and forthcoming from John Noē and East2West Press. Tentatively titles and subtitles and their estimated publication year are:

THE GREATER JESUS
His glorious unveiling
 (Est. 2012)

UNRAVELING THE END
A balanced scholarly synthesis of four competing and conflicting end-time views—Unifying 'One of the most divisive elements in recent Christian history'
 (Est. 2012)

BEHIND 'UNRAVELING THE END'
The author's doctoral dissertation and more
 (Est. 2012)

A ONCE-MIGHTY FAITH
Whatever happened to the central teaching of Jesus?
 (Est. 2013)

GOD THE ULTIMATE COMPETITIVE EDGE
Why settle for anything less?
Transcending the limits of self-motivation, self-esteem & self-empowerment in a tough competitive world
 (Est. 2013-14)

THE ISRAEL ILLUSION
Pulling back the curtain on the 'land of God' (Oz)
 (Est. 2014-15)

THE ORIGIN AND PURPOSE OF EVIL
Solving the problem of the presence of evil
 (Est. 2014-15)

THE SCENE BEHIND THE SEEN
A Preterist-Idealist commentary of the book of Revelation—unveiling its fulfillment and ongoing relevance—past, present & future
    (Est. 2015-16)

LIFE'S LAST GREATEST ADVENTURE
What really happens today immediately after you die?—you may be surprised!
    (Est. 2016-17)

'WARRIORS OF THE LAST TEMPLE'
The back story, theology, and script behind the movie
    (Pending movie release)

Also see: **PEAK PERFORMANCE PRINCIPLES FOR HIGH ACHIEVERS**
    (1984, revised edition 2006 – Frederick Fell Publishers)

Books Out-of-Print

BEYOND THE END TIMES

SHATTERING THE 'LEFT BEHIND' DELUSION

DEAD IN THEIR TRACKS

TOP TEN MISCONCEPTIONS ABOUT JESUS' SECOND COMING AND THE END TIMES

PEOPLE POWER

THE APOCALYPSE CONSPIRACY

What They Are Saying

The Perfect Ending for the World

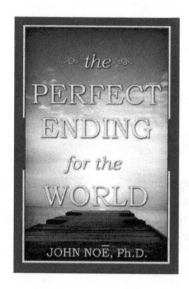

"I go home at night and your book is in a different place than where I left it. I think my wife is reading it too." **– Joe Perrott**

"I'm loving it . . . . the way you write is the way you speak and I learn much from people who speak my type of language, that is, easy to understand type." **– Gloria Lombardi**

"It is fabulous! You have given me so many tools in it to apologetically defend my view . . . . by far one of the best books on Preterism that I have ever read. . . . the perfect book to hand to people who are checking Preterism out and would like to know more." **– Sherrie Baker**

"This guy writes with a lot of confidence, but he has earned it. It's written in a style that should appeal to the average reader while still managing to cover the essential points . . . superbly organized." – **John S. Evans, Ph.D.**

"The Perfect Ending for the World" . . . is what I have been looking for . . . to begin to teach others but I never really knew where to begin. . . .your book has laid it out really well . . . like how it finished really strong and not just begging people to see it your way . . . In all my studies I have never seen eschatology presented this precisely." – **Mark Foreman**

"It's absolutely crystal clear! I am enjoying it so much." – **Bryan Davis**

"I . . . just love it. It answers SO many questions that are asked today by skeptics and sincere Bible seekers." – **Eddie Prather**

"I would call it 'life-changing' . . . . I felt relieved. A burden had been lifted that had troubled my father for years . . . . I congratulate you on making 'things' . . . make sense! . . . Good stuff and more importantly, 'Godly' stuff." – **Pastor Jim Allen**

"It truly is a brilliant book." – **Marty Angelo**

"Outstanding! . . . I read your new book very carefully. . . . the way you explained heaven and earth was the most understandable terms I have ever read. . . . Excellent job, John, looking forward to your next book." – **Steven Ames**

<u>For more: see reviews on Amazon.com</u>

Hell Yes / Hell No

Pro (+) & Con (-):

(+) "Fascinating study . . . . Being informed is strength. . . . free from error and how we have perhaps mishandled Scripture." – **Eddie Prather, Amazon.com review**

(-) "Sheer arrogance. No one before has understood God's plan until you . . . came on the scene." – **Roderick Edwards**

(+) "This book is not for the opinionated person who relies solely on what he has been taught . . . . It is not for the faint of heart . . . . earth-shaking book." – **Dr. Ben Ruth, Amazon.com review**

(-) "You're a Cross-despising, Scripture-trampling, puffed up pervert, John. You have NO business teaching anyone. . . . It's the Platonic Ideal of Poop. . . . It's written by John Noe, Ph. Duh." – **David Green**

(+) "The book is a real mental workout, and I like how you work so hard to get readers to look at both sides of the issue. So many of us are used to creating straw men out of those with whom we disagree that we find a balanced approach difficult to work through. . . . I am blown away by the subject and am really enjoying it . . . and learning a lot." – **John S. Evans, Ph.D.**

(-) "Until you can reconcile the clear, explicit language of Scripture with your claims, your views don't mean much. . . . your thoughts as it pertains to spiritual matters carry no weight." – **Paul Gates**

(+) "I like your style of writing, John; it is impressive for anyone wondering if you have done your homework. . . . I read Bell's book . . . thought it was a little too glib, not serious enough. You seem to be covering all the bases while we make up our minds." – **prefers anonymity**

(-) "I have very strong convictions against any sort of Universalism, and the ambiguity you seem to raise doesn't let me feel right. . . . [but] I am very interested to see what you have to say." – **prefers anonymity**

(+) "You have my attention; tons of questions but I'll finish the book first." – **prefers anonymity**

(-) "The issue is pretty clear to me. I don't need to rehash it, that is unless I need to explain why universalism and annihilation views are not compatible with the Bible." – **prefers anonymity**

(+) "Wow – . . . I cannot wait to see what you have to say in this book." – **prefers anonymity**

(-) "Unsubscribe me from all your e-mails." – **prefers anonymity**

(+) "Wow, John, you're bolder than I thought!" – **Mary Erickson**

(-) "I am not agreeing with this yet. . . . Where do you come up with this stuff?!" – **prefers anonymity**

(+) "I ordered it the minute I received your e-mail. I am <u>really</u> looking forward to reading it. I will make it a top priority, my friend!" – **Bob**
(-) "I'm not on board with . . . 'universal salvation' though. Too many verses condemning the wicked to 'everlasting shame and contempt' (Dan. 12:2, etc. . .)." – **prefers anonymity**

(+) "I hope this message gains momentum in spite of its controversy. Of course any biblical correction will be controversial. . . . I'm so excited that this message is getting out." – **Dana Salsbury**

(-) "I think that Scripture is clear that those who don't 'believe' will be eternally separated from God. How that is done, I don't care. Eternal separation from God is 'hell' in my mind." – **prefers anonymity**

(+) "This is a real tough topic, John. . . . You are about to start a firestorm." – **prefers anonymity**

(+) "You are the best person I know to have addressed this subject. I will order a copy." – **Larry Siegle**

(+) "I am very interested in what you have to say on this topic . . . I am very keen to read your latest. Thank you for alerting me to its publication." – **Barry Tattersall – Australia**

(+) "Thank you, Dear Brother. I will order it. . . . Like millions of Christians . . . I have grappled with the implications of the Gospel message for family members and friends who reject our Lord Jesus Christ, especially those who acknowledged Him and then denied Him." – **Paul Richard Strange, Sr.**

(+) "Sounds like an informative and interesting read. That is something I have thought about for a long time. . . . it would sure be 'fun' finding out what you think. I really liked your synthesis approach to the four views of eschatology." – **Michael Riemer**

(+) "Not enough people are ADMITTING, YET, that they have some problems with this hell issue as it is being presently taught. I would say it is THE issue coming on the radar for all of us." – **prefers anonymity**

(+) "Yes, I've read the entire book. . . . I want to commend you on your excellent style of writing . . . . well done brother! . . . I'm glad you got your thoughts down on paper, so we can begin the dialogue, and my, what a bunch of wonderful 'Universalists!' I never knew they existed, WOW!!!'" – **David Shulse**

(+) "I was reading it this morning and find it to be just what is needed in today's confusing world. . . . I love how you are setting the stage. . . . It is rich . . . and I love it!!!" – **Marty Angelo**

(+) "Thanks for the heads-up; I'll order it today! This has been a real issue in my life recently. . . . I'm excited to find out what you have concluded!" – **Bradley Stone**

(+) "I will order my copy from Amazon right away! I always appreciate your books. It is because of your books and others that I have seen prophecy in a much more balanced light." – **Pastor Jim Allen**

(+) "I trust you, John. There's a lot of stuff I wonder about . . . . you are on the verge of one of the biggies and I am interested in where you take this hell thing." – **prefers anonymity**

(?) "I thought about your book a lot today. The definitions you sent tell me this is potentially about a lot more than the debate about ECT [eternal conscious punishment] and Annihilationism. Does it address questions about the fate of those who never hear the gospel? That has always been a touching issue. All men are sinners, so all are worthy of death, but does God's grace in Christ reach some who never obey the gospel? I am sure there have been some great debates down through history on that one! Ambitious undertaking!" – **prefers anonymity**

Worst-of-the-Worst Comments:

"Although I have not yet studied your book, I have to say that I feel you have erred greatly in putting forward the notion of any sort of universal salvation. . . . The whole current and stream of scripture is against it." – **prefers anonymity**

"You cannot refute Scripture with mere assertions. You need to show exegetically, grammatically, and historically how the above two texts prove that Gehenna is merely nothing more than 'a [physical] valley in Jerusalem.' . . . It is you versus scripture. . . . you are not welcome selling your snake oil Universalism in the Preterist camp. Back off, and get away from us." – **prefers anonymity**

"You're the same Liar John Noe you've always been. Now go play with your Barbie Dolls, Coward. . . . you're a coward, a liar, and a fraud." – **prefers anonymity**

"I do not believe that his overall approach has merit. . . . the fact that it is so poorly written, argued and referenced IS a crucial factor in whether or not this book has merit." – **prefers anonymity**

More Positive Comments:

"Your book is creating quite a stir, and the review from Mitchell is obviously a big plus. This is an exciting time to be tuned in to serious discussions of biblical interpretation. . . . Anyway, keep firing on all cylinders." – **John S. Evans, Ph.D.**

"Your book arrived and . . . I am gripped! . . . this is the best presentation of the competing Christian visions of the full extent of the atonement I have ever read! . . . . You have handled this volatile manner in a highly responsible manner, and I believe that the benefits of reading it greatly outweigh any angst for any Christian, whichever side of the 'all' they find themselves. Any usefulness of these comments for this great kingdom debate would be an honor." – **Paul Richard Strange, Sr.**

"Recently, I read a book that has been more thoroughly engaging in regard to all of the issues gathered together than I think has ever been done before! Dr. John Noe . . . has provided what I see as an amazingly fair-minded presentation of the pros and cons of the views held among Evangelicals . . . . Dr. Noe's book . . . lifts the debate to a higher plane, and inspires all believers to stretch in our thinking! – **Paul Richard Strange, Sr. – blog post**

"I am half-way through your book! Wow! You love to live on the edge! (smile) . . . I find this fascinating and credible. . . . Genesis 18:25 . . . 'Will not the judge of all the earth do right?' . . . I think this verse is a 'standard-bearer' verse for what you are discussing in your book." – **Pastor Jim Allen**

"I am sending this out to my friends, and to the address list for our Greater-Emmanuel website. . . . You have done an excellent job. . . . May your work go far." – **Jonathan P. Mitchell**

"Noe's book presents arguments for both sides, so it is a good resource." – **Jonathan P. Mitchell**

"You're doing the right thing by speaking up for truth and writing well-reasoned arguments, regardless of the results. We just have to let go of the results and naysayers who aren't ready yet. I hope you don't take the 'con' stress too hard. . . .You're fighting the good fight and you're not alone! Not anymore. This message is too good to be kept down much longer." – **Riley O'Brien/Powell**

"It's interesting to read people's reactions. And I mean some are really reactions, aren't they?! – **Riley O'Brien/Powell**

"I suspect your book will go down as one of the best books for getting people to talk, study and argue over. It will shake the Christian world to pray, study, and ask the Holy Spirit to lead us and guide us into all truth, then we must be big enough to admit we have not been taught right." – **Gloria Lombardi**

"I'm reading your new book, about halfway through. Now I know why certain people are mad at you. . . . Your book explains about mankind basically making God's book say what they wanted it to say . . . . To me that is making the Bible corrupt and in man's image. A real turn-off. John, I really appreciate you and what you have done." – **Steven Ames**

"Great book! It really gets a Christian to think." – **Steven Ames**

"John, speaking as one who has seen the infighting . . . I commend you for publicly stepping into the deep end of the theological pool. – **Paige Marshall**

"Thank you for the wonderful book. I thoroughly enjoyed it and I think you have moved the discussion forward." – **Bill Benninghoff**

"Didn't really think I would like your book, "Hell Yes / Hell No! and thus did not purchase one. However a friend insisted I read his copy and I did. Finished it yesterday and have told other friends about it. Ordered my own copy today to lend to others as need arises. First off right out of the box it is well written. It has a sense of humor that is contagious. . . . What I found most compelling about the book is summed up in one word, 'introspective.' I cannot recall reading any book that made me look at myself more than this one did." – **Jack Gibbert**

"I mean 'lake of fire' that one blew my mind away! . . . very good!!!" – **James A. Burks**

". . . your excellent treatise in Hell Yes! Hell No!. . . . I just took a long time to read it – slowly, carefully, and with great delight. I have purchased some more copies and have begun to share them with others. I tell them that Dr. John Noe is the only scholar I personally know who deals with a controversial subject with such a comprehensive degree of excellence, and by that I mean his attention to the exegesis of scripture – exploring the original languages, the etymology of biblical terms, and the development of, changes and different understandings and expressions of a doctrine throughout the history of the Church including the fruit that such understandings and expressions bore in times past and currently bear in our era. Dr. Noe's works are thought-provoking, challenging and intriguing, a delightful exercise of 'iron sharpening iron.' At one and the same time, I have only read a mere handful of authors so even handed as to allow each opposing side of a doctrinal dispute to express their position in their own words without ad hominem attacks or bitter diatribes about the persons, or their opinions, with whom he may disagree. . . . One last note on the comments of those critiquing your book here, and speaking of "fruit," I noticed a clear distinction between those who agreed with you or were not sure but appreciated your scholarly work and the vicious, personal, slanderous attacks of those who either disagreed with you or seemed utterly disgusted that you dared to even question such a 'sacrosanct' doctrine as 'hell.' Interesting! . . . Love and appreciate you so much, Brother John!" – **Robert Preston**

A Critical Challenge Posted on Amazon.com:

Customer Review

A New Testament translator's Review, October 26, 2011
By **Jonathan P. Mitchell**

I concur with the six previous, positive reviews. John Noe's approach to this topic is even-handed and gives the reader a chance to use his or her own mind and spirit to reach an informed conclusion. The 374 pages are a good read for anyone that is interested in the Christian church's teachings about "hell" (a mistranslation, used for three different Greek words in the NT, as Noe points out) and God's judgments. You will find his research to be thorough, and the historical information which he presents on the early Christian beliefs about these things may surprise you.

I have read quite a few books about hell and judgment over the past 50 years, and John Noe's presentation is among the best. For a solution to the debate he presents a 7-point Synthesis, which you will find interesting. I have already recommended this book to my friends and to my readers. For serious Bible students, this book is a must.

Challenging Question

Initial post: Nov 2, 2011 11:47:47 PM PDT
Kelly N. Birks says:

Hello Mr. Mitchell. I noticed that you refer to yourself as a "translator" in your heading here. Not trying to start an argument, but I would like to know what translation boards have you been involved with? I assume then that you can read and translate Koine Greek? You give quite the sterling recommendation to Noe's book. *I know Dr. Noe and am wondering how far you may be willing to go to back up his work and abilities in the Greek New Testament on this subject?*

Thank you,
Dr. Kelly Nelson Birks
Reply to this post

In Reply

In reply to an earlier post on Nov 3, 2011 8:32:56 AM PDT
  Jonathan P. Mitchell says:

Dear Dr. Birks, I would simply point you to my translation that is offered here on Amazon: THE NEW TESTAMENT - GOD'S MESSAGE OF GOODNESS, EASE AND WELL-BEING WHICH BRINGS GOD'S GIFTS OF HIS SPIRIT, HIS LIFE, HIS GRACE, HIS POWER, HIS FAIRNESS, HIS PEACE AND HIS LOVE. You can read sample passages on my web site, under Jonathan Mitchell New Testament. The introduction will explain my presentation of multiple renderings. I began my study of Koine Greek in 1962 and spent 23 years in research for this project. I have a Masters degree in Anthropology, in which I also studied linguistics. *I would be happy to back up Dr. Noe's work, as I did a careful read of it.*

Respectfully,
Jonathan Mitchell

(**Bold** and *italics* above are mine)

What My Pastor(s) Thinks:

Several readers have asked, "What does your pastor think of your book, *Hell Yes / Hell No*?" So here is what he and one of Grace's associate pastors are saying, publicly (used with permission):

"You may not come to the same conclusion John Noē does in his book, *Hell Yes / Hell No* . . . but, you cannot fault his excellent biblical work, his thorough analysis, and open handed conclusion. To all those who say . . . show me what the Bible says . . . here's your book!"

Dave Rodriguez
Senior Pastor
Grace Community Church
Noblesville, IN

(Grace is a 3,000-attendance, mega-church located in a northern suburb of Indianapolis.)

"Whether agreement comes or not, as one interacts with John Noē's book, *Hell Yes / Hell No*, readers I trust will appreciate as I do his biblical exegesis, his engagement with church history, his balanced and fair treatment of all 'sides' and his gracious, yet bold spirit as he wrestles with theological issues that are pressing in our day."

David A. Bell
Associate Pastor – Young Adults
Grace Community Church
Noblesville, IN

For more: see reviews on Amazon.com

CPSIA information can be obtained
at www.ICGtesting.com
Printed in the USA
BVHW070104050222
627844BV00003B/78

9 780983 430322